Voluntary Work
in the Welfare State

MARY MORRIS

LONDON
ROUTLEDGE & KEGAN PAUL
NEW YORK: HUMANITIES PRESS

First published 1969
by Routledge & Kegan Paul Limited
Broadway House, 68–74, Carter Lane
London, E.C.4

Printed in Great Britain
by C. Tinling & Co. Ltd
Liverpool, London and Prescot

No part of this book may be reproduced
in any form without permission from
the publisher, except for the quotation
of brief passages in criticism

SBN 7100 6581 7

939715

361·7·   26/1/70

VOLUNTARY WORK IN THE WELFARE STATE

INTERNATIONAL LIBRARY OF SOCIOLOGY
AND SOCIAL RECONSTRUCTION

Founded by Karl Mannheim

Editor: W. J. H. Sprott

A catalogue of books available in the
INTERNATIONAL LIBRARY OF SOCIOLOGY AND SOCIAL RECONSTRUCTION
and new books in preparation for the Library
will be found at the end of this volume

For Charles Morris

Acknowledgments

I should like first to thank the late Mr. G. R. Dalby, Lecturer in the Department of Adult Education and Extra-Mural Studies in the University of Leeds, for all the help he has given me. I came to rely on his knowledge of voluntary work and on his sound judgment when we were working together on a previous book, *Social Enterprise*, and was therefore delighted when he agreed to read the first draft of this book. I have found his comments and criticisms most helpful.

The survey of voluntary work in Bradford described in Appendix III was carried out by students in the School of Social Studies in Applied Social Studies in the University of Bradford under the supervision of Mr. J. W. McCulloch, Lecturer in Research Methods. I am most grateful to the students, and especially, of course, to Mr. McCulloch, who not only planned and supervised the survey but analysed the results and helped me to prepare the report. In this connection I should like to thank the Leverhulme Trustees for their generosity in making a grant to cover the expense of the students who conducted the interviews.

I have been fortunate in being allowed to use the Library at the National Institute for Social Work Training, and am greatly indebted to the Librarian, Mrs. E. M. Holliday, for her patience – and her success – in helping me to find the books and pamphlets I needed; and fortunate, too, in having the book typed by Mrs. Mollie Hargreaves, who, in addition to deciphering my typescript and often my illegible handwriting, took such an interest in the subject that she was able to help me check quotations, notes and references.

So many people have given me the benefit of their specialized knowledge that it would be difficult to mention them all individually. Much of the information on which the descriptive parts of the book are based has not been published and had to be obtained from the officers of the voluntary bodies concerned. They have given freely of their time in person or by correspondence and have generously allowed me to share their knowledge. In thanking everyone who has helped me in this way, I should like especially to mention Miss M. Bucke, secretary of the National Old People's Welfare Council, Mrs. D. Cane, secretary of the Central Churches Group, Miss E. R. Littlejohn, secretary of the Standing Conference of Councils of Social Service, Brigadier D. Meynell, secretary of the Standing Conference of National Voluntary Youth Organizations, and Miss N. Rice-Jones, secretary of the British National Conference on Social Welfare, all of whom allowed me to learn from their experience, to have access to their files and even to use their offices while I was studying the material. I want also to record my debt to Miss Roché, the secretary of the Council of Social Service in Nottingham, who arranged for me to see at first hand some of the voluntary work being done in that city and who has kept me in touch with its development; and to Mr. R. K. Harrison, who allowed me to use material from his unpublished thesis.

To these and others who are closely involved in working with volunteers I owe a special debt, but the debt I owe to the volunteers themselves is even greater. For nearly forty years I have had the privilege of seeing volunteers at work over a wide field of social action. What I have learned from them led me to think it might be worth while to try and describe the extent and the value of voluntary work, and to them, therefore, my deepest thanks are due.

Mary Morris

Contents

Glossary of Abbreviations

A C E	Advisory Centre for Education
a e g i s	Aid for the Elderly in Government Institutions
a m e n d	Association for the relatives of the Mentally, Emotionally and Nervously Disabled
B A H O H	British Association of the Hard of Hearing
B R C S	British Red Cross Society
C A R D	Campaign against Racial Discrimination
C R A C	Careers Research and Advisory Centre
C M A C	Catholic Marriage Advisory Council
C C D	Central Council for the Disabled
C A B	Citizens' Advice Bureau
C A	Community Association
C S V	Community Service Volunteers
C A S E	Confederation for the Advancement of State Education
C S S	Council of Social Service
D E S	Department of Education and Science
D I G	Disablement Income Group
D P A	Discharged Prisoners' Aid
E S N	Educationally Sub-normal
F P A	Family Planning Association
F S U	Family Service Unit
G F S	Girls' Friendly Society
H M S O	Her Majesty's Stationery Office
I L E A	Inner London Education Authority
I V S	International Voluntary Service
J P	Justice of the Peace
L E A	Local Education Authority
L H A	Local Health Authority
L W A	Local Welfare Authority
M Y C S	Manchester Youth and Community Service
M G C	Marriage Guidance Council
M P	Member of Parliament
N A B C	National Association of Boys' Clubs

NACRO	National Association for the Care and Resettlement of Offenders
NADPAS	National Association of Discharged Prisoners' Aid Societies
NAMH	National Association for Mental Health
NAPV	National Association of Prison Visitors
NAYC	National Association of Youth Clubs
NCCI	National Committee for Commonwealth Immigrants
NCCOP	National Corporation for the Care of Old People
NCSS	National Council of Social Service
NFP-TA	National Federation of Parent-Teacher Associations
NFYFC	National Federation of Young Farmers' Clubs
NHS	National Health Service
NMGC	National Marriage Guidance Council
NOPWC	National Old People's Welfare Council
NSMHC	National Society for Mentally Handicapped Children
OPW	Old People's Welfare
PND	People Next Door
PPA	Pre-School Playgroups Association
P-TA	Parent-Teacher Association
RCC	Rural Community Council
RNIB	Royal National Institute for the Blind
RNID	Royal National Institute for the Deaf
SCF	Save the Children Fund
SSCVYO	Scottish Standing Conference of Voluntary Youth Organizations
SCNVYO	Standing Conference of National Voluntary Youth Organizations
UK	United Kingdom
UNA	United Nations Association
USA	United States of America
VSO	Voluntary Service Overseas
WRVS	(formerly W.V.S.) Women's Royal Voluntary Service
YMCA	Young Men's Christian Association
YWCA	Young Women's Christian Association
YHA	Youth Hostels Association

Introduction

Why voluntary work?

Voluntary work is undertaken for three main reasons; first, there are jobs to be done which cannot be or at least will not be done by paid personnel; second, the opportunity to give service meets a personal need felt by individual people; and third, voluntary action is a powerful force for social progress. These three reasons provide the explanation and the justification for the existence of voluntary work.

They are not, however, universally accepted and must therefore be considered critically if their validity is to be maintained. Criticism may take one or more of the following forms: it may hold that paid personnel are in fact doing everything necessary, or that where gaps remain they should quickly be filled by paid workers so that volunteers can be eliminated; it may deny the existence of a personal need to give service, or though recognizing it may not approve of meeting it through voluntary work; it may claim that volunteers do not in fact help to achieve progress, and that their influence on policy and practice is not desirable.

The purpose of this book is to examine the present position and future role of voluntary work in the United Kingdom and to analyse its value to the individual and to the community. Its limitations as well as its achievements will be considered and criticism as well as praise will be recorded.

Since human communities are continually changing and developing it is necessary to look afresh at frequent intervals at all aspects of life within them, and to see how far policies and methods of carrying them out which may have been right in the past have now outlived their usefulness.

It is not surprising that the massive changes that took place in this country with the coming of what is called the Welfare State should have led people to think that the days of voluntary action were over, since it was commonly thought that the State would provide for all the needs of all its members 'from the cradle to the grave'. This attitude to voluntary action, however, was short-lived, and it is now generally agreed that voluntary societies and voluntary workers are as active and as numerous as they have ever been. Some changes have taken place in the tasks undertaken and in the methods adopted in response to changing conditions and attitudes, but the voluntary element in much social provision has remained unchanged.

The general approval of voluntary action as a valuable part of community life is still mainly derived from the personal knowledge of ordinary citizens of what is happening in their own neighbourhoods. This local knowledge is supplemented through radio, television and the press by information about new developments in other places. Yet in spite of the wider knowledge that mass communications now make possible there is still comparative ignorance on the part of the general public of the nature and extent of voluntary work in the country as a whole. This ignorance is often shared by the volunteers themselves who tend to be concerned simply with their own work in their own districts. Both they and the wider public accept voluntary work as part of the natural order of things and give little thought to its extent or its importance. Yet this somewhat unquestioning acceptance of the fact of voluntary work is accompanied by widespread recognition of its contribution to the welfare of society, even though there is little knowledge of what this contribution is or ought to be. The vague approval of the ordinary citizen is reinforced by repeated public utterances from the leaders of opinion, praising the work of the volunteer and urging him to further efforts. These pronouncements are in line with the view of the general public that voluntary work is an essential part of the welfare state[1].

This general approval of voluntary action as 'a good thing for society' exists alongside the criticism to which attention has been drawn. The public as a whole pays lip service to the voluntary principle but some of its members object to certain pieces of work and to particular workers, and a few even

---

[1] That this is the public view is illustrated by the replies received to a question on the subject in a survey of voluntary work recently undertaken in Bradford. See Appendix III.

question the value of the principle itself[1]. These people feel that society as a whole suffers more than it gains from voluntary activities, and that individuals and groups who need help would in all cases be better served by statutory bodies and by paid workers. They do not always count the cost either in money or in personnel of replacing all voluntary effort by paid service nor face realistically the task of persuading the taxpayer to meet the extra cost.

Others who do not adopt this extreme position yet feel that much of the voluntary work that is being done is unnecessary, and that volunteers would be better employed in giving service of a different kind. Others again feel that voluntary workers are inefficient and unreliable and should be persuaded or even obliged to undergo some kind of training. Some critics also feel that opportunities for service are not sufficiently widespread through the community and remain largely the prerogative of the 'middle aged and middle class'.

These criticisms must be borne in mind in any consideration of the value of voluntary work. They cannot be answered simply by pointing to its general acceptance as an essential part of the life of the community. The vague approval of the public is not sufficient guarantee of its value, since this approval is based on limited knowledge and provides no answer to the fundamental questions raised by these and other criticisms. These fundamental questions to which answers must be sought are three:

1 What part are voluntary workers actually playing in social action today, and are they playing it well?
2 What is the value of voluntary work to the individual volunteer and to the community?
3 Should voluntary workers play any part in social action and if so what part should that be?

---

[1] An attempt to estimate how many such people there are was made in a survey undertaken by the Portsmouth College of Technology into *Attitudes towards Voluntary Social Work in the City of Portsmouth* (1965). A quota sample of the population was asked four questions designed to discover attitudes to voluntary social work. Eighty-six per cent of all responses were favourable (1918 as against 301). This compares with eighty-four per cent of the Bradford sample who answered 'yes' to the question, 'Is there a need for voluntary helpers in our country which runs Welfare Services?' (Appendix III). Reference to the Portsmouth survey is made on p.17.

The first question can only be answered satisfactorily by means of an inquiry into what voluntary workers are in fact doing in the main fields of social action. Such an inquiry should also throw light on the extent to which present provision falls short of what is needed by society, and therefore on the likely future demand for volunteers. It should show what kind of work will be required to meet the need and indicate how this might be allocated between statutory and voluntary bodies and between paid and unpaid workers. This inquiry forms the subject of Part I of this book.

The answer to the second question will involve consideration both of the satisfactions which the volunteer finds in his work and the motives which lead him to undertake it, and also of the role of the volunteer in a democratic society. This will be discussed in Part II.

The third question is in two parts and can best be answered in two stages. The first part can be answered here and now by a simple affirmative, since voluntary workers will always be needed so long as there are jobs to be done which cannot be or are not being done by paid labour. The second part – as to what their role should be – must be answered in more detail. This will be done in the final chapter of the book, and will involve discussion of the social needs of the community, of the total resources available to meet them, and of the tasks to be undertaken by voluntary workers.

The extent of voluntary work today

It is comparatively easy to obtain information about the work which is being done by the national voluntary organizations, since this is described in their reports and publications and is given some publicity in the press. It is possible, too, to find out what is going on in any particular place, since many local societies also publish reports and attract attention in the local press. It is more difficult to discover either nationally or locally how many volunteers are involved in the work of these societies, what they are like and how much time they give; and even if such figures could be obtained they would leave out of account the much larger number of people whose voluntary service takes the form of spontaneous neighbourly service and who are not attached to any organization[1]. It is more difficult still to estimate future demands for voluntary help and therefore to plan recruitment and training for those who are likely to be needed.

As far as the present position is concerned, some voluntary bodies are reluctant to admit that they are short of helpers, though there may well be a franker reaction in the field than at headquarters. The cynical may suspect that in some cases at least jobs may be cut to suit the volunteers available, rather than efforts made to find and train volunteers for the jobs that need doing. At the same time, it is only fair to record that some national voluntary bodies are becoming increasingly interested in training[2].

Though exact figures are not available, it is possible to obtain general indications about numbers from the head-quarters of the various bodies and from other sources, and this information will be presented later. But first an attempt will be made to define the voluntary worker and to look at voluntary work as a whole.

The voluntary worker

Voluntary workers or volunteers can be defined as people who undertake unpaid work for the community as a whole or for individual members of it. They may be male or female and of any age. They may be in full-time paid employment, or they may, like many housewives and pensioners, not be 'gainfully employed'. They may give as little as an occasional afternoon or evening or as much as seven days a week. Their skills and suitability for the jobs they tackle are varied. They may be qualified professional people giving unpaid service in the field of their expertise, or they may be unskilled helpers performing humble tasks like making tea and running errands. Unfortunately, too, they sometimes undertake tasks for which they are unsuited by temperament or qualification, and they are not always reliable and conscientious. These shortcomings

[1] The Bradford survey showed that four times as many people were giving neighbourly help as were voluntary workers in the social service agencies. See Appendix III.

[2] Training is an important part of the subject matter of the Aves Committee on voluntary workers in the social service whose report is expected in 1969.

can never be wholly eliminated since they are human failings common to both paid and unpaid workers, but they can be minimized in the case of volunteers as well as other workers when care and attention is paid to selection, training and allocation to jobs by the voluntary or statutory body concerned.

Categories of voluntary work

Voluntary work falls into three categories: *first*, public service which is undertaken as part of the business of running the community – local government, the magistracy, hospital management, membership of royal commissions, working parties, committees of inquiry and advisory bodies; *second*, work undertaken in social or community service, through a voluntary body or at the request of a statutory authority, and *third*, neighbourly help which is spontaneous and unorganized.

The second of these categories forms the main subject of Part I of this book but some reference will be made in it to the other two, since it is impossible to keep the three in watertight compartments. Unpaid public work is voluntary work in its own right but it is rarely undertaken in isolation from other voluntary service. Councillors perform much unpaid work in addition to their duties as elected members of local authorities; J.P.'s and members of hospital committees do not restrict their voluntary activities to those which they were appointed to undertake. Spontaneous neighbourly service cannot be altogether separated from the more organized work undertaken by volunteers with the voluntary and statutory bodies and its importance is constantly apparent. The contribution to the general well-being made by unrecorded acts of neighbourly help cannot easily be measured, but some idea of its extent can be gained from the evidence of a special survey recently undertaken in Bradford. This is described in Appendix III and discussed in Chapter VII.

In the second category, that of work undertaken through a voluntary body or at the request of a statutory authority, the field of action is so wide and the forms it takes so varied that any grouping of activities is bound to be somewhat arbitrary, and there will inevitably be some overlapping. In the interest of clarity, however, these multifarious activities must be grouped in some way, and the most convenient division is according to the statutory authority with which they are mainly concerned. Division in this way gives six groups: *First*, health and welfare, where statutory responsibility lies with the Department of Health and Social Security and with the health and welfare departments of the local authority. *Second*, hospitals, where it lies with the Department of Health and Social Security and with Regional Boards and Boards of Governors. *Third*, children and young people, where it rests with the Department of Education and Science and the Home Office and with the children's and education departments of the local authority. *Fourth*, care and aftercare of prisoners and their families, where the Home Office is the responsible department. *Fifth*, information and advice in which various government departments are interested, and *Sixth*, race relations, where the Home Office is the principal statutory body concerned.

These six groups cover the main forms of activity in the social service field in which organized voluntary work plays a part, and it is to this field that the descriptive section of this book will be mainly devoted. It will, however, include a final chapter about unorganized neighbourly help. It is well to remember, too, that there are other important ways in which voluntary workers can and do contribute to social well-being, notably by working for a cause, by participation in cultural and recreational activities, and by raising money on a large scale; and that the numbers engaged in these other forms of unpaid work are probably no less numerous than those directly undertaking social service through voluntary bodies.

It is difficult to draw a hard and fast line between what is and what is not social service, but some line must be drawn if any clear picture of the role of voluntary workers in social and community service is to emerge. This line is best drawn between organizations whose primary aim is social service and all the others. Political and trade and professional societies and pressure groups on the one hand and cultural and recreational societies on the other have all been excluded except in so far as they make provision in their activities for some particular group which needs help, such as the old, the young or the handicapped. Money-raising societies, whose main aim is to raise funds for such causes as relief work or research, have also been omitted, though reference is often made to the help of volunteers in raising money for the welfare work they are themselves carrying out.

Housing has also been excluded, but for a different reason. It has been excluded, not because the provision of suitable accommodation for everyone whatever his means is not a social service, but because this must depend on statutory rather than on voluntary effort. This does not mean that voluntary workers have no part to play, but their role is different from what it is in the other social services. New homes will be built and old ones upgraded mainly by housing authorities and private enterprise and not directly by voluntary effort. It is true that housing associations, which are largely run by volunteers, are giving some help to particular groups of people – the aged, the handicapped, the immigrants – who find it impossible to buy and difficult to rent a house, a flat or even a single room, and this is of immense value to the individuals and families concerned. But the main contribution that is being made by voluntary workers is in the field of public relations. By publicizing needs and exposing evils they are helping to create a public opinion which will put pressure on the responsible authorities to prevent exploitation of tenants and to provide more and better accommodation at a price those who most need it can afford. At the same time they are helping ignorant and often frightened tenants to claim their rights under the law. A recent report[1] by Shelter, a voluntary society devoted to helping housing associations to rehouse some of the most needy families, draws attention to terrible conditions of insecurity in which many people live and, while blaming exploitation by landlords on the one hand and the ignorance and fear on the part of tenants on the other, stresses that 'shortage' is the real enemy of the homeless, the unsuitably housed and the insecure tenant. Voluntary societies and the workers who support them cannot themselves meet the housing needs of more than a fraction of even the most urgent cases but their publicity and their example strengthen the hands of those who can. They can keep the problem constantly in the public eye, and until the shortage is overcome can help to protect the exploited and the insecure.

[1] *Notice to Quit.* [12th September, 1968]

Part I

Voluntary Workers
in Action

CHAPTER I

Health and Welfare

I

THE GENERAL PICTURE

Department of Health and Social Security

Health and welfare will be discussed separately from hospitals. Both come under the Department of Health and Social Security but they are the province of different statutory authorities at local level. Moreover, health and welfare itself covers so wide a field that it can most conveniently be considered in four separate parts, as is done in the Ministry's Blue Book *Health and Welfare, The Development of Community Care*[1]. These four parts are concerned with Mothers and Young Children, the Elderley, the Mentally Disordered and the Physically Handicapped. Voluntary work with people in each of these groups will be described in separate sections after the present position and future role of voluntary workers in health and welfare as a whole has been outlined.

On this subject much can be learned from the Ministry's Blue Books and Circulars[2], especially regarding the Ministry's views about the type of work which should be tackled by volunteers and about the proper relationship between statutory and voluntary bodies. Other sources of information are the National Council of Social Service which has sponsored conferences and inquiries, various guides to voluntary service

---

[1] *Cmnd.* 1973.

[2] *Health and Welfare, The Development of Community Care*, April, 1963 (*Cmnd.* 1973) *Ibid.*, June, 1966 (*Cmnd.* 3022). Circular 7/62 *Development of Local Authority Health and Welfare Services: Co-operation with Voluntary Organisations* (April, 1962). Circular 18/62 *Ibid.* (August, 1962). Circular 18/64 *Voluntary Effort in the Health and Welfare Services* (November, 1964). Circular HM/62/69 *Voluntary Help in Hospitals* (April, 1962).

3

and a number of special studies. These guides and studies are not in most cases restricted to the field of health and welfare, but cover a wider range of social and community service.

Blue Books and Circulars from the Ministry of Health

These include long lists of what volunteers can do and are doing; fifty-four different jobs are listed in Circular 7/62, thirty-six in H.M.S.O. 62/29 and fifteen main types of work are described in the Blue Book. No mention is made, however, of the numbers of volunteers likely to be wanted. The Ministry stresses the value of voluntary work and emphasizes that recruitment should be through the voluntary bodies – 'approaches should be made to voluntary organizations as such and not to individual members. Disappointments and difficulties have most often resulted from failure to observe this rule'. This, however, is a point on which there is considerable difference of opinion and further reference to it will be made later[1]. The Ministry urges local authorities to take voluntary bodies into consultation, also to tell them their requirements and also to give them grant aid[2]. It asks them to consider arrangements for securing co-operation, and suggests the setting up of joint committees for the purpose. It does not, however, ask for reports on what action has been taken and none have apparently been received.

In spite of this, however, it seems clear from the Circulars that the Ministry, no less than the voluntary bodies, hoped that the local authorities would take active steps to put these suggestions into practice. Circular 7/62 was issued to follow up a conference of hospital authorities, local authorities and voluntary organizations held by the Ministry in February 1962 in which the following national organizations took part: British Red Cross Society, National Association of Leagues of Hospital Friends, National Council of Social Service, National Old People's Council, St. John Ambulance Association and Brigade and Women's Voluntary Service for Civil Defence. The Circular states that 'the representatives of the voluntary organizations have emphasized that their constituent and

---

[1] See below, pp. 233 and 236.
[2] Circular 18/64.

local bodies will not fail to respond to a call for more voluntary workers' and goes on to say:

With this encouraging assurance, the Minister asks all local health and welfare authorities to give fresh thought to the work which voluntary organisations are already doing and to consider what further or other work they can suitably be invited to undertake ... Successful co-operation between statutory and voluntary bodies depends on regular consultation. The representatives of all the voluntary organisations have stressed this point and local authorities are asked to give it particular attention ... Local authorities are accordingly asked to consider the existing arrangements for securing co-operation with and amongst the voluntary organisations in their areas, and how these can be improved or extended to ensure that regular consultation takes place. A special joint committee may be the best method in some cases.[1]

A second conference with the same membership was held in June of the same year, and was again followed by a Circular[2] urging local authorities to take action:

There was again a general request from the voluntary organisations for more information from local authorities about ways in which their members could give voluntary service ... Enthusiasm will be lost if action is delayed. Local authorities which have not already done so are asked to make formal contact now with local voluntary organisations – by means of a preliminary conference if necessary – in order to make their own needs known.

It appears from this wording that the Minister was disappointed at the lack of progress made – a disappointment increasingly shared by the voluntary bodies.

The National Council of Social Service. Conference Report

It was from the voluntary side that the next move came. This took the form of a conference called by the Standing Conference of Councils of Social Service[3]. It was extremely well attended by both statutory and voluntary bodies and

---

[1] *Ibid.*, extracts from paragraphs 6, 7 and 8.
[2] Circular 18/62.
[3] Community Services for Health and Welfare. Co-operation between local authorities and voluntary organizations. 21 June, 1963.

there was a good discussion[1]. Many of those who were present expressed the view that there was sufficient trust and positive response to encourage hopes of active co-operation in the future.

In view of subsequent developments, or rather in view of the fact that so little has come of the high hopes expressed, it is interesting to note some of the pronouncements made by those in authority. The then Parliamentary Secretary to the Ministry of Health, Mr. Bernard Braine, drew attention to a number of specific tasks which he considered particularly suitable for voluntary effort and claimed that the more state provision was extended the greater was the scope for voluntary effort, and went on:

It is imperative, therefore, that we consider as precisely as possible the role of voluntary social service in the modern welfare state. The brief survey that I have given may suffice to provide the background against which your discussions today will take place. I think that there are three deductions that we can draw from this survey. First, the needs of those for whom the services are intended cannot be met by local authorities alone. There is here a vast and growing field for voluntary action. Secondly, voluntary effort nowadays must stand comparison with paid work. Not only must voluntary workers know how to do the job they undertake – and this argues the case for some kind of training – but the service they provide must be regular and punctual and the volunteer willing to undertake the humdrum routine tasks. Thirdly, if voluntary effort is to play its full part acceptable methods will be needed to enable the various organisations with their varying structure and different traditions to work together. The Minister of Health has suggested a special Joint Committee or committees to cover groups of services or different

[1] The list of delegates comprises eighty-six from fifty Health and Welfare Authorities, eighty-four from fifty-eight Cs.S.S. and rural community councils, and thirty-six from nineteen other voluntary bodies. The delegates from the local authorities were almost equally divided between aldermen and councillors on the one hand and officials on the other. It should be noted incidentally that many of the delegates from local authorities were also connected with voluntary bodies; of these one of the main speakers, Sir Alfred Owen, is an obvious example. In only one case, however, was the statutory and voluntary body actually represented by the same person; Newcastle-under-Lyme. Many of those present at this conference are examples of voluntary workers giving unpaid service both in public work and through voluntary bodies (see p. xviii above).

parts of a local authority's area. Clearly there is need for experiment here. I would not like to lay down any hard and fast rule this morning. This is something that must be worked out at local level in a way which would enable us to draw lessons from what is being done. But whatever method may be adopted, it is essential that it should be one under which all the bodies concerned feel able to work happily together[1].

So far the case was put in a way that was acceptable to the voluntary bodies, except that they cannot have liked the emphasis on 'humdrum routine tasks'. It is true that the conference report does not record this dislike[2], but anyone who is in touch with voluntary workers knows that it exists[3]. It is not so much that they object to 'humdrum and routine tasks' in themselves as that they want an opportunity of using their skills and their goodwill in more interesting ways as well, and want their organizations to have some say in policy making and in job allocation. This is the point on which the Parliamentary Secretary was challenged, for he had used these words:

It is for the local authorities to establish what the gaps are that need to be filled and to say what services they expect from voluntary effort, and they must be precise about this. It is for voluntary organisations in their turn to mobilise the resources to fill these gaps: they will be all the better equipped to do so when the need is shown to them plainly and the machinery for close and constant consultation has been established at every level and not merely at the top.

It is interesting to note, however, that he accepted at once the point made in the following challenging question from a member of a local C.S.S.

She had been surprised by this suggestion because she thought it essential that there should be consultation and a real exchange of views about plans between local authorities and voluntary organisations. Voluntary organisations often knew of gaps which local

[1] Conference Report, p. 5.

[2] Though one representative of a C.S.S. is recorded as saying 'She hoped that volunteers would not be thought of as cheap labour'.

[3] Reference is made to this in an article by Mrs Ruth Adams – *Sunday Times*, 24th October, 1965. 'It's really sad the way these people turn up willing and eager and all we can offer them is some dreary little job.'

authorities could meet and the identification of gaps and planning to fill them should be a combined operation.

Mr. Braine said that he accepted the point completely, and continued:

In Circular 7/62 the Minister of Health had asked local authorities to consider their existing arrangements for securing co-operation with voluntary organisations. He knew that voluntary organisations were aware of the importance of co-operation but he had been asking local authorities to make certain that they had machinery for effective and continuing co-operation and that it was working.

The fact the he accepted the point so completely though it ran counter to his pronouncement, surely shows that he had not thought through the implications of what he was saying. The acceptance of the point by the Ministry was, however, underlined later in the conference by the then Deputy Secretary Dame Enid Russell when she said:

consultation between the statutory authorities and the voluntary bodies must be two way; there must be what you might call 'cross fertilisation'.

The point was also taken by the Vice-Chairman of Staffordshire County Council, Sir Alfred Owen, in his address.

I think myself that we should have a partnership: voluntary service is not of inferior quality, it is not only there to fill the gaps left by the statutory services, it is an equal partner with them in the welfare state.

This statement by the representative of a local authority was most encouraging for the voluntary bodies, though later on in the same speech Sir Alfred recognized that his attitude was far from universal.

I can honestly say that in Staffordshire the voluntary organisations are recognised as part of the team by the county council although not by the municipal boroughs, who seem suspicious of them and fear that they are trying to take for themselves, work that should properly be done by local authorities. There is a feeling that voluntary organisations are intruders rather than members of a team.

In fact, very few local authorities seem to believe that

voluntary service is an equal partner, if their views are to be judged by their response to the circulars from the Ministry of Health.

Evidence from Councils of Social Service

What this response has been cannot easily be discovered from the Ministry, since no request for information on this point was made to local authorities. It has been possible, however, to find out something from the other end – that is to say, from the voluntary bodies. This has been done in an unpublished thesis[1] undertaken by Mr. R. K. Harrison from the University of Southampton with the full co-operation of the National Council of Social Service. The work is based on information received from fifty-seven of the seventy Councils of Social Service affected by the Ministry Circulars (the other thirteen did not reply). The omission of these thirteen and of the areas where no C.S.S. existed is unlikely to affect the general picture, since in the first case 'no reply' almost certainly means that no action has been taken, while in the second it can be assumed that local authorities in areas where there is no C.S.S. are not more likely than others to take their voluntary organizations into partnership. Moreover, the Cs.S.S. from which information was received cover the different types of authority (county borough, non-county borough and urban district) and also are widely distributed throughout the country.

The fifty-seven areas from which information was received were divided into five groups on the basis of the extent of developments in statutory-voluntary co-operation. Group 1 (13 areas): total inertia in both camps; Group 2 (14 areas): the local C.S.S. approached the local authority but could not induce them even to call a meeting; Group 3 (20 areas): a meeting was held with no subsequent significant improvement in co-operation. No less than forty-seven fell into these three groups. Group 4 (7 areas): significant improvements occurred but the C.S.S. was not adopted as the co-ordinating body; Group 5 (3 areas): the C.S.S. was so accepted and fulfilled the role effectively. It is impossible on this evidence to dispute Mr. Harrison's conclusion that more than four-

---

[1] *Voluntary Organizations and Statutory Authority*, November, 1964.

fifths of the areas failed to show any significant improvement as a result of the circulars[1].

This does not necessarily mean that there have been no developments in the use made of voluntary workers in these areas, but it does mean that there is little information available about such developments as have taken place, or about the number and type of volunteers likely to be needed in the future. Such information as there is comes from sources other than co-ordinating committees. It comes on the one hand from the Ministry Circulars, which suggest a large number and variety of jobs which could be done by volunteers, and on the other from certain voluntary bodies which, at national or local level, have themselves supplied information about openings and opportunities and have expressed their own ability and readiness to recruit and train the people needed to carry out these voluntary jobs.

Guides to voluntary service

The London Council of Social Service published in 1962 a booklet entitled *Some Opportunities for Voluntary Social Service in London*, which listed sixty-five types of work awaiting volunteers, and grouped the organizations making use of them into ten categories according to their main purpose. This booklet has been brought up to date at intervals and the most recent edition (1967) lists no less than 104 types of work and fourteen categories of organizations. Even allowing for some double counting when one type of work appears under more than one heading, this is a most impressive list and leaves no doubt that there are many opportunities for service in London.

The National Council of Social Service produced a considerably longer booklet, *A Guide to Voluntary Service*, by David Hobman, published by H.M. Stationery Office in 1964. This resembles the London guide in that it groups opportunities for service into categories, but differs from it in that it has no

[1] Mr. Harrison's contention is supported by evidence from Halifax, where the author conducted a brief inquiry on behalf of the National Council of Social Service, published as *Nacoss Occasional Papers No. 1. A Study of Halifax*, by Mary Morris. It is interesting to note, too, that in spite of Sir Alfred Owen's views his authority (Staffordshire) does not appear to have co-operated well. S. Staffs. was in Group 2 and N. Staffs. did not reply.

index of types of work. It is thus not possible to quote an overall figure to correspond with that given by the London guide and the total cannot be worked out from the information given since many types of work are available in two or more fields of service. In spite of this, it is a useful and comprehensive guide.

The following summary gives some idea of the wide range of opportunity for voluntary service covered by the guide. The information is grouped under fifteen headings: under *Marriage and the Family* ten associations which use volunteers are mentioned; under *Children* there are nine general headings of the type of work available; and under *Youth: Service by Adults* there are four. Under *Health* the list of fifty-four tasks given by the Ministry of Health in Circular 7/62 is repeated; under *The Elderly* there is a list of eighteen (most of which also appear in the Health list), under *Amenities* there are seven general headings and under *Community Organization* there are four. Under *Prisoners and After-Care* reference is made to seven organizations. Useful information is also given about opportunities for service in the Churches, through *Membership Organizations*, and with statutory bodies under the following headings – *Living Safely* (accident prevention), *National Savings*, *Civil Defence*, *Armed Forces Volunteer Reserves*. There is also a section on *Overseas Service*.

No special mention is made of unpaid public work in local government, hospital management or the magistracy, probably because these are fields in which the voluntary worker must be either elected or appointed and cannot himself simply decide to serve. Nor is there any discussion of the work of bodies specifically designed as pressure groups. It is true that some of the organizations which are noted do incidentally provide for the activities of reformers, but *ad hoc* bodies whose primary aim is to promote a cause are excluded. Such groups are usually formed by determined people who know what they want to do and how they want to do it and who do not expect to recruit supporters through a guide of this kind.

Other sources of information

Further information has been obtained from the voluntary bodies through a number of studies sponsored by the National

Council of Social Service and by various local Councils[1]. The first of these was *A Preliminary Inquiry into Recruitment and Training by Voluntary Associations in the Social Service Field* by G. M. Williams (1962). This was based on interviews with senior officers of nine national voluntary organizations: British Red Cross Society, Toc. H., Women's Voluntary Service, Soldiers', Sailors' and Airmen's Families Association, National Marriage Guidance Council, National Association for Mental Health, Invalid Children's Aid Association, National Children's Home, South Regional Association for the Blind. This short document does not give information about numbers – either actually at work or likely to be needed later – but it reveals a general satisfaction on the part of the national organizations with the present level of recruitment and lack of anxiety about the future. It is true that these societies did not know what additional work they might be called upon to undertake, yet two of them (the B.R.C.S. and the W.R.V.S.), which already employed large numbers of voluntary workers, had felt able to emphasize, at the Conference called by the Ministry of Health in February of the same year, 'that their constituent and local bodies will not fail to respond to a call for more voluntary workers' and were confident 'that an increased number of able and reliable voluntary workers can be forthcoming'[2]. Under the circumstances this must have been largely an expression of faith since they knew neither how many nor what kinds of volunteer they were likely to need, nor had they apparently given much thought to how they would be recruited. It appears, too, from the above quotation, that the national bodies were relying on people in the field to carry out the pledge given at headquarters[3]. In order to try and ascertain what this pledge meant in practice it was therefore necessary to have a look at what the voluntary bodies concerned were thinking and doing at local level,

---

[1] The British Federation of University Women also undertook (in 1966) a limited inquiry into the voluntary work being done by graduate women. See C. E. Arregger, *Graduate Women at Work*, Chapter 16.

[2] Ministry of Health, Circs. 7/62, paragraph 5.

[3] In fact a number of Cs.S.S. did take the lead in approaching local authorities about the formation of co-ordinating committees as suggested in the circular – see above, p. 9.

and this is what the *Preliminary Inquiry* suggests should be done. In fact, however, there was much less follow-up than had been hoped and only one small pilot survey was completed.

This was published by the N.C.S.S. in 1964 as *Nacoss Occasional Papers No. 1. A Study of Halifax*, concerned with the recruitment training and deployment of volunteers in the Social Services. While this was being undertaken on behalf of the N.C.S.S. research was also going on elsewhere. In Hampstead the C.S.S. produced two reports for private circulation on *Research into the selection, placing and training of voluntary social workers* (1966). In York the Community Council published *Voluntary Workers in York* (1965) and in Portsmouth the College of Technology, in conjunction with the Council of Social Service, carried out a survey with *Attitudes towards Voluntary Work in the City of Portsmouth* (1965). In the same year the Yorkshire Council of Social Service set up working parties on *Co-operation in the Health and Welfare Services* and the *Recruitment and Training of Voluntary Workers*. The former issued its report in September 1968, the latter hopes to complete its deliberations early in 1969. In Manchester Youth and Community Service (M.Y.C.S.), in conjunction with the Aves *Committee on Voluntary Workers in the Social Services*, undertook a survey to evaluate the extent of preparation and training for voluntary workers in Manchester. A full report was to be published in 1968. A student from the University, Mr. D. J. Rice, also undertook a survey entitled *Some Aspects of Voluntary Workers* which examined the records and structure of M.Y.C.S. The Nottingham C.S.S. has issued a number of reports about the recruitment, allocation and training of voluntary workers. This Council has made a special point of this aspect of its work and has successfully recruited and allocated volunteers for a wide variety of tasks, including old people's welfare, help in hospitals, care of unsupported mothers and neighbourhood work. A brief account of its achievements in this neighbourhood work is given in Chapter VII below. The N.C.S.S. has no knowledge of any other systematic inquiries on the subject which are being undertaken at the present time, but it has collected some interesting information from local Councils for inclusion in the forthcoming report of the Aves Committee. On the particular question of training there is some information available at national level as the N.C.S.S. publishes a list giving details of general courses, and the National Old People's Welfare Council devotes a section of its annual reports to the subject.

The local inquiries into the position of voluntary work not surprisingly reveal rather less confidence in their ability to 'deliver the goods' on the part of the people in the field than had been expressed by those at headquarters interviewed for the *Preliminary Inquiry*, and as time goes on they may become even more doubtful about the future because of the lack of effective machinery for working out with their local authorities what jobs they ought to be tackling, and how many volunteers they will need to recruit and train.

Halifax, Hampstead, York, Portsmouth, Yorkshire

The Halifax survey was based on personal interviews with representatives of nineteen voluntary organizations. The consensus of opinion among them seemed to be 'that there is likely to be a shortage of people prepared to undertake responsibility either as leaders of voluntary societies or as voluntary workers with rather special personal contacts with individuals, such as M.G.C., C.A.B., C.S.S., Samaritans, though there seem to be reserves of people prepared to do unskilled work if they do not feel too much is going to be expected of them.' The officers of the local authority, on the other hand, thought that there was an actual shortage for present needs, especially in the visiting services. Visiting, though certainly not 'unskilled', was not among the types of work for which the voluntary bodies themselves feared a shortage.

In Hampstead twenty-four organizations using volunteers were studied over a period of nineteen months. There was 'a constant though fluctuating demand for volunteers on the part of the organizations' and a 'steady flow of volunteers coming forward'. In spite of this, however, the organizations were by no means always sure how best to use the volunteers and there seemed to be increasing difficulty in fulfilling the more menial tasks. This conflicts with the evidence from Halifax where there seemed to be reserves of people for this kind of work. The Hampstead survey showed the value of a Central Bureau to bring organizations and volunteers together, to arrange informal training and to keep in touch with volunteers after placement.

The York survey was a more ambitious project. It aimed at covering volunteers connected with all the voluntary and statutory organizations in the town, and attempted to estimate the number of people involved. This was no easy task in view of the absence of accurate statistics, an absence which it describes as the main gap in its report[1]. 'It has proved extremely difficult to get answers to the questions that would have thrown most light on the subject in quantitative terms . . . Totals are available, but some of these are inaccurate, being estimates in some cases: in others, it was difficult to discover the proportion of members who were active. In addition there is considerable double counting due to some people's working in more than one organization. A direct approach to volunteers themselves is the only way to elicit this information accurately[2].

On the question of numbers it is interesting to compare the estimates reached in this survey of York with those given in *Social Enterprise*[3], an earlier study of Halifax, a town of roughly similar size. Though *Social Enterprise*, unlike *Voluntary Workers in York*, was not primarily a study of the place of voluntary workers in the community and was not directly concerned with making recommendations as to recruitment if their numbers were insufficient, it contains a certain amount of information about numbers which is comparable to that which is included in the York survey. The total given for York is 1821, made up of 429 men, 888 women and 504 whose sex is not recorded. The grand total is remarkably similar to that in Halifax (2,111), though here the sexes were more evenly divided (1,001 men and 1,110 women)[4].

---

[1] *Voluntary Workers in York*, p. 2.

[2] *Ibid.*, p. 85. An attempt to do this has been made in a survey recently carried out in Bradford. See Appendix III.

[3] *Social Enterprise.* A study of the activities of voluntary societies and voluntary workers in an industrial town, by Mary Morris, 1962. This is not to be confused with *Nacoss Occasional Papers No. 1. A Study of Halifax* (1964). Halifax was chosen for the second study because of the knowledge gained of the place during the author's work for *Social Enterprise*.

[4] *Op. cit.*, p. 90.

Though the two surveys are not strictly comparable, since they were carried out by different methods and did not both cover all the same organizations, the similarity is striking. The main differences were that the York survey included local authorities which make use of volunteers, whereas these were excluded in Halifax, and that the Halifax survey included youth organizations which were excluded in York. This second difference may account for the greater proportion of men in Halifax since youth organizations tend to attract more men than most others. Neither survey claims statistical accuracy for its figures – in both cases they are given as estimates based on the information available. In the case of Halifax the total was calculated from information derived from forty-four out of ninety-seven social service organizations questioned. In York the number of organizations among the seventy-five questioned which failed to reply is not given but it is clear that here, too, the satisfactory replies were limited in number.

The fact that similar difficulties[1] were encountered in both places and that the estimates in both are based on information subject to the same kind of limitations makes it seem likely that the actual total in each place may be as similar as are the totals in the two surveys. Admittedly, this is matter for speculation, not certainty, but fortunately the important question for the future is not how many voluntary workers there are now, but whether there are enough of them for present and future needs. On this the York survey makes some useful points. It concludes that the numbers appear to be adequate for the tasks at present undertaken but emphasizes that there is work that badly needs to be done for which there is a shortage of recruits. 'The shortage is not of volunteers as such, in the form of recruits to existing organizations; but of organizations, specifically geared to recruiting and, where necessary, selecting and training to provide readily available and suitable workers in fields not already covered.' This need for a central agency which was emphasized in the reports from Hampstead is thus repeated in *Voluntary Workers in York*, which does not tire of stressing its importance in every field

[1] For descriptions of what these difficulties were see *Voluntary Workers in York*, p. 2, and *Social Enterprise*, p. 81.

of voluntary service[1] and returns to the subject in the very first paragraph of its *Recommendations*:

Organisation is the key to further growth of voluntary work in York, both in any new fields that are tackled and in consolidating work that has already been started[2].

The Portsmouth survey[3] set out to investigate 'the capacity and desire of the ordinary citizen to render voluntary service'. It covered three types of service: organized through voluntary bodies, spontaneous as between neighbours and friends, and private within the confines of family relationships.

The quota-sampling method was used and the 622 people interviewed were chosen to represent as accurately as possible the population of Portsmouth over the age of fifteen.

Twenty-nine per cent of the men and thirty-one per cent[4] of the women in the sample claimed to be doing some voluntary social work. The age groups up to fifty produced more volunteers than their proportion in the sample; those over fifty less. There was little indication that volunteers were to be found in one social class rather than another.

Among men about half the work claimed was being done on a private basis and half through organizations, while among women only a quarter was carried out through organizations. The men were mainly engaged in 'community and general' work, the women in the fields of marriage, children and the family. Health services and old people's welfare seemed to attract both sexes equally.

Those interviewed were also asked if they were prepared to do some (or more) social work and to this 186 replied 'yes'. Of those, 117 were new volunteers. The authors of the survey suggest that their findings have the following implications for

---

[1] *Voluntary Workers in York*, pp. 40 and 55.

[2] *Ibid.*, p. 92.

[3] *Attitudes towards Voluntary Social Work in the City of Portsmouth.*

[4] It is interesting to compare these figures with those produced in the Bradford survey (see Appendix III) where very similar numbers seem to be involved, though in Bradford the third type of help 'within the family' was specifically excluded. There are, however, differences between the two towns as regards the proportion of volunteers both in the various age groups and in the social classes. Incidentally, the Bradford survey covered adults only while Portsmouth included a sample of everyone over the age of fifteen.

recruitment: the largest potential source of volunteers of both sexes is in the thirty-five to forty-four age group; young people are more willing than the old to volunteer; social work as an activity for preparing men for retirement seems unlikely to succeed; recruitment through societies and clubs will be more likely to succeed than appeals to the general public.

The great value of this survey is that it supplies definite information about the voluntary workers in one city. It estimates their numbers, sex, age and social class and gives some idea of the kind of work they do. In addition it draws attention to the fact that a large number of people who are not yet involved in voluntary work are prepared to volunteer – more than half as many in fact as those who were already involved – and makes suggestions about recruitment based on its findings.

The Yorkshire study, *Co-operation in the Health and Welfare Services*, is equally valuable, though in a different way. It is not concerned to estimate the number of voluntary workers nor to describe what kind of people they are nor to consider recruitment, matters which form the subject of the other working party set up by the Yorkshire Council of Social Service. The aim of this study is 'to explore the nature and extent of present co-operation between the statutory bodies and voluntary organizations in the sphere of health and welfare services within the geographical County of Yorkshire; to encourage consultation in order that present work may be consolidated and new work initiated; to consider any work relevant to such consultation' – a task of considerable magnitude.

The report falls into three parts. The first explains that it was the publication of the Ministry of Health's Blue Book *Health and Welfare* which gave the real impetus to its work, since this emphasizes in no uncertain terms the importance of a proper relationship between statutory and voluntary bodies.

The development of community care, as proposed in the local authorities' plans, and the rate at which it can go forward, will be greatly influenced by the relationship which is established and maintained between statutory and voluntary effort. This will largely depend on the arrangements for regular consultation and the use which is made of them[1].

[1] *Health and Welfare, Cmnd.* 1973 (1963), paragraph 153.

The report goes on to explain that it proposes to tackle its subject by studying the social services for the four groups whose needs had been outlined by the Ministry – mothers and young children, the elderly, the mentally disordered and the physically handicapped. It then gives an account of the statutory health and welfare services in Yorkshire and proceeds 'to attempt to assess co-operation between social service agencies, voluntary and statutory'.

The second part presents three studies of patterns of co-operation in individual local authority areas, and the third part consists of comments and conclusions prompted by the findings of the working party.

The picture which emerges from this study is one of immense variety. There is no uniform pattern of co-operation throughout Yorkshire either between the various statutory departments or between them and the voluntary bodies. Nor are there similar relationships in the various fields of community care between statutory and voluntary bodies in the same place. The variations both in attitude and practice led the working party to conclude that there was no single 'best way' of ensuring effective community care in every district.

The lack of uniformity makes it difficult to estimate the extent of co-operation which exists in Yorkshire as a whole, but it is clear from the findings of this report that it is considerable. It is often taking place at personal and grass-roots level in spite of the general absence of machinery designed to foster it. The Ministry's emphasis on the importance of regular consultation has not led to the setting up of the kind of machinery suggested in its Circulars, but although there seems to be little evidence of regular consultation between representatives of all the statutory departments concerned on the one hand and all the relevant voluntary bodies on the other, there are many examples of contacts between individual departments and particular voluntary bodies and also between officers and social workers in one field with their opposite numbers in the other which are both frequent and fruitful. Much depends, at ground level, on the attitude of key people on both sides. The key people on the statutory side may be elected members or officials or workers in the field: on the voluntary side they may be either representatives of organizations with concern for a particular category of need or individual volunteers in positions of influence.

The strength of the ties between people on both sides who are actually involved in giving service often achieves more in the way of practical co-operation than official meetings between people who are further removed from the field of action. Though it is disappointing that the Ministry's suggestions for regular consultation have not been more generally adopted, since this would strengthen the hands of those who are trying to work together in the field and would facilitate constructive planning for the future, it is satisfactory that this failure has not meant a general failure to co-operate. On the contrary the findings of the working party show that there is considerable co-operation at ground level and that where it is working well those in receipt of community care are reaping the benefit. What is needed is to bring this care everywhere and in every branch up to the level of the best. In some places the best way of doing this may be to strengthen and extend existing ground-level contacts: in others more official machinery may be essential. Where machinery for more general co-operation is planned this must be acceptable to the people who are actually doing the work if it is to be effective, and should therefore be built on the foundation of any successful informal co-operation that already exists.

A careful study of this report should help people both in Yorkshire and elsewhere to work out ways and means of strengthening the co-operation on which the future effectiveness of community care depends.

The information derived from the Blue Books and Circulars of the Ministry of Health, from the N.C.S.S. and from guides to voluntary service and finally from these special studies of voluntary work makes it clear that voluntary effort is an essential part of community care. Yet no definite picture emerges of what that part is now or what it should be in the future when the whole field of health and welfare is considered together. This is partly because, as the Yorkshire working party stresses, there is no uniform pattern of co-operation between statutory and voluntary bodies, either from one place to another or in respect of different branches of community care.

A somewhat clearer picture of what is actually happening and of what is needed for the future should emerge if each of the four groups – mothers and young children, the elderly, the mentally disordered and the physically handicapped – is studied separately. These studies form the subject of the next four sections.

2

MOTHERS AND YOUNG CHILDREN

Welfare services for mothers and young children can be divided into two groups – those which are provided for all through hospitals and local authorities and those which cater for special categories and are not universally available, which are still in the main provided by voluntary bodies.

Statutory services

It is now the statutory duty of the local authority to maintain and staff the maternity and child welfare service, and though voluntary workers are still attached to many of the clinics and centres they are no longer essential to their functioning.

The high standard of these services is a tribute to the voluntary bodies whose pioneering work convinced the public of the value and indeed the necessity of a universal statutory service if infant life was to be saved; what was achieved by groups of enthusiasts in different parts of the country showed what could be done to save the lives and improve the health of mothers and babies. Many of the pioneers were lay people, but from the first they had the support of individual doctors and nurses; and the foundations of a service run by professionals were early laid[1]. This meant that as and when the clinics became more widespread it was taken for granted that they should rely on trained medical and nursing staff, and throughout the period when they were operated by voluntary bodies

---

[1] Health visiting was first organized by a voluntary body – The Manchester and Salford Ladies Sanitary Reform Association, founded in 1862.

21

and partly staffed by volunteers the medical and nursing care was in the hands of doctors and nurses. This made it easier to dispense with the voluntary element when in 1946 responsibility for the service passed to the local authority. Some authorities made no use of voluntary workers, but many were glad to retain the services of members of local Babies' Welcome and Babies' Welfare Committees who had helped to run the clinics when they were under voluntary management, and many, too, recruited new volunteers.

An investigation undertaken in 1947 by the National Association for Maternity and Child Welfare Centres[1] showed that there was considerable variation both in the use made of voluntary help and in the esteem in which it was held. The majority of the local authorities which supplied information were glad to have volunteers for the general ordering of clinical and clerical work, and, to a lesser extent, for the weighing of babies, and the National Association concluded that the attitude towards volunteers was generally favourable, and that the demand for them would continue[2]. No information as to what has in fact happened is available from the National Association itself since it does not keep records of the numbers and activities of voluntary workers in the various regions. It is, however, in touch with a network of local associations which are run by voluntary committees, some members of which almost certainly help in the clinics. More information about helpers in the clinics can be obtained from the organizations which provide them, chief among which are the B.R.C.S., and the W.R.V.S. The B.R.C.S. are able to provide helpers with training in nursing and first aid, and in 1967 were giving regular help in 493 child welfare and pre- and post-natal clinics in England and Wales[3]. The W.R.V.S. 'gives help at ante-natal clinics and maternity and child welfare clinics, by weighing babies, making teas, doing clerical work'[4]. No statement is made as to the number of

---

[1] Now the National Association for Maternal and Child Welfare.

[2] See M. Rooff, *Voluntary Societies and Social Policy*, p. 71. This book contains a full account of the development of the maternal and child welfare movement.

[3] *Annual Report* for 1967, p. 51.

[4] *Women's Royal Voluntary Service Bulletin*, June, 1968, p. 21.

places where such help is given but the W.R.V.S. is known to be responsible for the distribution of welfare foods at 500 different points.

Altogether several thousand voluntary workers must be involved in various ways at the clinics of the local authorities and they must be helping considerably to lighten the load of the professional staff[1]. Yet, valuable and extensive though it is, this work is only of marginal importance since the service is not dependent on its existence. The position is very different in the case of work with special categories of mothers and babies, since here voluntary organizations and voluntary workers are playing a major role both in running existing services and in promoting new ventures.

Voluntary services

The three main categories for which some special provision is made are unsupported mothers, problem families and children under school age.

1 *Unsupported mothers*

Unsupported mothers, be they widows, deserted wives or single women, have always been and still are inadequately cared for, in spite of the efforts of voluntary bodies and interested individuals and of increasing support from statutory services. The efforts of the voluntary bodies have been concentrated on helping unmarried mothers, but it is well to remember that these are far less important numerically than widows and deserted wives. Of the 540,000 unsupported mothers in Great Britain, only 60,000 are unmarried while 175,000 are widowed, 55,000 divorced and 250,000 separated[2]. It is true that the unmarried mother is more likely to need help during

---

[1] But since the *Annual Report of the Ministry of Health* for 1965 (*Cmnd. 3039*) states, 'The number of premises in use as ante-natal and post-natal clinics and child welfare centres at the end of the year was 6,376', there must be a very large number where neither B.R.C.S. nor W.R.V.S. supply volunteers.

[2] See Margaret Wynn, *Fatherless Families*, p. 181, Appendix 1, and Anthony Denney, *Children in Need*, p. 184 et seq.

her pregnancy and confinement and that she, unlike the widow and deserted wife, will have to face the question of adoption, and it is these problems with which the national bodies are mainly concerned. But there is work to be done by volunteers not only with single women but also with widows and deserted wives. Though these mothers have had a husband at any rate for part of their lives and are likely to have some support from relatives and friends, and though they do not have to part with their children as do so many unmarried mothers, they usually have a very hard and often lonely life. Most widows are poor and their pensions are small, while deserted wives often receive nothing from their husbands and cannot draw a pension. Voluntary workers cannot do much to improve the financial position, but they can do a great deal to combat loneliness by neighbourly help.

Work for the unmarried mother is undertaken at national level by the National Council for the Unmarried Mother and her Child, the Moral Welfare Council and the Adoption Societies. These organizations apparently make less use of volunteers now that they employ more trained workers, though they are still dependent on them to a considerable extent. At local level, there are many groups concerned with the social needs of their own neighbourhoods, some independent, others attached to a church or women's organization, and these are often entirely run by volunteers. Though it is hard to discover how much they are actually doing, or to visualize what arrangements could be made to increase the extent and the quality of their work, it is clearly the case that too little is being done. More should be offered to the unmarried mother than material help, important though this is. If she is unsupported by the father of her baby or by other relatives she needs more than shelter, money and medical care: she needs understanding from the community, and personal support from at least a few members of it. This support is the role of the good neighbour, and therefore should not really need organizing, but neighbours do not always play their part without prompting. Fortunately many such mothers do receive spontaneous help, but many, too, are lonely and isolated during their pregnancies because it is nobody's business to befriend them, and are left to face the world alone after the birth of their babies because no one takes the opportunity to put them in touch with kindly help. The staff of Mother and Baby homes are not often able to give all the support that is needed, certainly after the mothers leave their care. Nor do the officers of the adoption societies provide long-term assistance since they are primarily concerned with the baby and the adopting parents. Moreover the great majority of unmarried expectant mothers do not go into homes – the Church of England Committee for Diocesan Moral and Social Welfare Councils estimates that only fourteen per cent wish to do so – and they also need help. They often need accommodation and they always need friendship.

Some valuable work is being done, still on a small and experimental scale, to try to meet these needs. It may be quite informal, with no office, staff or even committee, like the scheme at Cookham described in the *Guardian*[1] or an ambitious scheme like Family First, launched by a group of enthusiasts in Nottingham. The Cookham scheme was started by a vicar's wife who keeps a register of families prepared to take in pregnant teenage girls who have been disowned by their own people. These are girls 'who live away from home and their parents refuse to have anything to do with them when they become pregnant; so they disappear into London to hide or seek an illegal abortion'. The scheme started after the vicar and his wife had taken in a girl who had been thrown out of her home – 'the word went around the grapevine and since then there have been ten or more girls'.

Family First is 'a new trust which aims to bring new hope and fresh purpose to families who do not need charity but practical help to enable them to help themselves'[2]. Its initial scheme is to 'assist unsupported mothers by offering independent flatlets at an economic but non-profit-making rent and will include a nursery where children will be well cared for while their mothers work. Each mother will have full responsibility for her child and the running of her home'. It 'counts an expectant unmarried mother as a family unit and will offer accommodation to unmarried mothers who need it, not only for the few weeks before and after giving birth to

[1] *Guardian*, 21st July, 1966.
[2] *Family First Trust*, The Croft, Alexandra Park, Nottingham.

their child, but for several months before and as long as is needed after'. Widows and deserted mothers will also be eligible, and it is hoped that the project 'will provide valuable experience for future housing schemes which offer families maximum independence PLUS short-term support necessary for their long-term survival as family units'. Family First has secured grants from charitable trusts and is planning to become self-supporting. It has started without a paid warden, the management of the project being in the hands of a normal family living on the premises whose breadwinner husband goes out to work. The whole burden thus rests, at least in its early stages, on volunteers, and the pioneers of the project have not only worked hard themselves but recruited many helpers, have created great public interest and have, moreover, stimulated those who have themselves been helped to help others. This enthusiasm and mixing of helpers and helped is one of the most exciting features of the scheme. Clearly such schemes, and there are others[1], involve a tremendous amount of voluntary effort, both initially and later, and depend on people who are prepared to give time and effort not only to the business side but also in personal service as good neighbours and friends. These are ambitious schemes, but people of goodwill need not wait for something of the kind to be started in their neighbourhood – they can help lonely mothers by asking them to their homes, by baby-sitting and by offering temporary accommodation, though it is usually necessary to have some form of organization so that people who are anxious to help can be put in touch with those who need them. This may be very simple, as at Cookham, but even here the accommodation would not have been offered and accepted had there been no example set and no register kept.

Some opportunities for service to unsupported mothers can still be found in the well-established voluntary bodies which have been caring for them for years. This service does not usually take the form of personal contacts with mothers, but rather of committee work, money raising and rousing public

[1] Eighteen projects of this kind were known to the author (Jill Nicholson) of *Mother and Baby Homes* (1968), and others were being planned during the period of her survey.

interest. There are also opportunities in connection with running the Mother and Baby homes provided by voluntary organizations, and a considerable number of volunteers help in this way. Since the work of the homes is expected to stay for some time in voluntary hands[1] the need for help will continue. These volunteers are no substitute for trained workers, whose numbers are fortunately increasing both in statutory and in voluntary agencies. But trained workers are still in short supply and their time is limited; and though some mothers may prefer to seek help from them rather than from volunteers there must be many cases where friendship from an untrained helper could be a most valuable and appreciated addition. Adoption societies, too, make some use of volunteers[2], especially of church members. They may be consulted professionally as doctors, lawyers, teachers or social workers, they may help with interviewing prospective adopters, or provide transport, or give neighbourly help.

Personal service from good neighbours is greatly needed by unsupported mothers whether they be widows or deserted wives, lonely and bringing up their family single-handed, or unmarried women who have to decide whether or not to keep their children. If they keep their babies they will often need long-term support, and if they let them go both they and the adopting parents will often need more continuing care than can be supplied by the officers of the adoption society or local authority. It is not possible to give the number of volunteers who are now helping in these different ways, but it is certain that more are needed. Improvement in financial provision, in hospital care and in residential accommodation are all essential and must in the main come from statutory sources, but these alone are not enough. Greater understanding by the community and friendly support from its individual members are also needed, and these are the contribution of

---

[1] The importance of what is being done by the voluntary bodies is recognized by the Ministry of Health and taken into account in its future plans – see *Health and Welfare*, Cmnd. 1973, p. 12: 'the voluntary organizations experienced in this work will no doubt continue for a long time to make the major contribution'. Out of the 172 known homes, 138 are provided by Church organizations. (ref. Jill Nicholson, *op. cit.*, p. 17).

[2] D. H. Hobman, *Guide to Voluntary Service*, p. 16.

the volunteer. Only with the help of volunteers can contacts between residential homes and the community be strengthened and these contacts are of great value to both residents and staff[1].

2 *Problem families*

Some families are overwhelmed by the problems of everday living. Their difficulties may be due to one or more of many causes, such as bad housing, poverty, large families, ill health, mental incapacity, fecklessness, improvidence or crime, and the result is misery, hopelessness and debt. Help from outside is needed with budgeting, house cleaning, health advice, and caring for children, if debts are to be cleared, health improved and better housing found. A voluntary organization, Family Service Units, exists to render help of this kind. Though these units employ trained staff and are sometimes well supported financially by local authorities they rely on voluntary help for committee work and money raising and in some cases for personal service also. Their task is hard and often unrewarding since many of the families they serve are unable to manage without long-term and sometimes indefinitely continued help. The staff have heavy case loads and often need encouragement and active co-operation from members of the communities in which they work. The overall number of volunteers involved is small but more will be needed if the number of units grows. There are still (1968) only seventeen units in the whole country and an increase in their number will depend on increased voluntary effort. The few units already at work owe their existence to small groups of pioneers, and more pioneers will be needed if more are to be formed. But though comparatively few voluntary workers have so far been involved their efforts have been out of all proportion to their numbers. They have had to struggle to convince the public of the value of the work and they, like the staff, have had to persevere in the face of difficulties and disappointments.

3 *Children under school age: playgroups*

These are groups of children under school age 'who regularly

[1] Jill Nicholson, *op. cit.*, pp. 80 and 93.

play together, under the supervision of adults trained to be sensitive to their needs'[1]. They are especially valuable for children who live in high flats or overcrowded conditions and wherever there is special danger from traffic, and also for those whose mothers go out to work or who are ill and over-burdened. But there are few children anywhere who would not benefit from the opportunity of playing with others and with exciting toys.

The pioneer in this field was the Save the Children Fund (S.C.F.). Starting from small beginnings, during the second world war, the number of playgroups which they have planned and supervised had in 1967 risen to eighty. These groups have been started at the request of local people with a concern for the young children in their neighbourhood. Thus, though the groups are run and supervised by paid staff, they owe their existence to the action of volunteers.

The Fund has also started groups for the under fives in hospitals, and in the adventure playgrounds for older children which it has itself promoted[2], and in these some use is made of voluntary help.

In spite of the development of its work in these different ways the Fund realizes that what it can do is small in relation to the need, and feels that the provision of supervised play facilities should no longer be left to a charitable organization[3]. Its evidence to the Plowden Committee[4] was doubtless a factor in that committee's recommendations for an increase in nursery schools and classes.

Some mothers, however, are not prepared to wait for the government, and action by a handful of enthusiasts has resulted in a nation-wide movement – The National Association of Pre-School Playgroups.

These groups were started in 1961 as the direct result of one mother's letter to the press welcoming inquiries 'from mothers and teachers who would like to create their own solutions to

---

[1] *What about Playgroups?* Issued by the National Association of Pre-School Playgroups, 87a Borough High St. S.E.1.

[2] See below, p. 100.

[3] See *The Neglected Age Groups*, by Eglantine M. Jebb, reprinted from the *World's Children*, 1964 Summer Quarterly of the S.C.F.

[4] *Children and their Primary Schools*, H.M.S.O. (1967), Chapter 9.

their problems' and there are now (1968) some 3,000 of them caring for children between the ages of two and a half and five for at least one day a week.

The groups are almost entirely dependent on voluntary effort. Although about three-quarters of the supervisors receive some payment, this is usually only a nominal amount, and they are supported everywhere by unpaid helpers. Volunteers also work hard at raising money, and are responsible, too, for arranging parent meetings and training courses and for liaison work with local authorities. The work of the association itself is also largely in the hands of volunteers, since there are only two part-time staff to deal with press publicity, contact with the 4,000 members, and the·despatch of the magazine[1].

This movement is an attempt by parents to fill the gap left by the scarcity of nursery education, and was in the first place a self-help project. But it is much more than this. It is true that most groups owe their existence to the efforts of parents on behalf of their own and their neighbours' children, unlike those sponsored by the S.C.F. which are usually started at the request of individuals and committees concerned with the children of others; but many of these parent-formed groups include a few children who cannot afford fees, and the movement as a whole is outward looking. Efforts are being made by the more enterprising groups to help parents in under-privileged areas, and at national level to press for the extension of nursery education, for which they do not consider their playgroups are an adequate substitute[2]. Moreover, much of the work of the association is carried out by mothers whose own children have passed the nursery age.

The rapid growth in the number of groups shows what can be achieved by voluntary effort where the need for a service is keenly felt, and there seems little prospect of its being met by statutory means. But though 3,000 groups in seven years is a

[1] Ref. letter to the author from the business manager of *Contact*, the magazine of the P.P.A., 25th September, 1968.

[2] *What about Playgroups?* The Chairman of the Executive of the Association in a letter to the *Guardian* (26th September, 1966) writes: 'While we recognize the important community service that playgroups can provide, both for children and their parents, we strive to bring to public notice the needs of children under five, and these include part-time and full-time nursery schools and classes.'

fine achievement, the very success of the movement creates a challenge for the future. If so many have been formed by local initiative, why not more? Even if there are more, and there may well be groups unconnected with the national association, the total number is certainly small in comparison with the need. Children everywhere would benefit from the opportunities that are now open to those who attend existing groups. The need is especially great where there are difficult living conditions or invalid or working mothers, but it exists everywhere. The great majority of children in this age group need to be able to play together under supervision in groups of this kind, where there are no nursery schools or classes for them.

Moreover, the value is not restricted to the children. Parents, and especially mothers, benefit, not only by having more leisure and a little much-needed respite from infant company – they gain from contacts with the outside world. The problem of the isolation of the young mother is emphasized by Hannah Gavron in *The Captive Wife*[1]. The working-class mother in her survey no longer enjoyed the 'street life' which, as the author says, depends on 'a stable population, familiar with the area and its inhabitants, a street-level front door, reasonable safety from traffic, and perhaps most important of all a large number of home-based women, available during the day'. The street used to provide the opportunity for social intercourse as well as a place for play. 'Children's play was a constant source of worry to 77 per cent of the mothers involved in trying to keep their children under five happy in two rooms.' Clearly mothers in this situation would benefit enormously from playgroups. They would be freed from anxiety about their children's lack of play, they would gain from the contacts made through the groups, and would be free for at least a few hours a week to enjoy outside interests and to lessen their feeling of isolation. Those who are helping to provide playgroups for their own and their neighbours' children, and more especially for the children of less privileged mothers, and those who are pressing for the extension of nursery education are doing as much for these isolated women as for their play-starved children.

[1] Pp. 132-3, 1966 edition – now (1968) also in a Penguin. See also A. Denney, *Children in Need*.

Family planning

This is another service which is still largely in the hands of voluntary bodies and which makes considerable use of volunteers. It differs from work for unsupported mothers, for problem families and for playgroups in that it is not restricted to special categories of people, but resembles it in not being everywhere available. Its necessity and even its desirability is even now by no means universally accepted, and in some places voluntary committees have to struggle for financial support and recognition; yet its help is sought by rich and poor, healthy and sick, married and unmarried, though public opinion is still divided as to whether it should be provided for the latter. It has recently become available under the Health Service, though the necessary machinery has not yet been set up everywhere[1]. Under the new arrangements the part played by voluntary bodies and unpaid workers will change, and as in the case of other services pioneered by voluntary bodies and taken over by the State it will change in different ways in different places.

The Family Planning Association is the body responsible at national level for the work of some 340 clinics which are controlled by 270 branches. It is possible to give a more accurate account of the work of volunteers in this association than in almost any other, since it set up a working party to review the aims and objects, constitution, organization and services of the Association, to consider how these might be brought further into line with present requirements, and to make recommendations to the National Executive'[2], which

---

[1] Under the National Health (Family Planning) Act 1967 local authorities are directed by the Minister of Health to make arrangements for the giving of advice on contraception. The implementation of this act is now (early 1968) under consideration by local authorities who are asked by the Minister to plan the provision of services jointly with representatives of hospital authorities, general practitioners and the Family Planning Association, or other voluntary bodies concerned to ensure the availability of a comprehensive service in all areas. (Circ. 15/67, Ministry of Health, 31 July, 1967).

[2] *Family Planning in the Sixties* – As a result of the recommendations of this report an extensive reorganization has taken place and there are now about 700 clinics run by fifty-one branches. The reorganization will probably lead to the employment of a greater number of paid workers, but it is unlikely to lead to a decrease in the number of voluntary workers, and as the service expands more will be needed.

reported as recently as 1963. This working party, under the chairmanship of Professor F. Lafitte, undertook a most detailed review and published a lengthy report. Although the work of the volunteer is only a small part of the field under review, this part, like the rest, has been treated in sufficient detail to make it a most valuable source of information. A whole chapter is devoted to the branches and their workers. It estimates their numbers and describes who they are, and what they do. From this it appears that there are 5,330 active workers[1], all but 530 of whom are women, mostly in the 40–50 age group[2]. They are for the most part middle class – nine in every ten come from the non-manual classes – and the majority (six in every ten) of committee members are non-employed wives. In fact the chief reservoir of unpaid labour is 'the wives of business or professional men, generally of fairly high social standing, with time and resources to give voluntary service'[3]. Quite a number of the professional staff also give some unpaid service[4]. An interesting point is the extent to which voluntary clinic workers and committee members are the same people. More than half the members of the governing bodies are clinic workers, while two-thirds of the clinic workers are members of their governing body.

The work they do is well described in their clinic handbook which devotes a special section to 'layworkers' and gives guidance as to what they do and how they should set about it. Starting with the sentence 'The patient's well-being is the first consideration' it goes on to stress the importance of a kindly atmosphere and the confidential and private nature of the work. Most of the points made are relevant to other forms of social work, but they are not always sufficiently stressed in training nor always well observed by either professional or voluntary workers. The handbook mentions the three main tasks which are undertaken by volunteers – reception and interviewing, sales and checking of stock, and keeping of records, and describes

---

[1] *Op. cit.*, Chapter 5, p. 5.

[2] The information about age comes from a letter to the author from the secretary of the F.P.A. (9th Jan., 1967).

[3] *Op. cit.*, Chapter 5, page 12.

[4] *Op. cit.*, Chapter 4, page 12.

briefly what each involves, setting out in shortened form the relevant material in the Lafitte report.

The Lafitte report itself is a most valuable source of information on the whole subject of voluntary workers in one special field of social work – no other group of volunteers has yet been analysed and described in quite this way. It is not, however, possible to treat the workers in the Family Planning Association as typical since the kind of work it does is in some respects so different from other forms of social work. The value of the Lafitte report for the study of voluntary workers as a whole is not that it provides data from which general conclusions can be drawn, but that it is a model of the kind of inquiry needed in other fields of social work.

This brief account of what is being done to help mothers and young children shows that although many thousands of volunteers are actively and usefully involved, only a fraction of the need is being met. Much more could and should be done by volunteers. They can back up professional workers, by acting as good neighbours to unsupported mothers, and they can help to fill the yawning chasm left by inadequate provision of opportunities to play for all young children who need them. These are two directions in which the extent of what needs to be done, and what could be done by volunteers, is almost unlimited, but in other directions, too – as in the care of problem families and in family planning – more help is also needed.

3

THE ELDERLY

Sources of information

There is more information available about voluntary work with the elderly than with mothers and young children because a national organization, the Old People's Welfare Council (N.O.P.W.C.) is in direct touch with Old People's Welfare Committees throughout the country and these in their turn are, to a greater or lesser extent, aware of what is going on in their own districts. The N.O.P.W.C. was formed in 1940 'to bring together in consultation national voluntary organizations working for the welfare of old people, with representatives of government departments, local authority associations, local old people's welfare committees and individuals with special experience, to study the needs of old people and to encourage and promote measures for their well-being'. It seeks to assess every three years the extent of the services provided for the elderly by the voluntary organizations, its most recent survey having been carried out in 1965[1]. It also publishes a useful quarterly bulletin and has been responsible, with the National Council of Social Service, for many valuable publications about old age. Another organization, the National Corporation for the Care of Old People (N.C.C.O.P.), undertakes research into the subject, some of which bears directly on the use of voluntary workers. Research on many different aspects of the subject is also undertaken by other research institutions, by universities, by local authorities and hospitals, by O.P.W. committees and by other miscellaneous organizations and individuals[2].

The survey of services for the elderly undertaken by the N.O.P.W.C. was carried out by means of a questionnaire to 1,486 O.P.W. committees[3] throughout the United Kingdom. The questionnaire was in two parts, the first covering staffing and finance and the second services provided. Unfortunately the response rate was not high[4], since only 57·8 per cent of

---

[1] *Survey of Services for the Elderly provided by Voluntary Organizations*, 1965, N.O.P.W.C., 26, Bedford Square, W.C.1.

[2] For details see *Old Age*, a Register of Social Research, published by the National Corporation for the Care of Old People, 1960 and Supplement, 1964.

[3] The discrepancy between this figure and those given in the *Annual Reports of the N.O.P.W.C.* (1,537 in 1965 and 1,528 in 1966) is due to the fact that some of the organizations listed in the reports were clubs and not committees, and also to the fact that some smaller committees in Scotland were not included in the survey (see *Survey*, p. 6). The figure 1,486 was that of committees known to the national body on 31st December, 1964. The latest published figure is 1,552 (for March, 1968) (see N.O.P.W.C. Annual Report for year ending 31st March, 1968, p. 4.)

[4] The reasons given by the author for this poor response are, first, a general reluctance on the part of the committees, especially those with no paid staff, to answer questionnaires, combining a feeling that they 'don't see the point of them' with a view that doing unpaid work is enough without filling in forms about it, and, second, that the officers to whom the job of filling in questionnaires falls are often uncertain as to how to do it properly.

the committees returned one or other or both parts, 52·6 per cent the first, and 50·3 per cent the second. Moreover, the quality of the response is described as 'rather poor' and the comment is made that in many cases care was not taken in reading the questions and in many more they were totally ignored. No claim is made that the statistics accurately represent the picture for the whole country, but what is claimed, and justifiably, is that 'the material shows the range and scope of voluntary contribution in this sphere of social service'[1] and 'presents a general picture of the work for interested members of the public and those planning future services'[2]. This is true in spite of the fact that the evidence received was often sketchy and that no information whatever was received from nearly half of the local committees known to the N.O.P.W.C.

The published report of the survey unfortunately makes little reference to the workers who are making this 'voluntary contribution' – in fact they are only mentioned in connection with the visiting service in two short paragraphs[3] and no reference at all is made to volunteers other than visitors. It is therefore necessary to consult the unpublished material for the information needed to fill in the picture, and even then the evidence must be treated with caution because of the low response rate. It is necessary to consider how far conclusions based on information from the respondent areas can be taken to apply to those which did not reply to the questionnaire. Can it be assumed that the non-respondent committees were as active as the others and just did not bother to reply, or, on the other hand, is it more likely that they were considerably

---

[1] *Survey*, p. 1.

[2] *Ibid.*, p. 2.

[3] 'The average number of visitors employed by these services falls somewhere in the range of 20-25. Thirty-four areas (mainly the more populous ones) recorded over a hundred visitors. A fairly high proportion (26·1%) said they did not know the numbers of visitors'. (*Survey*, p. 15). There is also an important reference to volunteers in the Conclusions (p. 19); 'This service seems to be growing in importance . . . several old people's welfare committees are appointing visiting organizers to cope solely with the matching of old people and volunteers and the record-keeping which is so essential here. This service needs a steady supply of volunteers if it is to operate successfully.'

less active, and for that very reason less anxious to reply? The view of those responsible for the survey, who in addition to conducting the inquiry have considerable knowledge from personal contacts and from correspondence, is that the number of voluntary workers in the non-respondent areas is about half that recorded by those which did reply. They believe that the non-respondent committees are with few exceptions less active than the others, and that their visiting services are less well organized. They feel, however, that this does not necessarily mean that the number of visitors in proportion to the population over 65 is always smaller in these areas than in the others, since visiting of an unorganized kind is often widespread, though unrecorded by the local O.P.W. Committee. The absence of statistics for the non-respondent areas makes it impossible to calculate accurately from this survey the number of voluntary workers in the whole country either in the visiting service or in any other field of old people's welfare, but there are fortunately sources other than the N.O.P.W.C. survey from which useful information can be obtained about achievements and needs. These supplement the evidence of the survey and help to build up a picture of the present position and to form an estimate of future needs for the country as a whole.

A detailed survey of visiting services in twenty-four areas was carried out for the N.O.P.W.C. in 1964[1]: a report on clubs for the elderly based on work in Lancashire and Derbyshire in 1961–4 was issued in 1964[2], and a government social survey of Meals on Wheels was carried out for the N.C.C.O.P. in 1960[3]. These are only three of the publications which deal with these particular services, and do not by any means exhaust the material available. There have been studies of nutrition by the King Edward's Fund[4] and booklets and statistics by the Women's Royal Voluntary Service (W.R.V.S.)

---

[1] Winifred M. Bayes, *Visiting Services for the Elderly*. An inquiry into Methods and Organizations undertaken for the N.O.P.W.C. in 1964.

[2] E. E. White, *Clubs for the Elderly* (N.O.P.W.C., 1964).

[3] A. Harris, *Outlines of a Survey on the Meals on Wheels Service*. Summary of a report by the government social survey (N.C.C.O.P.), 1960.

[4] *Report of an investigation into the dietary of elderly women living alone* (1956). Seventeen of the sixty women who took part in the survey received domiciliary meals.

and reports by the British Red Cross Society (B.R.C.S.) and other voluntary bodies. These and other sources of information help to define the picture of voluntary work derived from the N.O.P.W.C. survey.

The N.O.P.W.C. survey sought information about voluntary workers partly by asking a direct question about volunteers and partly by asking about services wholly or partly dependent on voluntary work. Except in the case of visiting, the questions about services did not ask for the number of volunteers involved, but a rough estimate can be made on the basis of the service provided, particularly where additional information is obtainable from other sources. These, as well as the replies to the survey itself, have been taken into account in the following discussion of the various services.

Visiting

It appears from the survey that there were in the respondent areas some 17,000 unpaid people working as visitors directly for O.P.W. committees and 38,000 voluntary visitors known to the committees but not necessarily working for them. On the assumption that there were half as many in the non-respondent as in the respondent areas the total for the whole country will be 57,000. Arguments in support of these figures are given in Appendix 1.

These are large numbers, but they fall far short of requirements if all elderly people who need and want a visitor are to receive one. There are bound to be different views as to how many fall into this category and the position will not be the same everywhere. There is certainly a tremendous difference in the proportions actually being visited in different places. Evidence for this comes from the detailed survey[1] carried out by Miss Bayes in twenty-four areas where the numbers visited by the responsible organization varied from one in fifteen to one in 300, though in the latter areas there were other organizations with visiting services and the total number being visited was not known. From a special study of two areas, Guildford and St. Austell, where one in fifteen was being visited and where the service had been based on a survey of

[1] *Visiting Services for the Elderly.*

need, Miss Bayes concludes, 'it would appear that the maximum need for visiting is approximately one in 15 to one in 20'[1]. Even if the lower figure is accepted no less than 330,000 of the 6,600,000 people over sixty-five will need visitors. Since the number of elderly people allotted to each visitor rarely exceeds four and is often less, well over 100,000 visitors will be required to meet this need.

This figure is based on the assumption not only that every volunteer will visit three elderly people, but that they will all be able to visit as often as required and will moreover be conscientious, reliable, and acceptable to those they visit. Clearly such assumptions cannot be made, and though Miss Bayes concludes 'I was generally impressed by the high standard of the services and the efforts that were being made everywhere to give friendship, security and practical help to the elderly', it would be unrealistic to assume that voluntary visiting, as at present organized, is adequate in quality any more than in quantity, especially in view of evidence pointing to serious shortcomings. It is impossible to ignore the views of authorities such as Jeremy Tunstall and Frazer Brockington. In *Old and Alone* Jeremy Tunstall has studied the minority of old people whose condition takes one of the following forms – living alone, social isolation, loneliness and anomie[2]. His conclusions are based on interviews with the 195 who form this minority out of a total sample of 538 men and women over sixty-five drawn at random from the lists of general practitioners in four areas – Harrow, Northampton, Oldham and South Norfolk.

The picture he draws is a gloomy one. This is particularly serious where visiting is concerned since this is one of the best methods of combating loneliness. He found that only one per cent of all old people in his sample and two per cent of the 'socially isolated' had received a voluntary visitor in the week prior to the interview[3]. Very little visiting was done

---

[1] *Op. cit.*, p. 13.

[2] Tunstall describes social isolation as 'having few social contacts' and loneliness as 'feeling alone'. Anomie he describes as the feeling 'of being cut off from the broad social values of society', as 'despair, hopelessness, discouragement, personal disorganization, demoralization or disheartenment'. *Op. cit.*, pp. 17-21.

[3] Jeremy Tunstall, *Old and Alone*, p. 288.

by the clergy[1]. Some was being undertaken by youth clubs and sixth forms, but Tunstall found little evidence of its effectiveness and is sceptical of its value. Most schemes were being run by O.P.W. committees, the W.R.V.S. and other voluntary bodies, but here again he was unable to discover from his survey much about how they worked in practice. His general impression of the inadequacy of voluntary visiting is reinforced by the findings of a study of a scheme in Hornchurch from which he quotes[2]. This was conducted by Stephen Baran in 1963. The place was chosen because it appeared to have an unusually vigorous visiting programme, but Baran is led to conclude:

On the whole Hornchurch Old People's Welfare Association visiting of old people seemed to be of mediocre quality in its conception, in its execution and its end result ... Substantial numbers of those visited denied being lonely, were not living alone, were physically able, and had numerous social contacts during the day. Many were indifferent or antipathetic to visitors who nevertheless continued to go to see them. There seemed to be little follow-up once visiting had begun to see if it was doing good[3].

He found that only just half those visited had a 'positive reaction' while fourteen per cent were actually hostile. In spite of these criticisms, however, Baran acknowledges that the survey shows how necessary voluntary workers can be since 'old people often see hardly anything of the statutory agencies'[4]. Tunstall himself thinks that voluntary work will never bring the major development in services for old people which he advocates.

A special study of the over-eighties by Frazer Brockington and S. M. Lempert[5] also reveals the inadequacy of the volun-

---

[1] On the other hand the Bayes survey (*Visiting Services for the Elderly*, p. 10) mentions a trend towards recruitment of visitors from the churches, and F. Brockington and S. M. Lempert in *The Social Needs of the Over-80's* (p. 26) report that 19·7 per cent of the men and 29·3 per cent of the women covered by their survey of over-80's in Stockport were visited by the clergy.

[2] This study is described by Stephen Baran in *New Society*, 25th February, 1965, in an article entitled 'A friendly chat is not enough'.

[3] *New Society*, 25th February, 1965.

[4] *Ibid.*

[5] *The Social Needs of the Over-80's.*

tary visiting service, for it shows that even in this age group only a small proportion (7·6 per cent of the men and 10·9 per cent of the women) receive visits from voluntary societies. The authors comment: 'It seemed that voluntary societies had little knowledge of where to find old people in need of a visitor just as the old people had little knowledge of where to find them'[1]. In spite of this comparative failure they pay tribute to the N.C.C.O.P. and the N.O.P.W.C., and to the local O.P.W. committees[2].

The evidence of these surveys is disturbing, and it is undeniable that more ought to be done to relieve the loneliness of the 'old and alone' but it is doubtful whether enough can be done without voluntary help. More statutory help is certainly needed but this in itself will not necessarily lessen the part that should be played by volunteers in friendly visiting.

With all its shortcomings the visiting service, as it exists today, brings comfort and company to thousands of lonely people. Many of the visits are deeply appreciated and lasting friendships are often formed. It is difficult to see how any statutory service, however well organized and widespread, could ever make unnecessary the neighbourly contacts of friendly visitors. What is needed, surely, is not the replacement of volunteers by paid professionals, but the improvement and extension of the voluntary service side by side with greatly increased statutory provision.

Clubs

Some general information about voluntary work in clubs can be obtained from the survey carried out by the N.O.P.W.C., and a more detailed picture of the position in Lancashire and Derbyshire from *Clubs for the Elderly* by E. E. White[3]. Some figures for that part of the work for which the W.R.V.S. and the B.R.C.S. are respectively responsible are given in the W.R.V.S. *Bulletin* (June 1968) and the *Annual Reports of the B.R.C.S.*

According to the survey carried out by the N.O.P.W.C.

---

[1] *Op. cit.*, p. 26.
[2] *Op. cit.*, p. 82.
[3] A report to the National Old People's Welfare Council.

there were in 1965 some 5,000 clubs in the respondent areas, which means that there were at least 7,500 in the whole country. The argument in support of this estimate is given in Appendix 1 which also lists the various organizations responsible for running the clubs.

Seven thousand five hundred for the whole country works out at an average of one club for every 842 people over sixty-five years of age. This compares with one for 750 in Lancashire and one for 605 in Derbyshire[1]. These figures may reflect a genuine difference between these two counties and the country as a whole, but they may mean that the estimate of a total of 7,500 is too low. According to those with personal knowledge of the field, the second alternative is the more likely, though there are no statistics to prove it. It is certain, however, that whatever the total provision may be it is not uniformly spread throughout the country, as the available figures for Lancashire and Derbyshire show. It is clear, too, that demand and need also vary, since the extent to which the social needs of the elderly are met by family and neighbourhood varies from place to place. There is unfortunately no evidence as to whether or not there is most provision where the need is greatest.

Though overall provision depends primarily on the number of clubs, it depends, too, on hours of opening, and on this the N.O.P.W.C. has received some useful information which shows that though the majority still only meet once a week, there is a definite trend towards five-, six-, or even seven-day opening.

The value of frequent opening is obvious not only because it means that existing clubs can cater for a larger number of members who only wish to come once or twice a week, but because they will be making provision for those who need a regular social centre. The report of the N.O.P.W.C. stresses that this need is becoming increasingly recognized. 'Those

[1] *Population over 65* (12% of total population) Registrar-General's figures (1961 census)	*Number of clubs*	*Ratio of clubs to People over 65*
Lancashire 600,000	800	1/750
Derbyshire 96,000	160	1/605
U.K. 6,321,000	7,500	1/842

responsible for clubs are also becoming increasingly aware of the need to open for members on seven days a week as in this way they can play an important part in combating loneliness'[1]

These clubs are almost entirely dependent for their formation and functioning on voluntary workers. There is no information about numbers in the published report of the N.O.P.W.C. survey nor in the White study but it is possible to make a rough estimate on the strength of the experience of people working in the field. This shows that four non-member volunteers per two-hour session and six per club is a general average. The average per club is higher than that per session not only because about a quarter of the clubs have more than one session, but also because of the voluntary service of members. Many clubs are run entirely by members and most receive help from them as well as from outsiders. On the basis of six per club there are about 45,000 people giving voluntary service once a week in the 7,500 clubs in the country.

The attitude to service and control by members varies from club to club. 'All types of management prevailed amongst the clubs: every degree from complete autonomy for the members to complete authority for the leaders'[2]. The W.R.V.S. likes to keep control in its own hands[3] while the N.O.P.W.C., though it concedes that there is still a place for the autocratic club, sees more value in democratic methods and draws attention to the clubs which neither are nor need to be under the aegis of any outside body.

Different types of club suit different people, and since most are well patronized, it must be assumed that most meet the needs of at least some of their members. It is another question how far the club movement as a whole meets the needs of all the elderly people who would welcome opportunities for the kind of social intercourse which it can provide. There is little hard evidence on this subject. It seems that fifteen to twenty per cent of retired people in most areas are in membership[4], but that only about 6·6 per cent attend even

---

[1] N.O.P.W.C., *Survey*, p. 18.

[2] White, *op. cit.*, p. 93.

[3] *W.V.S. Clubs for the Elderly*, Notes for the Guidance of Leaders, 1965, pp. 3–4.

[4] White, *op. cit.*, p. 18.

as often as once a week[1]. The extent of unsatisfied demand cannot be accurately known since this only becomes evident when a suitably situated club has been opened. Some people do not attend because there is no club near their homes, or no vacancy in those which are accessible. Others are not attracted by what the clubs have to offer, others again are too frail to attend, while many simply do not feel the need for such gatherings. A small survey carried out in Salford in 1961–2 'to discover what proportion of the elderly attend clubs, what they think about the clubs and how they spend their time' showed that half of those who did not join were deterred either by family or other interests or by poor health, and that nearly a quarter were not interested[2].

Yet the facts that those who do attend generally seem to enjoy and appreciate their club and that waiting lists are common, in spite of a generally low level of convenience and amenity, make it likely that more and better provision would increase the overall membership. Many who stay away might be glad to go if hours of opening were increased and if more transport were provided. More varied activities and better accommodation might well attract people to whom what is now offered does not appeal. A higher standard of buildings and equipment is urgently needed, if clubs are to play a more important part in meeting the social needs of the elderly. Though this question does not directly affect the work of volunteers, it is one on which they can have an important influence. People who are giving regular service in the clubs are those best able to draw the attention of the public to

---

[1] Tunstall, *op cit.*, p. 218

[2] See White, *op. cit.*, pp. 99–101. Eighteen per cent of the sample were members, and the others gave the following reasons for not joining:

	%
Infirmity or poor health	25
Not interested/don't want to	20
No time – family and home	19
Disapproval of some aspect of clubs	14
No time – other interests	5
Lack of information about clubs	4
Other	13
	100

shortcomings and to press for better accommodation. It is a vital function of the voluntary worker to use his personal knowledge of the conditions and needs of those with whom he works as a weapon on their behalf.

Meals

(a) Meals on Wheels

Some information about meals on wheels can be obtained from the survey carried out by the N.O.P.W.C., but much more detail is available in the Harris Report of a survey[1] undertaken in 1960 for the National Corporation for the Care of Old People by the Government Social Survey and it is on this that the following account is based. References throughout are to the shortened version whose essence is 'the same as the original', and not to the original report which is 'a very detailed document which supports all statements with much statistical evidence'[2].

There were at the time of the survey 4,094 volunteers giving an average of 2·33 hours per week. The total number of hours given was some 9,528 which was 90 per cent of all the time spent. (The other 10 per cent was paid for.) Time spent on the preparation of meals and by drivers loaned by local authorities was not included in this estimate[3].

The number of recipients was 20,595 but they were not evenly spread throughout the country as schemes were unevenly distributed. Since the existence of schemes was related not to need (as determined by the number of old people and especially of the housebound in the various areas) but to the existence of voluntary bodies able to collect funds and volunteers, it could be assumed that an unsatisfied need existed wherever there was no scheme in operation. On this matter the survey makes the following point: 'If the demand in areas not at present covered by a meals-on-wheels service is similar to that where the service is in operation, it can be calculated that the number of additional potential recipients

---

[1] A. Harris, *Outline of a Survey on the Meals on Wheels Service.*
[2] *Op. cit.*, p. 1
[3] *Ibid.*, pp. 26-7.

in areas not covered is a minimum of 17,500 making the total of about 38,000 an increase of 85 per cent'[1].

There was also an unsatisfied need among recipients, to meet which a yearly total of 6,000,000[2] meals was thought to be necessary, whereas the actual total was estimated to be only about 1,250,000.

The author of the survey was extremely doubtful whether voluntary organizations could meet the need since nearly half the organizers stated that they could not find the volunteers to enlarge their schemes. 'It would seem that the possibility of voluntary organizations being so expanded as to meet the full demands of all older people in need of meals on wheels is doubtful since the number of meals needed would be a minimum of four times the number at present served'[3]. The difficulty of recruiting the necessary helpers was greater in some parts of the country than in others, and as the service was dependent on voluntary organizations and on volunteers it tended to be least adequate where it was most needed. 'The proportion of areas with the highest economic status covered by a meals service is more than twice as great as would have been expected from the distribution of administrative areas in England and Wales, and the proportion of schemes in areas with the lowest economic status is about half what would have been expected'[4]. It seems likely from the facts set out in the survey that this inequality can only be remedied by statutory action, and by compulsory instructions to local authorities; for if such provision is permissive only and not compulsory the poor areas which need statutory schemes most will be least likely to have them.

In discussing future costs, the survey clearly indicates that more support from local authorities will be needed. This is what it says:

Were they empowered themselves to provide meals services they would very probably wish to take over the administration and the supply of meals, leaving voluntary organizations to serve meals and

---

[1] *Ibid.*, p. 25.

[2] The author also mentions that even a total of 6,000,000 would *not* really meet the need (*op. cit.*, p. 25).

[3] *Ibid.*, p. 27.

[4] *Ibid.*, p. 23.

maintain social contact with the recipients. With the full support of the local authorities behind them and adequate finance it should be possible to recruit more helpers and thus more nearly to meet the demands throughout the country[1].

What is not said is what would be the cost to local authorities if they were to provide the service themselves compared with the cost of expanding provision along existing lines. This would depend in parts on the extent to which labour would still be supplied on an unpaid basis, either through the voluntary bodies or by direct recruitment of volunteers. It would depend, too, on the degree of expansion undertaken. Any service which a local authority is obliged by statute to provide must be made available to everyone falling within the categories laid down. Recipients of the service could not as at present be chosen at the discretion of the voluntary body, nor could a restriction of the services be easily justified to the ratepayers by a shortage of volunteers. Even if the provision of the services were permissive only and not obligatory it would almost certainly have to be more widespread than at present if it were run by the local authority. This is no reason for failing to make the service an obligation on local authorities, since this is probably the only way of ensuring just distribution, but it must be recognized that a change of this kind will greatly increase its cost. This is an important service but local authorities are obliged to consider it as only one part of their welfare provision for the aged, and may well hesitate to raise sufficient money to cover it adequately.

But although the survey made no estimate of the cost of increasing the service and did not suggest how it should be met, it stated categorically that a massive increase was needed if the unmet need was to be fulfilled, and estimated that the number of meals needed would be a minimum of four times the number then being served – a yearly total of 6,000,000 as against the then estimated number of 1,250,000. At the same time it expressed doubts as to whether the service could continue to rely even to the extent it did on the voluntary organizations and their voluntary workers: 'it is possible that the number of voluntary workers will decrease since younger

[1] *Ibid.*, p. 28.

women are more inclined to take up or continue in paid employment'[1].

What in fact has happened? Has the recommended increase taken place, and if so how far is the service still dependent on voluntary organizations and on unpaid workers?

By 1967, the first year for which the Ministry of Health collected these statistics, the number of main meals served during the year was 11·3 million. Of these about 3·6 million were provided under arrangements organized by local authorities and about 5·5 million by the W.R.V.S., the rest being provided in a variety of ways by other bodies such as O.P.W. committees, the B.R.C.S. and the Salvation Army[2].

This increase has involved an increase both in the number of recipients and in the number of meals per recipient. The number of recipients has grown from just under 20,000 in 1960 to 95,000 in 1967 and the proportion of recipients who receive meals twice a week or more has grown in the same period from sixty per cent to about seventy-six per cent.

Though the part played by the local authority has increased tremendously more than two-thirds of the work is still in the hands of the voluntary bodies and the number of voluntary workers is now very large indeed. In 1960 there were 4,094 voluntary workers in the schemes for which the voluntary bodies were responsible and the total number of meals served was 1,250,000 per annum. At that time each voluntary worker served an average of 300 meals a year. On this basis there must now be over 25,000 volunteers engaged in serving the 7·7 million meals which are delivered by the voluntary bodies. This is only an approximate figure, but it is likely to be an under- rather than an over-estimate for England, Scotland and Wales because the Ministry of Health figures, unlike those in the Harris Report, do not include Scotland, and because no account has been taken of voluntary workers who may be helping in schemes run by local authorities.

The number of workers has certainly increased tremendously from the 4,000-odd recorded in the survey carried out in 1960, and the number of meals now being served goes far beyond its estimate of minimum requirement. This estimate

[1] *Ibid.*, p. 27.
[2] *Annual Report of the Ministry of Health for 1967, Cmnd.* 3702.

of need has been shown in the intervening years to have been too modest, and the Ministry of Health, in its annual report for 1966, stated that there was still room for expansion, especially at week-ends. 'There is still room for a considerable expansion of meals services, not only to reach larger numbers of old people, but also to increase the number of days a week meals are served. In very few areas indeed are they available on seven days a week.'[1] Though the report for 1967 does not repeat this comment it emphasizes that provision varies greatly in different parts of the country. This must mean that in some areas at least it is still inadequate.

Certainly most people working in the field think that expansion is urgently needed. This view is forcibly expressed in statistics taken from *The Aged in the Welfare State*[2], by Peter Townsend and Dorothy Wedderburn, which show that at a time when 70,000 old people received a meal once a week, a further 250,000 did not and would like to do so. Although both the number of recipients and the number of meals per recipient have increased since this study was made, this estimated demand for the service is still far from being met.

Meals

(b) Lunch/dinner clubs

The meals service for elderly people provided by voluntary effort is not restricted to meals on wheels though the majority of meals are served in this way. Lunches, dinners and teas are also provided in special clubs and in some of the social clubs as well. The Harris study was only concerned with the 459 areas where there were known to be meals-on-wheels schemes, and of these eighty-seven had lunch clubs also. The N.O.P.W.C. survey recorded the existence of lunch or dinner clubs in twenty-two per cent and of social clubs serving mid-day meals in 15·1 per cent of respondent areas: in some places there were as many as five or six clubs of these kinds. 'Four municipal boroughs recorded as many as five clubs of this sort (special

---

[1] *Cmnd.* 3639, p. 30.
[2] Undertaken in 1962 and published in 1965. The figures quoted in the text are on p. 136.

lunch clubs) and one municipal borough and one county borough recorded six clubs with these facilities.'[1] The total number of clubs serving dinners in the respondent areas was 583, so on the assumption that there were approximately half as many of these clubs in the non-respondent areas as in those which replied to the questionnaire there must have been about 874 centres in the country as a whole. The report of this survey gives no details of the number of days per week on which these meals are available, nor of the number of recipients, nor of the likely number of voluntary workers involved at that time.

It is, however, possible to estimate the extent of voluntary help at the present time on the basis of figures published by the Ministry of Health. In 1967 nearly five million meals were served in lunch clubs, etc., the largest providers being the local authorities (2·3 million), O.P.W. committees (one million) and the W.R.V.S. (0·9 million). Information supplied by the W.R.V.S. and from other voluntary bodies suggests that each volunteer serves on average ten club meals per week or 500 in a fifty-week year. On this basis there must be some 5,400 volunteers engaged in serving the 2·7 million club meals per annum for which the voluntary bodies are responsible[2]. If this number is added to the 25,000 helping with meals on wheels there are no less than 30,400 volunteers involved in the meals service as a whole.

In view of the importance of an adequate service, both through meals on wheels and through dinner clubs it is satisfactory to note that more local authorities are now providing meals themselves as well as assisting voluntary bodies to do so. Whether expansion along present lines will go far enough to meet the need, and how far it will affect the continuing need for voluntary workers cannot yet be estimated. This will depend on the policy of local authorities and whether they are prepared to meet the cost of providing more and more of the service by paid labour. Clearly a greater expansion for the same cost will be possible if continued use is made of voluntary help. Unless and until the local authorities can themselves provide an adequate service the contribution of

[1] N.O.P.W.C., *Survey*, p. 15.
[2] See Appendix I, pp. 243–4.

the volunteer will be essential. It is true that the service as at present operated does not fully meet the need, but it has grown five-fold since 1962[1], and its growth shows how much can be done by voluntary bodies and by unpaid workers.

These three services, visiting, clubs and meals, have been described in some detail because they affect the largest number of elderly people and attract the most voluntary workers. But there are other services in this wide field of social welfare which are also dependent to a greater or lesser extent on the help of volunteers and on the action of voluntary bodies. Seven of these services in addition to the three already described were included in the survey carried out by the N.O.P.W.C. – Boarding out, Chiropody, Employment, Holidays, Homes, Housing and Laundry – and the following account of them is based on that report.

Boarding out

This is not widespread and there appears to be little reliable information about it. Only 6·7 per cent of the respondent areas had schemes, or fifty in all, so the number of voluntary workers involved is small, possibly no more than 100 to 150 in these fifty schemes and perhaps 200 if the non-respondent areas are included.

Chiropody

This is now the recognized responsibility of the local authority, but at the time of the survey a voluntary service was still being carried out in 269 (36 per cent) of the respondent areas, and in a further 103 cases was provided by a voluntary organization and financed by the local authority, while in forty-two more a comprehensive service was provided by a combination of the two. This means that there were 414 schemes dependent on voluntary help in the respondent areas alone and therefore probably at least 600 in the country as a whole.

There was thus a considerable volume of voluntary work

---

[1] This comparison is made in the Seebohm Report (*Report of the Committee on Local Authority and Allied Personal Social Services, Cmnd.* 3703, 1968, Appendix F, para. 183).

involved in the chiropody service, though less than when the voluntary bodies were bearing the whole brunt of it. Direct evidence from the O.P.W. committee in one county borough shows that their scheme involved at least five volunteers giving regular weekly service, so if this is in any way typical the total figure for 600 schemes will be about 3,000.

Employment

Only forty-three (5·7) of the respondent areas had workshops, so that although these may all involve large numbers of volunteers in setting up an organization and also perhaps in the day-to-day running, the overall numbers will not be great; perhaps 400 to 500.

Holidays

Four hundred and eighty-six (65 per cent) of the respondent committees recorded the existence of holiday schemes, the great majority of which were organized by the voluntary bodies. Here considerable voluntary work is involved both in preliminary organization and at the time of the holiday when volunteers, often with Red Cross or St. John training, accompany the group. Car drivers also help by providing transport both for holidays and for outings. At least ten or twelve volunteers are needed to make the arrangements and to carry through each group holiday, so here again there are several thousand people giving voluntary service, some for a few hours every week throughout the booking season, others full time at the period of the holiday. A rough estimate would be 750 schemes for the whole country and ten volunteers per scheme, viz. 7,500. This is a valuable service for the frail who are unable to arrange holidays or to enjoy them safely on their own, but is unnecessary in the case of the very large number who are able and anxious to make their own plans, either separately or in groups, and who are doing so in increasing numbers. But in many cases it was a holiday organized by a voluntary body and run by volunteers that broke the ice for people who would not otherwise have ventured to arrange their own, so that the value of the schemes goes beyond those who now make use of them, to many others who are enjoying holidays which they have arranged themselves.

Homes

The information in the survey relates only to voluntary homes opened in the previous three years, so that it gives an incomplete picture of the extent of voluntary work in this field, since even long-established homes continue to rely on a group of helpers not only for committee work and money-raising, but also for personal contacts with the residents. The N.O.P.W.C. cannot supply a list of homes since to keep such a list up-to-date would take staff time which it cannot afford. It is, however, able to give some general information. In its Annual Report for 1965 it stated that there were between four and five thousand homes with places for 105,000 residents, more than two-thirds of whom were in homes run by local authorities. The others were partly in non-profit-making homes and partly in homes run as business concerns, but the relative numbers in each type were not known accurately. Moreover, not all homes are registered, some because they are exempt – as in the case of those for which the B.R.C.S. is responsible – and others because they evade registration. For all these reasons it is impossible to give the overall number of homes run by voluntary bodies, and consequently to estimate the number of voluntary workers involved, but it is safe to say that they must run into thousands. Some estimate can, however, be made of the number involved in the newly-formed voluntary homes since there is some information about these in the N.O.P.W.C. survey. One hundred and eight were recorded by the respondent committees and each of these must be involving sustained work on the part of a group of at least ten or twelve. It is probably not an underestimate to say that a thousand people were giving voluntary service in the setting up and running of these 108 new homes in the respondent areas, and another 500 in those which did not reply. For old and new homes together the number of voluntary workers may well be 4,000 or 5,000.

These homes, though undoubtedly valuable in helping to increase provision for those who need residential care, are not, in the view of the authors of the N.O.P.W.C. survey, the best direction for the expenditure of voluntary time and money, which they think are better devoted to housing.

Housing

Facts given in the report of the survey are sketchy. Twenty per cent of the respondent areas were said to make some provision of this type but no details of the number of schemes per area are given, though it is stated that while a few of the larger ones mention nine or more, the bulk record only one. Evidence from the unpublished material shows that the total number of schemes was 372[1]. Each scheme involves considerable work in planning and administration and probably at least 5,000 volunteers must have been helping with this work at the time of the survey. This is a field where developments are urgently needed and where volunteers can well take the initiative. It is encouraging to note that they are in fact doing so and that forty-seven housing associations for old people were formed and affiliated to the National Federation of Housing Associations in 1967[2].

Laundry

Only 167 (22 per cent) of the respondent committees recorded this service, and in more than half the cases where information was available the service was provided by the local authority (eighty-two) or a hospital (in fourteen cases). In a quarter it was arranged through reductions at launderettes, etc., and in less than a quarter direct by voluntary bodies. None the less, all these services, even those provided by statutory bodies and by launderettes, involved voluntary work on organization – the launderette scheme in one large county borough for instance involved a morning a week by one or two volunteers for the issue of concession cards. If this is typical of what is happening in other places, several hundred volunteers must be involved in the launderette concession schemes, and many

---

[1] See Appendix I, p. 244.
[2] N.O.P.W.C., *Annual Report* for the year ending March, 1968.

more where the scheme is operated as well as organized by the voluntary body. The total for the country as a whole may well be 1,000. There is certainly a great need for the expansion of this service, either directly by the local authorities, or in co-operation with voluntary bodies.

Future plans

The survey also asked for information about other activities and future plans. Nearly half the respondent areas (365) gave details of new developments. There were plans for 547 new schemes of many different kinds. The highest proportion, nearly a third, were for developing meals services, followed by plans for clubs and visiting – the three branches of old people's welfare which already involve the largest number of volunteers, and whose successful development depends on the recruitment of many more.

Publications

The final question asked in the survey concerned publications, and asked O.P.W. committees whether they (a) produced a leaflet/booklet on the services provided for old people, and to this 185 replied 'yes' and (b) an annual report which is available to the public, and here considerably more (404) said 'yes'. Though these publications are probably mainly the work of paid staff, where this exists, they are usually partly dependent on unpaid help even in these cases, and where there is no paid staff, must be entirely produced by volunteers. Possibly 1,000 voluntary workers give help of this kind.

The overall picture

The total number of voluntary workers who are giving regular service of at least two hours per week in the field of old people's welfare is about 155,800. This is an approximate figure, the sum of estimates made on the basis of information derived from various surveys and reports. The estimate for the various branches are: Visiting, 57,000; Clubs, 45,000; Meals, 30,400; Boarding out, 200; Chiropody, 3,000; Employment, 500;

Holidays, 7,500; Homes, 5,000; Housing, 5,000; Laundry, 1,000; Publications, 1,000.

These figures refer to 1965 except in the case of meals where it has been possible to obtain figures for 1967 since the number of meals served was recorded by the Ministry of Health in its annual report for that year.

These are conservative estimates. Where the information has been drawn from the N.O.P.W.C. survey alone, the figures for the country as a whole have included estimates from the non-respondent areas which were on the low side, and, moreover, considerable progress has been made in all fields since the survey was carried out. None of the figures quoted includes committee members and fund raisers unless the people concerned are active in other ways as well. If these had been included the totals would have been much higher. On the other hand, the totals would have been lower if allowance had been made for double counting. Many people undoubtedly give voluntary service in more than one branch of old people's welfare, and this necessarily reduces the total number of workers, though it does not affect the number of 'worker sessions'.

One hundred and fifty-five thousand is an impressive number and shows how large a part voluntary work is playing in welfare services for the elderly. Yet these services, especially those for the 'old and alone', are far from adequate, as studies of the subject by Tunstall and others have clearly shown. Reference has already been made to their comments about visiting, but their criticism is not confined to this one branch. It extends to the whole field of both statutory and voluntary provision, for Tunstall concludes that the welfare services, whether statutory or voluntary, fail all along the line to meet the needs of the elderly, and gives convincing figures to show how far supply falls short of demand. Only 4·4 per cent of all the old people in the country had a home help from the local authority, and a further nine per cent had private domestic help while another 5·9 per cent were not receiving, but wanted domestic help[1].

Only 1·1 per cent of all old people received meals, while five times as many have an unmet need. In the four areas

[1] Jeremy Tunstall, *Old and Alone*, p. 214.

specially investigated only four per cent even of the 'socially isolated' received meals[1]. A somewhat higher proportion attended clubs – 6·6 per cent of all old people had attended an Old People's Club in the week prior to the survey, and twenty-three per cent had attended a club of some kind during the previous month. In the four areas the corresponding figures were 7·8 per cent and 25 per cent, and of the socially isolated in these areas 10 per cent belonged to an Old People's Club, but another 12 per cent said that they would like to do so[2].

There are thus considerable gaps between provision and the demand revealed by Tunstall's survey of the four areas, and the need is certainly greater than the expressed demand. As far as home helps are concerned many people still do not know who is eligible nor what the service will involve in the way of investigation or of cost, while others dread an invasion of their privacy, and need reassurance as well as information. In the case of clubs, demand is often only expressed after a club is open. There is seldom difficulty in recruiting members even to clubs for which there has been no previous demand, though introduction by a friendly neighbour is often necessary for people who hesitate, through fear of the unknown, to take advantage of a service which they afterwards appreciate.

The gaps in these services – domestic help, meals, clubs and also in visiting must be filled, and much will depend on the local authorities. It is true, as Tunstall points out, that their powers are not being used to the full, though it does not necessarily follow, as he suggests, that 'if there is to be a major development and a more professional spirit in the future, voluntary and untrained workers will inevitably play a smaller role'[3]. Major developments in local authority provision are certainly needed but it is well to remember that the considerable improvement that has already taken place has not led to a decrease in the number of voluntary workers. The number of social workers and health visitors and home nurses, though still too small, has increased, and more of

---

[1] *Ibid.*, pp. 217 and 285.
[2] *Ibid.*, pp. 218 and 222.
[3] *Ibid.*, p. 294.

their time can be devoted to the elderly[1]. The home-help service has also expanded and though far from adequate is largely devoted to the same age group[2]. Meals on wheels and luncheon clubs and centres are being provided in greater numbers though they fall short of the need. The possibilities of useful development are so great that even a very well-disposed society may be unable to meet all the needs by paid labour, and even if an adequate supply of social workers, home helps and servers of meals were available and could be financed from rates and taxes, there would still be much that the unpaid good neighbour could and should be doing, especially in the field of friendly visiting and help with social clubs and outings. Experience shows both that basic provision by paid workers needs the supporting services of volunteers, and that the presence of volunteers helps to spur on the statutory authorities to expand their provision and improve its quality. There is no better way of making society raise the priority it is prepared to give to services for the elderly than by making it aware of their needs, and this the volunteer is well placed to do. An increase in the number and quality of voluntary workers should have the result of increasing the pressure for better statutory provision, and at the same time would involve more people in personal contact with those who are old and alone. Personal involvement of this kind is an essential part of real community care.

4

THE MENTALLY DISORDERED

Mental illness and deficiency are not now treated as crimes, but they are still viewed with suspicion by the general public.

---

[1] According to *A Survey of Manpower Demand Forecast for the Social Services*, by Kathleen Gales and R. C. Wright (N.C.S.S.), 49 per cent of those attended by home nurses in 1961 were elderly as against only 32 per cent in 1953 (p. 71), and some 10 per cent of the elderly will need supporting services (p. 68).

[2] The Seebohm Report (*Cmnd.* 3703, Appendix F, para. 252) states that care of the elderly accounted for over three-quarters of all cases where such help was given.

Though the mentally sick are no longer shut away in closed institutions for indefinite periods, and though the feeble-minded are not now treated as laughing stocks as they were when every village had its 'idiot', neither group is readily tolerated as fellow members of the community. While it is true that knowledge about the high incidence of mental illness and about the improving prospects for its cure is increasing, ignorance is still widespread. This is the background against which must be viewed the official policy of the Ministry of Health, based on the recommendations of the Royal Commission of 1957[1] that mental patients should as far as possible live at home and not in institutions. 'It is usually best for the mentally disordered person, whether adult or child, to live at home where this is possible'[2].

The willingness and ability of relatives to provide a home depends to a large extent on the support they receive from the welfare services of the local authority, but it depends, too, on the attitude of the community as a whole. This is recognized by the Ministry in these terms:

The aim of enabling the mentally disordered to take their part in the life of the community cannot be realized without the co-operation of the public. To foster acceptance of the mentally disordered in the community is thus an integral part of the local authority's duty to make arrangements 'for the purpose of the prevention of mental disorder, the care of persons suffering from mental disorder and the after-care of such persons...[3]' In no other aspect of health and welfare is it so necessary to demonstrate the existence of the need in order to be able to meet it. The participation of voluntary organizations in all kinds of work for the mentally disordered is all the more valuable for this reason[4].

With this task of demonstrating the need the voluntary bodies have been especially concerned. Active members of organizations for mental health who realize something of what

---

[1] *Royal Commission on the Law relating to Mental Illness and Mental Deficiency,* 1954-57, *Cmnd.* 169, H.M.S.O. (1957).

[2] *Health and Welfare,* The Development of Community Care, *Cmnd.* 1973, (1963), para. 86.

[3] Section 28 of the National Health Service Act 1946, as extended by Section 6 of the Mental Health Act 1959.

[4] *Health and Welfare,* para. 101.

mental illness means and of what can be done to overcome it are playing an important part in creating the change in public opinion necessary for the acceptance of the mentally sick in the community. They are helping to educate public opinion, and are constantly pressing for better statutory provision. At the same time people who are prepared themselves to give personal service are helping in a positive way to make community care a reality. Medical attention and professional assistance from social workers cannot meet the whole need of the mentally sick and subnormal, nor of the families who are living with them and caring for them by day and by night. Voluntary workers can help by neighbourly support on a person to person basis, by visiting and befriending the patient, by occasionally relieving the family of his care, by organizing clubs and outings and other occupational and recreational facilities, and especially by giving friendly support to patients without families when they come out of hospital. This is a form of social provision where personal service to individuals and small groups is especially needed, which means that it is expensive in time and manpower. In consequence it will always be among the most difficult forms of service to provide on a paid professional basis, and one therefore where voluntary help is greatly needed. At the same time it is work which demands skill and patience, and cannot be tackled by inexperienced people.

Help of this kind may sometimes only be needed for a short time, since mental patients often make complete recoveries, but sometimes, and especially in the case of the subnormal, it will be long-term and even life-long. Though the care of these patients falls mainly on their families, it is often a burden too great to be borne without outside help. Reading between the lines of the Ministry's 'plan' it is clear how inadequate statutory provision is, and indeed can ever be, for meeting the needs of the subnormal who are living at home. 'Mentally subnormal children who do not need treatment in hospital normally live with their parents and attend a local training centre'[1], states the 'plan'; but there are some for whom there are no places in the centres, and those who do attend are at home at week-ends and in holidays, while for the under-fives there is little

[1] *Ibid.*, para 89.

or no statutory provision. Clearly there are tremendous opportunities here for voluntary workers to help the harassed parents. The need is even greater in the case of adults for whom, on the admission of the Ministry, the provision 'lags behind that for children'[1].

The task of the voluntary worker is therefore two-fold. He must seek to influence and inform public opinion and press for better statutory provision, and he must take an active part in personal service.

The mentally ill

Voluntary work for the mentally ill was pioneered by the Mental After Care Association[2] which was for many years the only national body concerned with mental health. Founded in 1879 to provide homes in which discharged patients could be rehabilitated, it later expanded its work to include the care of patients out on trial and the provision of hostels and holidays. It was built up by the effort and interest of voluntary workers who placed recovered patients with individual householders, but no longer uses volunteers to help with rehabilitation since its main efforts are now concentrated on the type of patient who needs the services of qualified workers. While it co-operates with the voluntary workers in other organizations, it now has none of its own apart from those who serve on its committees and help with money-raising.

Today the main organization which offers opportunities for voluntary service in the two-fold task of influencing opinion and giving personal help is the National Association for Mental Health (N.A.M.H.). Founded in 1946 by the amalgamation of the Central Association for Mental Welfare, the Child Guidance Council and the National Council for Mental Hygiene, it has done much to bring about changes in the attitude of the public. The main emphasis of its work has been on education and research, but it also runs a number of homes for special groups of patients and encourages the work

---

[1] *Ibid.*, para. 98.

[2] For an account of its work, which has been mainly concentrated in the London area, see M. Rooff, *Voluntary Societies and Social Policy*, especially pp. 93-96 and 116-19.

of local associations. Its professional staff is small and the local associations rely heavily on volunteers. Its achievements are considerable, but much remains to be done, and it is actively interested not only in the recruitment of paid staff for hospitals and local authorities but in encouraging more members of the public to undertake voluntary work. The importance of active participation by members of the public in the care of the mentally sick is emphasized in *Mental Health and Mental Illness* by Nesta Roberts. The necessary aftercare, she says,

cannot be provided solely, or, indeed, even largely, by psychiatrists and psychiatric social workers. The kind of help needed by large numbers of discharged patients is not complicated therapy but the friendly interest and support of somebody with sufficient knowledge of mental illness to understand something of their difficulties in re-adjusting to life in the outside world and not to be dismayed at their occasionally bizarre behaviour[1].

It is true that this kind of help will involve professionals – doctors, mental welfare officers, health visitors, social workers – but it must involve friends and neighbours also. Only if voluntary workers back up the services of hospitals and local authorities will mental patients and ex-patients and their families enjoy real community care.

Another attempt to see that 'this essential part of the plan' (for community care) is really carried out was made in Mental Health Week 1967 when attention was focused on *Work to be Done*[2], a booklet issued by the N.A.M.H. describing careers in mental health, and on the encouragement of voluntary work[3].

What kind of help can the community give, and how far is it in fact being given at the present time? The necessary first stage is acceptance of the mentally sick by the community, and here considerable progress has been made, thanks to modern medicine and treatment, to the policy of the open door and to the education of public opinion. The next stage,

---

[1] *Op. cit.*, p. 75. See also the *Guardian*, 6 April, 1967. 'This friendly interest . . . does not yet come to any great extent. It is an essential part of the plan, and it is not really being carried out at all.'

[2] By Paul Vaughan (1967).

[3] See *Social Services Quarterly*, Spring, 1967, p. 142.

and here much less has been done, is the active participation of individuals by personal service. It must be admitted that the picture here is one of challenge and opportunity for the future rather than of present achievement. Something, however, is being done, and it is well to look at and attempt to evaluate this, both to pay tribute to the pioneers and to show along what lines progress could and should be made.

Some idea of the numbers and activities of voluntary workers in this field can be obtained from the records of the organizations concerned. The N.A.M.H. now (1968) has sixty-eight local associations with a membership of about 4,500. It is not claimed that every member takes an active part by personal service – some concentrate on committee work and on raising money, while others do little more than pay subscriptions and take a vague interest in the work. But there is a large group who are actively engaged and they often achieve considerably more than what they actually carry out personally since they involve their families and friends and make known to a wider public the needs of the mentally sick and what can be done to help them. The range and volume of work undertaken by the local associations is evidence that a large number of volunteers are involved. Most associations run social clubs and befriending services both in and out of hospital. In addition to this basic work of bringing the patient and ex-patient back into the community by personal contact with neighbours individually and in groups, seven associations are providing hostels and homes while others are pioneering with a consultation service for young people, with play groups for emotionally disturbed children, with sheltered workshops and in other ways. Pioneering and experimental work such as this is in the great tradition of voluntary action and should pave the way for action by the State.

Service by volunteers takes many different forms. It may be professional advice and the giving of skills, or acting the good neighbour in family, club and hospital which is the essential contribution of the lay worker. Unfortunately these activities, promoted and run by volunteers, are still thin on the ground, and the benefits they confer are only available to a few. Clearly many more voluntary workers are needed to pioneer and consolidate, if all who need their help are to receive it, and if provision everywhere is to be brought up to the standard of the best.

A recent development which shows clearly the isolation of mental patients and their families is the move on the part of a group of relatives to unite for mutual understanding and support[1]. They agree that the new approach to mental illness is the right one but stress the burden that it lays on the family. The formation of this movement for self-help should strengthen the appeal to the general public to play a greater part in helping relatives to bear the burden which the policy of community care has laid upon them.

The mentally subnormal

Self-help and mutual aid by the relatives of those concerned have been the main aims of voluntary work for the mentally subnormal, and it is the relatives who have taken the lead in pressing the claims of this group of people. In the case of children it is naturally the parents who are primarily concerned, and where good provision exists this is often due to parental effort to meet the need themselves and to persuade the statutory authorities to improve facilities. Parents who take the lead are helping not only their own but other children, and their self-help expands into community service both when they help the children of others, and when they involve non-parents by their examples and influence.

The National Society for Mentally Handicapped Children is an organization for helping parents with the problems that having a subnormal child presents. It helps to create local parent groups and keeps them informed of developments in treatment and care. Together with these groups it strives to influence public opinion to accept the subnormal into the community, for though it is now recognized by the experts that even the severely handicapped do not usually need to be segregated in their own interest, the reluctance of the community to accept them means that many are still confined and isolated in institutions. Those whose handicap is less severe are gradually being trained so that they can work and live in society, but

---

[1] 'Amend' (Association for the relatives of the Mentally, Emotionally and Nervously Disabled), c/o 39, Queen Anne St., W.1. (See the *Guardian*, 26 April, 1967.)

even they rely heavily on their families, and those without relatives need accommodation and supervision. Training is the responsibility of the State, and considerable improvements have been made in the number and standard of centres for children of school age. But their quality is still very uneven, and some children even of this age still have to wait for a place, while provision for school leavers and adults is most inadequate, and is almost non-existent for those under five[1]. The needs of the mentally subnormal are not being adequately met from statutory sources, and more and better provision is needed. But even if the standard of all training centres were brought up to that of the best, and even if proper arrangements were made everywhere for adults and young children, such statutory provision will never be enough. Those without relatives are in special need of friends and social contacts, and even those who have relatives need more in these directions than families alone can provide, and the families, too, need the support of neighbours. These are families with a continuing burden since the subnormal child does not cease to be a responsibility when he ceases to be a child. In some cases parent groups have managed to break the barriers of community mistrust and persuaded the neighbourhood to participate in the life of the subnormal. What can be done is illustrated by the story told by Anthony Denney of a local society which against all the odds formed, financed and ran a nursery group with remarkable success. Examples such as this, which are still all too few, illustrate 'the fact that the community itself, once alerted to the children's needs, is capable of shouldering the responsibility of meeting the needs'[2].

[1] See *Educating our Handicapped Children*, the report of a working party on special education (1966-7) set up by CASE (the Confederation for the Advancement of State Education), which concludes: 'It is evident that the needs of the present generation of handicapped children are not being fully met' (p. 22). It reveals that there are nearly 10,000 ESN and over 1,000 maladjusted children awaiting places in special schools (p. 15). Among its recommendations it is emphasized 'that education and training of all children between the ages of 2 and 18 should be the responsibility of the D.E.S.) (p. 4) and that early ascertainment is of vital importance. A brief account of CASE is given on pp. 96–7 below. Further reference may be made to Stanley Segal, *No Child is Ineducable*.

[2] Anthony Denney, *Children in Need*, p. 45.

There are at the moment 356 local Societies for Mentally Handicapped Children, ranging in size of membership from two dozen to over 400, only six of which have paid secretary-organizers. The 33,000 members are of both sexes and all ages. They are mostly, but not quite all, parents of mentally handicapped children, some social workers, and a few ordinary people wanting to interest themselves in a 'good cause'. They are thus primarily 'parent groups'. Their activities vary, but all raise funds both for their own projects and for those of the national body. The following services are provided and paid for by the local societies: Welfare Visitors, Information Officers, Youth Club Activities, Swimming Coaches, Facilities for Holidays, Paid Secretaries, Day Nurseries, Special Care Crèches or residential short stay provision, own meeting place or Social Centre, and Workshop facilities. Some of these activities such as the club work and the crèches use voluntary helpers other than members, but the main brunt of the unpaid work and of the money raising necessary to pay such staff as they employ and to support their central office falls on the members themselves. This is essentially an organization which draws its strength from the activities of local self-help societies. They support the national body in its work as a pressure group and as an educator and in its experimental projects, but their main concern is with local work. Their capacity to develop this depends on their own initiative and leadership rather than on outside guidance. This independence means that most of the local society work is impressively healthy, but it means, too, that it is less widespread and often less effective than it might be if more could be done nationally to encourage the formation of new groups and to extend the work of those already in existence.

The information supplied by the National Society for Mentally Handicapped Children and by the National Association for Mental Health gives some idea of what is being done by voluntary workers in this difficult field. At the same time it shows how much remains to be done and how great is the need for more voluntary action. Action is needed to press for more and better statutory provision since voluntary provision is no permanent substitute. It is needed, too, to educate the public, and to supplement the work of hospital and welfare

authorities in supporting and befriending the mentally disordered and their families.

5

THE PHYSICALLY HANDICAPPED

The physically handicapped do not suffer to the same extent as
the mentally ill from the fear and misunderstanding of the
public, but they, too, have great difficulty in being treated as
ordinary members of the community. Their disability often
makes it impossible for them to lead a normal life – some
cannot work or join in recreation and normal social intercourse, while all are subject to the handicap of being different
and being treated as such: even if they are kindly treated, this
differentiation is often resented, and what they need most
often is simply the opportunity to lead as normal a life as their
disability permits. In the words of Dame Georgiana Butler:

Normality! That is the goal to which every disabled individual,
without exception, passionately aspires and which all, in their
degrees, can achieve if given the right encouragement and opportunity[1].

Unfortunately this encouragement and opportunity is
often denied[2].

The care of the physically handicapped both in institutions
and at home is laid by statute on public authorities, but
voluntary bodies and voluntary workers are also involved,
and without their co-operation the provision made would be
even more inadequate than it is. They have a most important
part to play not only in continuing and expanding the services
they are already giving, but in drawing the attention of the
public to the urgent needs of this neglected group of people.
For only in the case of the blind has there been general aware-
ness of the need for help – the deaf and those with other handi-

---

[1] Quoted in *News Review*, Central Council for the Disabled (Spring, 1967),
page 12.
[2] A moving account of what it is like to be physically handicapped is
given in *Stigma*, edited by Paul Hunt. This is a series of articles by twelve
disabled people describing their feelings, their difficulties and their needs.

caps have been comparatively neglected by all but small sections of the public.

People who are too severely handicapped to live at home or who have no relatives able and willing to care for them have to live either in hospital or in some other institution. There is such a shortage of accommodation suited to their needs that they often find themselves in wards designed and run for an entirely different type of patient. The young are especially liable to suffer in this way since there is little special accommodation for them and they often have no choice between a geriatric ward, or, if they are lucky, an institution such as a Cheshire Home which, though much more suited to them, may be a long way from friends and relatives.

Voluntary workers can help those who are living in institutions in many ways – they can visit the lonely, they can provide trolley shops and libraries, and organize activities and entertainments. Most important of all, they can press for better financial provision and more domiciliary help, so that those who are able to do so can live outside. It has been estimated that no less than a third of those who are now permanently in hospital could live at home if better provision, financial and otherwise, were made for their community care[1]. No one is better placed to press the claims of the handicapped and chronic sick than the voluntary worker who sees at first hand how restricted are their lives, however devoted the medical and nursing care which they receive.

Fortunately only a minority are in institutions, and the great majority are living at home. Here there are tremendous opportunities for voluntary work, in spite of the fact that responsibility for providing adequate services rests with the statutory bodies. Local authorities are given power 'to make arrangements for promoting the welfare of persons who are blind, deaf or dumb, and other persons who are substantially and permanently handicapped by illness, injury or congenital deformity[2].' They keep registers of all handicapped people who seek their assistance, but there is no compulsory registration, and except in the case of the blind (who are now entitled

[1] See the evidence of a survey made by the Oxford Regional Hospital Board in 1963 (ref. D.I.G. memo to Minister of Health, Oct., 1966, p. 6).
[2] *Health and Welfare* (Cmnd. 1973), para. 102.

to a pension at the age of forty) the figures do not give a true picture of the number of people involved[1]. This is partly because by no means all handicapped people need or would use the services provided by local authorities under these powers, but it is also because the services have been slow to develop especially in the case of handicaps other than blindness. Schemes for the blind were made mandatory in 1948, but it was only in 1960 that they became so for the deaf and dumb and those with other handicaps, the so-called 'general classes'. While the provision of schemes was permissive, only little was done in most places beyond what was already being carried out by the voluntary bodies, and even now when provision for all groups has been mandatory for six years, it is uneven and often inadequate, in spite of the part still being played by voluntary help. As Phyllis Willmott says in her *Consumer's Guide to the British Social Services* (1967):

The combined resources of LHA and LWA services, supplemented by voluntary effort, are now meant to provide 'community care' for any disabled, chronically ill or mentally disordered people who need help to carry on living as normally as possible. In fact, almost everywhere 'community care' is at present more of a humane idea than a practical reality[2].

The needs of the handicapped are described by the Ministry of Health under four headings – assistance in coping with handicap; accommodation; rehabilitation employment and occupation; and recreation. Voluntary bodies are still providing some of the services which help to meet all these needs, and voluntary workers are helping not only in the voluntary but also in the statutory section.

The services are so numerous and so varied that it is difficult

---

[1] There were 259,683 (5·6 per 10,000 population) on the registers at 31st December, 1961. Of these 96,591 were blind. 'The registers contain virtually all blind persons and thus give a reliable picture of the extent of blindness in the population. For the other classes of the handicapped the registers indicate neither total numbers nor even the numbers who require welfare services, for until recently the services for these classes were largely undeveloped by local authorities, and even when they are fully developed, by no means all will require them.' (*Health and Welfare, Cmnd.* 1973, paras. 102-104.)

[2] *Op. cit.*, p. 171.

to estimate the number of volunteers involved and to discover what kind of people they are and what they do. Some idea of the number of organizations involved can be had from the fact that the Directories compiled by the N.C.S.S[1]. and by Phyllis Willmott[2] each list about forty societies directly concerned with physical handicaps – the societies mentioned in both lists are in most cases the same, though a few occur in one only so that the total is well over forty. Moreover neither list includes any purely local societies, nor do they cover homes and hospitals under voluntary control, and these should be included to complete the picture[3].

These organizations are for the most part concerned with one special handicap – blindness, deafness or one of the disabilities of the 'general classes'. They are often composed mainly of the sufferers themselves and of their relatives. This combination of self-help and service of others is an important feature of work with the handicapped. Such work is not only valuable in itself but has the further merit that it is evidence of the desire and capacity for independence of those concerned. Their activity on their own behalf and in the interests of their fellow sufferers helps to make their needs more widely known, and shows that they wish to be treated as far as possible as normal people. In order to achieve this aim they have the same two-fold task as that facing workers with the mentally sick: they must press for better statutory provision and inform and educate the public, and at the same time they must help themselves and those like them in a practical and personal way.

The blind

The active participation of the handicapped themselves has been a feature in the development of welfare for the blind, but the general public, too, has long shown a special interest in their needs. The voluntary organizations set up to help them have been generously supported with money and service,

---

[1] *Voluntary Social Services*, N.C.S.S. (1966).
[2] *Op. cit.*
[3] See pp. 74–5 below for details of the membership of the Central Council for the Disabled.

and successive governments have supplied funds for statutory provision. Moreover individuals in all walks of life have given personal help to blind people living in their midst. Help of this kind is always needed however much is done in the way of pensions, education, employment and welfare.

These services were in the main provided by voluntary bodies until 1948 when they were made mandatory on the statutory authorities. After that date some voluntary bodies have continued their previous work by acting as agents for the local authorities, while others have turned their attention to needs which were still unmet. Work of great value is still being done, and considerable sums of money are being raised by voluntary effort, and though the welfare of the blind today is less dependent on such efforts than it was, the part played by volunteers is still impressive. Among the activities listed by the Royal National Institute, money raising has an important place. Voluntary money is not now needed to meet the basic needs of the blind, but it is essential if the services provided by the voluntary bodies are to be kept going. These include the work of St. Dunstan's for ex-service men and women, guide dogs, the National Library, reading, repairing gramophones, tape recording, transcribing braille, training, provision and servicing of wireless sets, Sunshine Homes, schools, residential homes and rehabilitation centres. In all these activities voluntary workers play an important part, both by performing special tasks such as tape recording and transcribing braille and by rendering personal service to the residents and staff in the school and homes in their neighbourhood.

The volunteers are a representative cross section of the community and their ages range from Brownies and Guides to retired people. It is clear that there is a wide concern for and desire to help the blind and that voluntary work carried out through the organizations is supplemented by much unorganized personal service. Though this is unrecorded there is no reason to suppose that it is less widespread today than it has ever been, and certainly it is needed still. A pension, a job and the ability to read braille do not rule out the need for the support and friendship of sighted people for such things as helping with household tasks and shopping, reading newspapers and letters and for social contacts.

The deaf

The deaf have received less help than the blind both from the State and from the public, and are more isolated because of difficulties of communication. In the case of children, early ascertainment is of vital importance, and those who are considered after assessment to be too deaf to be taught in ordinary schools are educated in special schools for the deaf and partially hearing, which are run by the L.E.A.'s and recognized by the Department of Education and Science. The welfare of the adult deaf is still largely in the hands of voluntary bodies, sometimes acting as agents for the local authorities, who have been legally responsible since 1960. Until that time most welfare work and much education, training and research were carried out by the voluntary bodies, and they are still actively engaged both nationally and locally. The Royal National Institute for the Deaf (R.N.I.D.) is the protective association for the deaf, the deaf-blind and the hard of hearing. In addition to its general functions of giving advice and undertaking research and publicity, it runs a number of homes and has a welfare department. It does not itself make much use of voluntary workers except for committee work and money raising, because untrained people cannot communicate with the profoundly deaf, but its officers recognize the importance of voluntary work both for personal work with the hard of hearing, and also for informing the public about the problems of deafness. For it is most important that the general public, and especially the deaf themselves, should be kept informed as to how the disability can best be overcome. There has been considerable progress in electrical and electronic devices for 'getting through' to the deaf, but these cost money and the public must be persuaded that the provision of the right kind of aid for each patient is a fair charge on public funds. The deaf themselves need reliable advice to protect them from un-scrupulous sales promotion, for they are often so anxious to overcome their disability that they spend money they can ill afford on aids which turn out to be useless. Voluntary workers can help them to seek this advice and can sometimes dissuade them from undertaking unwise commitments.

The work in the field is in the hands of some one hundred

independent organizations either acting as agents for the local authorities or working alongside them. The quality and extent of their work, and of that carried out directly by the authorities, is uneven, and progess has been slow both because of insufficient knowledge of the numbers and needs of the deaf and because of an acute shortage of trained personnel. Voluntary workers serve on the committees of these local societies, and raise money for their projects and do a little visiting and club work, but this personal service is limited by the problem of communication in the case of the profoundly deaf. With the hard of hearing, on the other hand, this difficulty can be overcome, and volunteers can do a great deal to break down the isolation of this group of deaf people. In this connection social clubs are playing an important part.

The British Association of the Hard of Hearing (B.A.H.O.H.) was formed in 1947 by the Hard of Hearing Organizations throughout Great Britain. It is run by the hard of hearing and their friends, and now, in 1968, has a membership of some 8,500 in 208 clubs of various sizes. It has played a valuable part in shaping government policy for the hard of hearing and in bringing their needs to the notice of a wider public. Its activities include the study of aids to hearing, special courses, holidays, lip-reading and clear speech championships, promoting activities in the younger age groups and in scientific, social and vocational matters. Through its clubs especially it has helped people who were going deaf to regain self-confidence.

The work of the association is dependent on volunteers, and many more are needed. Local representatives are to be appointed to undertake welfare work with the hard of hearing, especially with regard to difficulties of communication. 'Such voluntary work has great potential since such helpers may be able to provide greater personal attention and sustained help than a statutory welfare worker could give to an individual case'[1]. Recruitment and the provision of training are problems which the association feels could be overcome by suitable

---

[1] This quotation is from the report prepared by the B.A.H.O.H. for the British National Conference on Social Welfare (April, 1967). The report is a useful source of information on the problems of the hard of hearing and how voluntary workers can help to solve them.

publicity and financial help, for both of which it looks to the local authorities. In the case of training it believes it could itself provide the necessary courses if the volunteers and the money were forthcoming. Work with the hard of hearing offers great opportunities for voluntary workers of the right kind – people, who may themselves be handicapped, who are prepared to tackle the problem of communication in order to help those who are isolated to overcome their loneliness, and to join in the ordinary life of society.

The general classes

Participation by people who are themselves handicapped is an important factor in the welfare of the 'general classes' and action by them and by their relatives is a vital force in the drive for a better deal for all disabled people. They form the main strength of the societies concerned with one special disability which have sprung up to supplement the work of those other charitable bodies which have a less specialized interest.

Both types of organization are members of the Central Council for the Disabled (C.C.D.) (formerly the Central Council for the Care of Cripples) which is the national co-ordinating body for all agencies, statutory and voluntary, which are working for the welfare of the physically handicapped. As its original name suggests, it is primarily concerned with the crippling disabilities, but some aspects of its work overlap with that of the societies for the blind and deaf, and also with that for the mentally disordered. Its aim is to 'develop voluntary services for the welfare of the physically handicapped' and its activities include 'The investigation of the causes of disablement and the promotion of measures for their elimination. The encouragement of the formation of local associations. The organization of schemes for the treatment, education, training, employment and general welfare of the disabled.'[1] It has 272 affiliated organizations of which 114 are counties, county boroughs and London boroughs, and about fifty are county and local associations. Some are societies concerned with a special disability, such as the British Epilepsy Association, the British Polio Fellowship, the British Rheumatism and Arthritis

[1] *Voluntary Social Services*, N.C.S.S. (1966), p. 49.

Association, the Haemophilia Society, the Multiple Sclerosis Society, the Muscular Dystrophy Group and the Spastics Society. These seven do not by any means exhaust the list of societies of this type, but they are among the most important and influential. The other hundred-odd affiliated organizations include hospitals, schools, training centres, clubs, groups concerned with special problems such as transport, and general bodies, like Councils of Social Service, with an interest in the handicapped. There are in addition about 150 individual members and twenty-five associate societies[1].

These various types of organization are all dependent to some extent on voluntary help. The societies concerned with a special disability, because they were promoted by sufferers and their relatives, have had the support of people who knew from personal experience what the disability meant. People of this kind give long and devoted service to their fellow sufferers and are often most successful in persuading the public to help with money and service. A number of these societies have been remarkably successful at fund raising and are able not only to employ paid staff but to make grants for education and research.

The local associations are also largely dependent on voluntary workers, though they, too, usually have some paid staff. The extent and quality of their work varies considerably – at their best and most active they are the main force for the welfare of the handicapped in their areas, at the least they provide useful additional services to supplement those supplied by the specialized societies and from statutory sources.

It is now the local authorities who are ultimately responsible for making arrangements for promoting the welfare of the handicapped but they may, and often do, use voluntary organizations as their agents. These organizations include some which are specially concerned to help the handicapped and others, like the B.R.C.S. and the W.R.V.S., for which such work is only one of many activities. All supply volunteers from their own members and supporters for the work carried out at the request of the local authority, and in some cases the authorities also recruit volunteers themselves.

It is not possible to give an accurate estimate of the total number of people who are giving voluntary service to the

[1] Ref. C.C.D., *Annual Report* 1966–7.

handicapped, nor of the extent and value of their work, since no records are kept by the C.C.D. of the numbers working in the local associations and these vary not only from place to place, but from day to day. Some local associations and some of the specialized agencies may be in a position to supply statistics, but these could not be used as a basis for calculating accurate figures for the whole country since even where records are kept they are not always up to date, and the methods adopted vary. But though accurate figures for the country as a whole are unobtainable some indication of their magnitude can be given by considering one or two examples chosen at random from the work of the county associations and specialized agencies, and by quoting from the reports of the two main general welfare agencies which supply volunteers for work with the handicapped – the B.R.C.S., and the W.R.V.S.

One county association for example, is known to have 140 voluntary workers, each one of whom is responsible for a local committee, while another has organized 'holidays for the handicapped' which are being widely copied. These are entirely staffed by volunteers who devote part of their own holiday to helping people who are too disabled to manage away from home without help. One of the specialized agencies has ninety branches, each of which is served by at least three or four active workers; a volume of activity which cannot be held exceptional since the handicapped themselves and their friends and relatives are known to undertake a wide range of personal service as well as money raising on behalf of sufferers from a particular disability. If numbers such as these are multiplied by the number of county associations and specialized agencies the total of voluntary workers runs into many thousands.

The annual reports of the B.R.C.S. and W.R.V.S., give some useful figures which help to fill out the picture. No less than 1,035 holidays for 4,886 handicapped persons were organized or assisted by Red Cross members in 1966 and 364 clubs met weekly throughout the year[1]. Each scheme and club must involve several workers, probably a minimum of three or four. The grand total of hospitals and convalescent homes in which members help either in nursing duties or in

____
[1] *Annual Report*, 1966, p. 55.

welfare is 3,371[1]. Not all the patients in these institutions are handicapped, but the number who are is considerable, and many thousands of Red Cross workers are involved in their care, not only at the bedside, but with reception duties, canteens, trolley shops, libraries and escort services. Clearly the B.R.C.S. undertake a very large volume of work for the handicapped, and it is work for which the great majority of its volunteers have been specially trained and which they are therefore well equipped to carry out.

Though the W.R.V.S. do not undertake nursing duties, they, too, play a valuable part in general welfare both in hospitals and in the community.

W.R.V.S. helped with refreshments, diversional therapy and entertainments in approximately 200 Local Authority Clubs for the Disabled and took full responsibility for a few W.R.V.S. Clubs. Helped in homes, read, wrote letters and provided escorts for the blind. Provided mobile libraries and visiting schemes. Ran holiday centres for severely disabled guests in Essex and Surrey[2].

It also assists at Training Centres for the Mentally Sub-Normal and arranges outings through its *Spare a Mile* scheme.

These are examples of what is being done by two of the organizations concerned, but they are only two among many. Members of churches and of women's organizations, Toc H, Rotarians and Lions are among the many who give voluntary service to the handicapped in hospital and at home[3].

All this voluntary service, though of considerable value, is inadequate to meet the needs, and great expansion is urgently required both in statutory and in voluntary provision. This urgency is recognized by the Ministry of Health not only because of the value of expanded services to those who receive them, but also because of their influence on public opinion:

In general the expansion of services and the development of public

---

[1] *Ibid.* This total is made up as follows:

Hospitals (nursing)	1,207
Other establishments (nursing)	596
Hospitals (welfare)	1,029
Other establishments (welfare)	899

[2] W.R.V.S., *Bulletin*, June, 1968.

[3] For more information about the work of volunteers in hospitals, see the section on hospitals below, pp. 82–95.

interest go hand in hand and the one interacts with the other . . . By developing their services, local authorities and voluntary bodies will encourage the public to extend their help to all groups of the handicapped[1].

This help from the public is of vital importance for the success of community care. It is needed both to increase pressure on the authorities to improve provision and to educate public opinion to accept and approve the increased expenditure involved. Help is needed, too, and will continue to be needed however much is provided by the State, in making life easier and pleasanter for people suffering from disabilities which prevent them from doing and enjoying so many of the things which those who are not handicapped can do and enjoy. Driving cars for outings and social intercourse, pushing wheel chairs, reading to the blind, communicating in their language with the deaf and dumb, visiting those who are housebound and in hospital, arranging clubs and holidays – these are just some of the ways in which volunteers are helping, and could greatly increase their help.

Recent developments

These activities are important to make life easier and pleasanter, but it is important, too, that the material conditions under which these handicapped people live and work should be improved. Here, too, voluntary workers can help since they can press on the public the claims of the disabled. Since their goal is normality, their fundamental need is to live and work as normal people. This means an adequate income on the one hand and aids to living – at home, with transport and at work – on the other. It is to achieve these things that a new organization, the Disablement Income Group has been formed. Founded in 1965 by a small group of disabled people and their friends it has spread rapidly and by 1967 had twenty-one local branches and over 2,000 members. Its aim quite simply is to improve the social and economic conditions of the disabled and in particular to secure 'the provision by the State of a modest basic income, with special supplementary allowances,

---

[1] *Health and Welfare (Cmnd.* 1973), para. 127.

for all disabled persons ordinarily resident in the U.K., whatever the cause of disablement, and irrespective of previous national insurance contributions'[1].

In support of this claim D.I.G. draws attention to statements by the Minister of Health 'that people with permanent disability should be enabled to live at home, wherever this is at all possible' and that they 'shall have the maximum opportunity of sharing in and contributing to the life of the community so that their capabilities are realized to the full, their self-confidence developed and their social contact strengthened'[2] and rightly points out that the first aim can often not be realized because of inadequate income, while the second, too, is also often impossible because of poverty. Housewives would be among the chief beneficiaries if a pension were granted irrespective of insurance contributions, and this extra income would make it possible for many wives and mothers to run their own homes instead of being sent to institutions and having their children 'in care'. This would not only mean happiness and well-being for many divided families, but would cost the taxpayer less than state provision for mother and children. Keeping families united by making it possible for the disabled person to live at home is the first need, but wider social contacts are also necessary and these, too, cannot be enjoyed when poverty is added to disablement.

This is the case that D.I.G. is bringing forcibly to the notice of the public. It is a pressure group and a provider of personal help and advice. Started and run by volunteers, it is a good example of what can be done by dedicated voluntary workers, unassisted by powerful friends and without financial backing. Its branches are entirely run by voluntary people, as are its advisory panels and its national executive. At headquarters it has a small paid secretarial and clerical staff with an hon. sec. (full-time) and an hon. medical social worker (part-time) and other voluntary helpers. These volunteers may be disabled or able-bodied, and come from all walks of life, though the majority are from the professional, upper and middle classes.

[1] *Memo* submitted to Rt. Hon. Douglas Houghton, M.P., Chancellor of the Duchy of Lancaster, Autumn, 1965.
[2] *Memo* to the Minister of Health, the Rt. Hon. Kenneth Robinson, M.P., October, 1966.

On this point the hon. medical social worker writes: 'It seems that mainly the poorer, lower-class disabled need our advisory service, and are unable to help themselves or do anything for other people – and the better-educated people are the ones who write to M.P.'s, papers, form branches, etc.'[1]. She feels that there is a great opportunity for non-practising people from the social work field (perhaps like herself with a young family) to associate with a local branch of D.I.G. and undertake the specialized work of enquiring into local provision of services for the disabled and of exerting pressure at local level. She also feels that there is a continuing need for volunteers to man the existing services for the disabled and chronic sick and to develop them further.

D.I.G. has been remarkably successful in a short time in enlisting the interest and support of other organizations[2], and in encouraging them both to extend their personal service to the handicapped, and to support the aims of D.I.G. itself. As far as personal service is concerned, it is evident from the correspondence received by D.I.G. that there is considerable demand for schemes of the good-neighbour type, which are sometimes run under the auspices of a local church, youth club, Rotary Club or Community Service Volunteers. They may provide meals when Meals on Wheels does not function, help with gardening, home repairs and decorating as well as visiting[3]. The existence and efficacy of such schemes is still extremely limited, yet most people are unaware of the extent of the need and of what they themselves could do to meet it. D.I.G. suggests that local authorities should encourage and co-ordinate voluntary helpers so that every disabled person in their area is contacted, visited and given the opportunity

---

[1] Letter to the author, 25th May, 1967.

[2] The following have shown a lively and in many cases practical and helpful interest: Ladies' Circles, National Council of Women, British Federation of University Women, Business and Professional Womens' Clubs, Women's Institutes, Women's Organizations of the three main Political Parties, Standing Conference of Women's Organizations, Married Womens' Association, Mothers' Union and Young Wives and Young Wives' Fellowship, National Council for the single woman and her dependants, Townswomen's Guilds, Inner Wheel, Individuals of the W.V.S. and the Red Cross. Ref. *Random Notes from D.I.G.*, para. 15.

[3] See *Memo* to Minister of Health, 1966, p. 5.

of accepting help[1]. If this were done people would at least know what the needs were and what part could be played by voluntary work. They would have some idea as to where they were most needed and what they could best be doing. At the same time the gaps in statutory provision would become more widely known, and this would strengthen the hands of those who are pressing for a better deal for the handicapped. This better deal will only be achieved if the public as a whole is prepared to pay the price, and this they will only be when they realize the extent of the problem. Those who become involved in personal service to the handicapped and know their needs at first hand are those best able to educate and influence public opinion, and anything that is done to increase their number and activity brings nearer the improvement in the material conditions of those they are seeking to help.

One of the most important ways in which those with first-hand knowledge can help is with employment. They understand the capabilities as well as the needs of the disabled and can influence the attitude of employers and fellow workers. This attitude varies from grudging fulfilment of a statutory obligation by employing a quota of disabled people on lowly tasks to real enterprise in using them for skilled jobs which they can tackle if allowance is made for their disability. The employer who provides good opportunities for disabled people, and the worker who tolerates and assists them are helping to raise their living standards and to increase their satisfaction in their work. Anything that voluntary workers can do to increase the number of enlightened employers will be making possible an improvement in the material conditions of those handicapped people who are fit enough to work.

It is hardly necessary to add that no improvement in material conditions through better jobs for those who can work, and more generous financial help for those who cannot, will render superfluous the personal service of friends and neighbours. This will always be needed to ensure that disabled members of the community are able to lead the fullest life of which they are capable.

[1] *Ibid.*

CHAPTER II

Hospitals

Discussion has so far been concentrated on the work of volunteers in the health and welfare services of the local authority but they are active, too, in the hospitals, and these were also included in the conferences of statutory and voluntary bodies called by the Ministry of Health in February and June, 1962[1].

The conference of February was followed by a circular, *Voluntary Help in Hospitals*[2], which asks management committees and Boards of Governors 'to take the initiative by reviewing the voluntary service given at all their hospitals and considering ways in which greater use can be made of help from the voluntary bodies', and further suggests both that approaches should be made to the voluntary bodies which are making or could make a contribution and 'that there should be continuing meetings with the representatives of the voluntary organizations which take responsibility for providing help at particular hospitals so that the current working and development of the services can be discussed and improvements or extensions made'. It includes a list of some forty types of work illustrating 'some of the services given to hospitals by voluntary bodies'[3].

The suggestions to hospitals made in this circular are similar to those addressed to local authorities, and the same points are emphasized in both cases. First, that 'the approach should be to the responsible body and not to individual members' and secondly that there should be 'continuing meetings'. It is clear from the circulars that the Ministry intended both that

[1] See pp. 44–5 above.

[2] H.M. (62), 29th April, 1962.

[3] These are grouped under four main headings: personal care of the patient, personal needs of the patient, recreation and occupation and general work for the hospital.

voluntary service in hospitals should increase, and that the voluntary organizations should have a say in policy making and not just be asked by the statutory body to deliver so many pairs of hands.

In order to estimate how far these intentions have been carried out it is necessary to discover what voluntary work is actually going on in hospitals and what measure of co-operation has been achieved between them and the voluntary bodies. The information available on both these matters is limited, and an estimate can only be made by piecing together material from a variety of sources as was done in the case of health and welfare.

In the case of hospitals there are five main sources, in addition to government circulars. *First*, general sources, such as Councils of Social Service and Guides to Voluntary Service; *second*, studies of particular places; *third*, schemes in individual hospitals; *fourth*, the National League of Hospital Friends; and *fifth*, the Trevelyan Report[1]. The first two have also been consulted in the case of health and welfare.

General sources of information. Councils of Social Service and Guides to Voluntary Service

The conference called by the Standing Conference of Councils of Social Service[2] did not include representatives of hospitals. It is true that the Parliamentary Secretary stressed the fact that the two plans, for hospitals and for the health and welfare services of the local authorities, were complementary, and drew the attention of the representatives of the latter to the importance of their relation with the hospitals, referring them to the Blue Book *Health and Welfare. The Development of Community Care*[3]. The importance of this part of his speech, however, lay in its emphasis on co-operation between the two branches of the statutory services, and not in any statement it contained on the role of volunteers in hospitals. Moreover, there was little reference to this role in the discussion, not surprisingly since the subject of the conference was community and not

[1] *Voluntary Service and the State*, 1952.
[2] See pp. 5–9 above.
[3] *Cmnd.* 1973.

hospital care. Hospitals were also omitted from R. K. Harrison's *Voluntary Organizations and Statutory Authority*[1].

Information about Councils of Social Service and voluntary work in hospitals must therefore be sought at local level. In a number of places Cs.S.S. are taking steps to recruit volunteers for this kind of work. In Leeds the Hospital Service Bureau, in Nottingham the Voluntary Work Agency and in Manchester Youth and Community Service, have made special efforts in this direction. In these and other places where the initiative has been taken by Councils of Social Service plans have been worked out in consultation with the hospitals in the area, and care has been taken to find people who were suitable for the jobs that needed doing and to keep in touch with them after placement.

Guides to Voluntary Service such as those published by the London Council of Social Service[2] and by the National Council[3] give a general picture of opportunities for hospital work. The former gives particulars of hospitals where voluntary helpers are welcomed, and the latter includes hospitals in its health section.

Special Studies: Halifax, Hampstead, York

Though the *Preliminary Inquiry into Recruitment and Training by Voluntary Associations* does not itself cover hospitals it suggests that they should be included in any further survey that might be undertaken, and the pilot study of Halifax[4] which followed includes a brief account of the work of the Hospital Friends. At the time of this study the Friends had not been invited to consultations by the Management Committee concerned but felt that the chairman of the House Committee 'was more receptive to voluntary work' than the Management Committee. Useful contacts existed with hospital secretaries and matrons, but the moves had come mainly from the Friends' side. There appeared to be no machinery for consultation except the Friends' own committee to which the

---

[1] See p. 10 above.

[2] *Opportunities for Voluntary Social Service in London* (1967).

[3] D. Hobman, *Guide to Voluntary Service* (1964).

[4] *Nacoss Occasional Papers, No. 1.*

matron was invited, and the success or otherwise of the work depended on the personal attitudes of hospital staff, particularly matrons. The Friends numbered about 120 voluntary workers at this time and undertook a wide variety of jobs.

The Hampstead *Research into the Selection, Placing and Training of Voluntary Social Workers* is based on a small number of interviews with organizations using volunteers and with volunteers themselves. Though not confined to hospitals it is particularly interested in them and quotes the case of St. Thomas's, London, which had 126 volunteers and used them in practically all departments.

Voluntary Workers in York describes in some detail the work being done by voluntary labour in and for the hospitals in the city. First there was the National Hospital Reserve which was administered by the Deputy Group Secretary: its target of 500 had been surpassed with ease as there were 617 on roll at the time of the survey. Then there was the Red Cross and St. John which recruit, train and allocate volunteers for particular tasks, and finally there was a large group of other voluntary bodies, most of which were represented on a League of Friends, which supply volunteers for a variety of tasks, such as work in canteens, libraries and trolley shops, which require less specialized training. It appears that there was no machinery for regular consultation between the hospitals on the one hand and the multiplicity of voluntary bodies on the other, and that the latter were not even well organized themselves, in spite of the existence of the Friends, since all were 'anxious to remain independent and provide their services as separate organizations'[1]. This created difficulties both for the intending volunteer, who did not know where best to offer his services, and for the hospitals, which did not know where to apply for help. The impression gained from reading this report is that there is considerable activity and goodwill but that much valuable human potential is wasted because of the failure to bring together the tremendous opportunities for voluntary work in hospitals and the large number of people anxious to do it. This, apparently, 'is one field in which it seems comparatively easy to recruit volun-

---

[1] J. Kamer, *Voluntary Workers in York*, p. 50.

teers'[1]; and it is certainly one where work is waiting to be done. Brief reference to voluntary work in hospitals is also made in the studies of Portsmouth and Yorkshire which were described in Chapter I[2].

These studies of voluntary work, like the reports of those Councils of Social Service which recruit and place volunteers, show that voluntary work is playing some part in the life of hospitals in the places concerned. They do not, however, give details of its nature and extent, nor do they describe the unpaid service of committee members. More information about the kind of work that is being done and the number of people involved can be obtained from those hospitals which are themselves making special efforts to use volunteers, and from the National Association of Leagues of Hospital Friends, and a detailed picture of the wider field of voluntary service including management is available in a study undertaken by John Trevelyan.

Schemes in hospitals

Fulbourn, Cambridge, was one of the first hospitals to plan and carry out a 'volunteer programme'. A report[3] was issued in December 1965 describing what had been achieved during the two years since the appointment of a full-time organizer 'whose sole responsibility was the recruitment, placing and training of volunteers'. A mere statement of fact – the increase in numbers from fifty-two to 359 and in the variety of tasks undertaken – is impressive enough, but more important is the beneficial effect on the hospitals as a whole. The report concludes with these words:

It is the opinion of all staff that the volunteer programme has made an important contribution both to the hospital atmosphere and to the after-care of patients and that it is one of the most important developments of recent years. All hope that it will be possible to ensure its continuing and extending development.

[1] *Ibid.*, p. 41.

[2] See pp. 17–20 above.

[3] *Report from organizers of voluntary services to Nuffield Provincial Hospitals Trust* (Cyclo.) (1965).

The lessons to be learned from this successful venture are clearly set out both in the report by the organizer herself, and in an accompanying paper which gives the views of the staff and shows why a full-time officer was necessary for the development of a programme of this kind. Her work 'has made clear why the volunteer programme did not expand before 1963 and has largely overcome the difficulties so that the programme has grown very effectively'. Only a special officer can supply the time and the skills needed for the recruitment, placement and training of volunteers, and, even more important, can hope to overcome what the report describes as 'unrealized general and social factors' such as the ignorance of the public and the lack of understanding of each other among the volunteers and staff.

Another interesting scheme has been started at St. Thomas's, London. Here, too, recruitment improved dramatically with the appointment of a special officer. Although much time was devoted to preparatory work both with the nursing staff and with others in the hospital, and though it was the policy to proceed slowly, no less than 120 volunteers were at work each week within a year of the appointment of an organizer. The Clerk of the Governors writes in his first report on the scheme:

Despite the previous gloomy prognostication and the self-imposed limitation on the area of recruitment, the embarrassment has been that the number of volunteers has grown faster than the hospital can absorb them. The fact that there are volunteers available, and indeed anxious to work in most hospitals, is demonstrated by the immediate response which has been made as a result of the introduction of the voluntary scheme to the Lambeth Hospital[1].

The success of the scheme at St. Thomas's has led to similar schemes being introduced not only at Lambeth, which is in the same group, but also in two others, and it is spreading to other places.

The success of these schemes led the King Edward's Hospital Fund to undertake an investigation into the use of organizers of volunteers in hospitals[2]. When the survey started in February 1967 thirteen hospitals were known to employ such

[1] *St. Thomas's Hospital. Voluntary Service in the Welfare State.*
[2] Jan. Rocha, *Organizers of Voluntary Service in Hospitals* (1968).

organizers, and since then several others have followed suit. The survey was based on interviews with hospital staff, volunteers, patients and with the organizers themselves, at which questionnaires seeking information and opinions about the work of the organizers were filled in. The report describes the evidence in detail and includes a long list of conclusions and recommendations. The main factors which prompted the hospitals in the survey to appoint organizers were:

the need to co-ordinate existing voluntary services; the desire to increase voluntary help; the example of the schemes at Fulbourn Hospital and St. Thomas's Hospitals and of the many American and Canadian schemes; the desire to promote community involvement in the hospitals [and the appointment of an organizer] has always resulted in greatly increased numbers of volunteers, not only through the Organizer's own recruiting efforts but also because her presence encourages organizations which hitherto have not been involved with hospital work to supply volunteers.

The final conclusion from the survey is that it 'has shown how desirable it is to have one person on the staff responsible for the co-ordination and encouragement of the local voluntary organizations and individual volunteers'[1].

Many other hospitals besides those employing organizers provide examples of work being done by volunteers. There has, however, been little general publicity on the subject, and articles in the national press appear infrequently, so that it is not easy to estimate how much is actually going on. For every scheme that attracts the notice of the public there may well be dozens whose work is unrecorded and is known only to those who take part in it and to the patients and staff whom they serve. Mental Health Week, 1966, provided an opportunity for an article in the *Guardian*[2], and the special supplement to *The Times* on 14th January, 1966, devoted to the Westminster Hospital, made possible an account of the work of its Friends by their chairman who wrote:

'. . . we provide shop trolleys, film shows, television, stethoscopic radio earphones and we give furniture and pictures for sitting-rooms

---

[1] *Op. cit.*, pp. 12, 13 and 15.

[2] *Time to Spare*, by Nesta Roberts. The *Guardian*, 7th June, 1966. This article describes the Fulbourn Scheme.

and corridors as well as other comforts. Our regular ward visits are popular and successful.

This is probably a typical list of activities of a successful Association of Friends. The emphasis here is still somewhat on money-raising, which does not feature at all in schemes such as those at Fulbourn and St. Thomas's. It plays no part either in the valuable work being done by the 'Playladies' who carry out voluntary duties in the children's ward of Whittington, North London. This scheme, described in the *Times Educational Supplement* of 9th February, 1966, was started by a local mother two years before and became an established success. The Playladies 'read to small patients, chat and play games with them or are ready with a much-needed comforting cuddle at tearful and near-tearful moments'. This, like the schemes which employ an organizer, shows how much voluntary workers can contribute to the well-being of patients and staff, and how important it is that such work should be established and encouraged in an increasing number of hospitals.

The National Association of Leagues of Hospital Friends

General information about the work of volunteers in the hospitals all over the country comes from the National Association of Leagues of Hospital Friends. In 1964 their membership increased by the affiliation of thirty-eight new leagues to a total of 661 and there were in addition unaffiliated leagues of which the national body has no record.

In the same year the national association set out to discover some facts about the membership and financial efforts of affiliated leagues. Only thirty-seven per cent of the 661 replied, but between them they served 762 hospitals and had a membership of 388,667, of whom some 20,876 were giving active personal service. They raised and spent on these hospitals the sum of £392,825 during the previous financial year and had spent over three million pounds since 1948[1]. The national association estimated that these figures both for personal service and for money raised would be doubled if returns had been received from all affiliated leagues. By 1968 the

---

[1] *Annual Report*, 1964–5, p. 9.

number of affiliated leagues had risen to 722 and the number of active workers to over 30,000.

The Trevelyan Report

A detailed picture of the whole field of voluntary service in British hospitals is given in this study, which was undertaken in the early years of the National Health Service. Although the information it contains is in some ways out of date, it remains the most complete study of the subject that has yet been made.

It was carried out with the help of an advisory committee of seven drawn from the National Council of Social Service, the King Edward's Fund and the hospitals. Starting with a discussion of the place of voluntary service in society it proceeds to give the historical background of the hospital service and the story leading up to the National Health Act of 1946. It then describes in detail the partnership between the state and voluntary service:

the first example in this country of a public service which is financed almost entirely from public funds being operated by a government department and voluntary service in partnership[1];

and discusses the type of work done by unpaid people and the time they give to it. It estimates that members of Regional Boards give on average eight to ten hours per week[2] and members of Management Committees six to eight hours[3], and that there are no less than 10,000[4] men and women who serve on these and on the Board of Governors of Teaching Hospitals and on the various sub-committees. There is no reason to suppose that these particular figures are out of date, since the machinery for running the hospitals has remained largely unchanged. Great changes have occurred however in the extent of voluntary work other than service on committees and in the numbers of people engaged in it.

Though the Trevelyan Report does not attempt to estimate

---

[1] *Voluntary Service and the State*, p. 33.

[2] *Ibid.*, p. 38.

[3] *Ibid.*, p. 42.

[4] *Ibid.*, p. 65.

the number of these other volunteers, it draws the following general conclusions from the evidence available:

it is true to say that at the present time, although there is a national health service financed almost entirely by public funds, there is more voluntary service given to the sick and infirm than ever before[1].

The evidence takes the form of descriptions of the work of the various societies, both national and local, which are active in this field and of the variety and extent of the services carried out by volunteers, and gives an overall picture of what they are doing to help the sick and infirm both in the different kinds of hospital and outside – in the home, in transport, in the care of the elderly and in the after-care of discharged patients.

The investigators were clearly impressed by what they saw and heard of voluntary service in hospitals, but recognized the problems which it presents. Chief among these was that of 'obtaining enough suitable people to do the work'[2]. This is simply and undramatically stated, but the two words 'enough' and 'suitable' go to the heart of the matter in this as in all voluntary work. The statement continues: 'The recruitment and training of voluntary workers is of vital importance'. This is an obvious sequence since successful recruitment would create an improvement in both numbers and quality of volunteers, while training also helps to raise their quality and may render people who would not otherwise come up to the standard required more 'suitable' for the work.

Voluntary work in hospitals today

The need for more voluntary workers was clear at the time of the publication of the Trevelyan Report, and it is still clear today. It is less clear however how great this shortage is since an estimate could only be made after detailed inquiries at each hospital as to what work is left undone for want of voluntary help. It is a fact, however, that the distribution of services dependent on volunteers is extremely uneven, and

[1] *Ibid.*, p. 71.
[2] *Ibid.*, p. 84.

that amenities such as canteens for out-patients and visitors, libraries and shops, and personal services such as reception, visiting and entertainment of patients, are non-existent or inadequate in many places.

These variations are more likely to be due to the attitude of management and staff than to the lack of potential volunteers. For the evidence from York[1] and other places is that hospital work is one field for which recruitment is comparatively easy, largely because of the favourable image and glamour of the hospital world. If this is true hospitals need only state their requirement to a willing public to receive sufficient offers of help of all kinds, and this in fact has happened in the case of hospitals with organizers of voluntary services. The evidence of these places certainly shows the value of having a special person whose job it is to appeal to the public for their help.

Members of the public are ready and indeed anxious to give voluntary service in hospitals – what is needed is valuable in itself for the personal service given to patients and their relatives and to the staff, but it is valuable, too, in an even more important way, that it forms a link between the hospitals and the community. Volunteers can be, in a very real sense, the watchdogs of the public, by making known the conditions in which patients and staff live and work. They can pay tribute to the staff in the very many cases where tribute is due, and they can draw attention to needs and expose failings. They can sometimes do this as individuals, but they can do it more effectively as groups. Patients' associations, supported by relatives and friends, can help to get general standards raised, and organizations like *Mother Care for Children in Hospitals* and *Aegis* (Aid for the Elderly in Government Institutions) can influence national policy and produce reforms.

Mother Care has helped to secure a general relaxation of visiting rules on children's wards and to make possible the admission of mothers with their children, while *Aegis* has exposed serious conditions in some of the big old hospitals. Both in the press, and more especially in a recent book *Sans Everything*[2], it has made accusations of neglect, unkindness

---

[1] J. Kamer, *op cit.*, p. 41.

[2] By Barbara Robb (1967); see also article by Lena Jager in the *Guardian*, 9th July, 1967.

and even cruelty which have led to committees of inquiry set up at the request of the Minister of Health. Though the findings of these committees[1] did not substantiate allegations of cruelty on the part of the staff, they did reveal the existence of conditions which were far from satisfactory, and make it clear that vigilance on the part of the public has an important part to play in securing better care for patients, especially those in long-stay geriatric and mental hospitals. There is no better way of assuring this vigilance than by voluntary service in the wards. *Aegis* hopes to introduce 'a new concept of caring for the aged, opening up, at last, the immense resources of organized voluntary help'[2] and suggests practical ways in which the volunteer could help. 'The voluntary services could be called upon to visit. Hosts or hostesses could be appointed to the wards to help the relations between patients and visitors and to organize social life, including outings.'[3] It also stresses the value of volunteers in helping to ensure that patients are receiving proper care: 'It must be emphasized that, apart from the human need of the old to have contact with their families and friends, a plenitude of visitors would make it harder for any of the staff so disposed to neglect or ill-treat the patients.'

It is not only in cases where unsatisfactory conditions should be exposed that the presence of volunteers is needed. These cases are few indeed compared with the many where voluntary helpers are working alongside the staff for the benefit of the patients, and by learning about difficulties and problems at first hand are able to interpret the hospital to the public and involve the community in further activity on its behalf. Such action is welcomed by many of those who are responsible for

---

[1] *Findings and Recommendations Following Enquiries into Allegations Concerning the Care of Elderly Patients in Certain Hospitals*, Cmnd. 3687, July, 1968. The public concern felt at the alleged abuses described in the book was not altogether allayed by the publication of this report, and it was followed by some unfavourable press comment. D. A. N. Jones, for example, writing in *The Sunday Times Magazine* for 29th September, 1968, says: 'No one I have met in the service is satisfied with the Ministry's whitewashing report on the abuses revealed in that book. They all think that it contains much truth.'

[2] Robb, *op cit.*, p. xvi.

[3] *Ibid.*, p. 111.

running the hospitals – in the words of the chairman of a Regional Board, 'The very fact that there are people in the community who want to come and help, who care enough to give up their free time, is in itself of therapeutic benefit to the patient and a great encouragement to the staff.'[1]

The role of volunteers as a link between the hospital and the community is important now, but it will be more important still if the administrative structure of the health service is altered in the ways suggested by the Green Paper on the subject[2]. The change suggested will involve a much smaller number of boards and committees and there will thus be fewer members of the public appointed with direct responsibility for the running of the hospitals. Whatever the advantages of the proposed new system there will be in it a danger of remote control since those responsible will lack the personal contact now enjoyed by members of management and more especially of house committees. If house committees were abolished a link between the hospital and its neighbourhood would be lost. It may be true that some members of these committees do not take the personal interest in patients and staff which their office should demand and sometimes tend blindly to support an official view in the face of public criticism, but they had and have the opportunity both to contribute personally to the welfare of the patients and to ensure that complaints and anxieties on the part of the public are dealt with properly. For every one who neglects these opportunities there are many who seize them and who carry out their duties conscientiously and well. House committees are not the only means through which service of this kind can be given, but they provide machinery for it, and if they are abolished something of value will be lost which must be supplied in other ways. The most obvious way is by increasing the number and activity of voluntary workers other than committee members, and positive steps should be taken to bring this about.

Some volunteers will come forward without special encourage-

---

[1] *Address* by Mrs. Isabel Graham Bryce, chairman, Oxford Regional Hospital Board, to the Annual Conference of the Royal Society of Health (1968).

[2] *National Health Service. The Administrative Structure of the Medical and Related Services in England and Wales*, H.M.S.O. (1968).

ment, but if active participation by members of the public is to be the rule rather than the exception more organizers of voluntary workers will be needed. The experience of hospitals where such officers have been appointed shows that recruiting can be more successfuly carried out by the institution itself than by voluntary bodies in the community. This raises important questions for the future of those voluntary bodies which regard recruitment, allocation and training of volunteers as one of their functions. If the pattern which seems to be developing in hospitals is followed in other fields the position of voluntary bodies is bound to change. It will change not only in relation to the hospitals and to the health and welfare services but wherever statutory authorities or institutions undertake their own recruitment.

The future of voluntary bodies as agents for recruitment, and the advantages and disadvantages of their involvement in the process will be discussed in the final chapter, after the present position of voluntary workers in other fields of social service has been described.

CHAPTER III

Children and Young People

Work with children of all ages offers tremendous opportunities for voluntary service both by adults and by the young people themselves. What is being done in this field can be considered under three main headings, roughly distinguished by the age of the child: – babies and young children, children of school age, and young people who have left school.

Some account of the work with babies and young children has already been given[1]. Many different voluntary bodies help to meet their needs in co-operation with the health and welfare services and with the children's departments, and all make use of volunteers. Children of school age are attracting increasing attention from the voluntary bodies, both in participation in the work of the schools and in provision for children outside school hours. On the one hand there are associations such as the Confederation for the Advancement of State Education (C.A.S.E.), the Advisory Centre for Education (A.C.E.) and Parent-Teacher Associations (P.-T.A.'s) which are all primarily concerned with the schools, and on the other hand there are organizations catering for the leisure-time needs of school children by means of play groups, play centres and in other ways. Finally, there is the Youth Service, which is mainly for children who have left school, and includes work by adults for the young, and work by the young themselves, both at home and overseas.

1 *School children*

C.A.S.E., A.C.E., C.R.A.C., P.-T.A.'s[2]

The active interest of voluntary bodies in the schools themselves

---

[1] See above, Chapter I, Section 2.

[2] See *Reports on Education* (issued by the D.E.S.), No. 19 (Feb., 1965).

is a comparatively recent development, though out-of-school activities have long been their concern. The Confederation for the Advancement of State Education (C.A.S.E.) is a national body linking 125 local associations (A.A.S.E.'s) which seek to improve the quality of state education in co-operation with their education authorities and by stimulating public interest. They seek representation of parents on education committees and on governing bodies. The Advisory Centre for Education (A.C.E.) provides an information service, issues the quarterly *Where?* and has started a National Extension College. The Careers Research and Advisory Centre (C.R.A.C.) helps students and their advisers with educational and career decisions. These three organizations, which are all of recent date, are largely dependent on the enthusiasm and hard work of volunteers. Paid staff are either non-existent or kept to a minimum and the work depends on the active participation of members of advisory committees and workers in the field who are all unpaid. The actual numbers involved may not be very great, but in C.A.S.E. at least there must be several hundred responsible for the day-to-day work of the 125 local associations. The honorary secretary gives the membership as 8,000 and the active membership as ten to twenty per cent of this[1].

Parent-teacher associations (P.-T.A.'s) – also a recent development – call on the services of many more volunteers. They are concerned with individual schools rather than with general educational problems, and exist at the school level to foster closer links between home and school. Their national federation (N.F.P.-T.A.) was formed in 1956 to encourage the growth of the movement. Though it reports a steady increase in numbers it does not know how many actually exist as no official record is kept of those which are unaffiliated, but there are certainly more than the 570-odd which belong to the federation[2]. The value of the work being done by the local associations varies greatly from school to school, depending

---

[1] Ref. letter to author of 21st April, 1966. See also *Education*, 8th April, 1966.

[2] 370 affiliated direct to the N.F.P.-T.A. and 200 through local county federations, of which there are 13. Ref. letter to the author from the hon. sec. of the N.F.P.-T.A., 30th September, 1968.

on the personalities of the parents and teachers who run them; but at least they form some kind of link between home and school and often raise money for much-needed amenities, while at the best they play an active part in what is being done in their school. Through them parents can get to know the teachers, and understand what they are trying to do for the children, and can themselves study problems of health and education. As the chief speaker at their ninth annual conference (1965) said: 'P.-T.A.'s are still in their infancy but their influence is rapidly growing and . . . the movement could certainly become a great creative force with a tremendous growth of responsibility'[1].

Once a P.-T.A. is formed there does not seem to be much difficulty in recruiting members since both parents and teachers have a direct interest in the child whose education they share, but it is never easy to find the key people who are both keen and competent enough to do the necessary preliminary work of securing 'the willing co-operation of Head Teachers, Staff and Parents'[2] so that the association can be successfully launched, and who are prepared to go on giving voluntary service as officers and committee members to ensure its continuation as an active organization. It would be an exaggeration to count all the members of all the hundreds of P.-T.A.'s as voluntary workers since most of them probably do little more than attend occasional meetings and perhaps help with money raising, but every association which functions at all must have some half dozen who give time freely to promote its objects. Though this adds up to a considerable total, the number of P.-T.A.'s is small indeed compared with the number of schools in the country. Many more should be formed, and those which exist should be strengthened and improved, for their potential value goes far beyond the provision of amenities – they are capable of providing a real link between home and school and could spread through the community information about the schools and help to create the public interest and concern that is needed to improve them[3].

[1] *The Parent Teacher*, Autumn, 1965, p. 13.
[2] Circular issued by the N.F.P.-T.A'.s on forming a Parent-Teacher Association.
[3] See *Reports on Education*, No. 19 (February, 1965).

There is general agreement about their value. The Plowden Report[1] pays tribute to their work. The National Union of Teachers is 'unreservedly in favour', the Department of Education and Science and a number of diocesan education authorities encourage support, yet they exist in only a small proportion of the schools in the country. The decision as to whether or not a P.-T.A. should be formed rests with each local headmaster and it must therefore be assumed, as the *Guardian* comments[2], that 'most choose to do without the unquestionable advantages'. It is apparent that official blessings are not enough, and that energetic action on the part of members of the public will be needed if the number and influence of P.-T.A.'s are to expand.

P.-T.A.'s, like C.A.S.E., A.C.E., and other bodies concerned to press for educational advance, are a comparatively new field for voluntary work and one where great developments are possible if the necessary volunteers are ready to take action.

An important step forward was taken in October, 1967, when a new body, the Home and School Council, was formed by C.A.S.E., A.C.E., and the N.F.P.-T.A. The chairman, Michael Young, writes: 'The two halves of the child's life, home and school, will never make a whole unless the parent is invited in and properly informed'[3]. The new Council will campaign for the formation of P.-T.A.'s or other parent groups in every school and for the appointment of parents as managers and governors. Though there is a paid officer in the field, the management of the Council rests with its honorary members and the success of its work at school level will depend at every stage on the voluntary service of parents and teachers.

Out-of-school activities

The provision of out-of-school activities has long been the

---

[1] *Children and their Primary Schools*, H.M.S.O., 1967, Chap. 4. While recognizing that they may be 'of the greatest value' the report stresses that they are not necessarily 'the best means of fostering close relationships between home and school'.

[2] 16th January, 1967.

[3] *Observer*, 28th October, 1967, and *Where?*, January, 1968, p. 5. The address of the Council is 57 Russell St., Cambridge.

concern of voluntary bodies and has always attracted large numbers of volunteers. Play groups for the under-fives and play centres for children of school age are run by both local authorities and voluntary bodies and in both cases much of the work is done by unpaid helpers. In the case of play groups, the driving force often comes from the parents. These may start with two or three mothers taking turns at caring for one another's children with their own, but as the groups expand they include the children of others, and what began as self-help and mutual aid develops into community service, and volunteers who are not parents join in the work. Much help is given also by people who are not parents in the case of play centres, which from the start are open to all the children of a neighbourhood.

The main national organizations responsible for play schemes which use voluntary workers are the Pre-School Playgroups Association, the Save the Children Fund and the National Playing Fields Association[1]. The first is entirely concerned with children under five[2], the second with all age groups[3] and the third mainly with school children and young people who have left school. These three bodies are in touch with many local schemes, but even so they represent only a part of what is going on. There are other groups which have sprung up spontaneously as the result of local initiative whose activities are little known beyond their own neighbourhoods. One such is the Playleaders Scheme in Nottingham which was started by an enthusiastic group in a park in a downtown area and has spread to other parks in the city. In London the Council of Social Service is actively engaged in promoting and running play centres and so are the Notting Hill Adventure Playground Association and International Voluntary Service (London Group) as well as the Save the Children Fund[4]; schemes are also being run by borough Councils of Social Service, by the churches and by other local groups. There are Play Parks and One o'Clock Clubs (for younger children)

---

[1] Ref. David Hobman, *A Guide to Voluntary Service*.

[2] See above, pp. 29–31.

[3] *Ibid.*, p. 29.

[4] See *Opportunities for Voluntary Social Service in London* (London C.S.S., 1967).

in many of the London parks and a number of adventure playgrounds. Though these are all staffed by paid playleaders supported by the local authorities, they also partly depend on voluntary help. Volunteers, moreover, do not restrict their work to helping in centres organized and staffed by statutory and voluntary bodies, but are actively concerned with launching new projects. One of the most recent ventures is a summer project undertaken in Notting Hill in August, 1967[1]. Organized by an independent committee it is an attempt to solve the problems of a twilight area and includes the setting up of play groups, opening of play streets, school playgrounds and church halls. Advice and material help was sought from the local authority, and volunteers aimed at getting 'intensive play' under way. This is just one example of pioneering work for the school-age child which is now being undertaken by voluntary workers, and there must be many others.

Some are waiting to take shape until the necessary action is taken by enterprising pioneers and planners. The action needed is described in an article in *New Society*[2], on the work of the London School Care Committees, which suggests that there is a large pool of personal service which could be used to better advantage, and outlines a scheme by which this might be achieved. A scheme of this type which involves training and reorganization is, the article maintains, the only way 'to provide adequate coverage for London's thousands of school children, and it might well afford a useful model for other big cities'.

Care committees

No account of voluntary work with school children would be complete without mention of this care committee service. Unique to London it has long played and still plays an important part in the provision of welfare. It evolved from the machinery set up to provide meals, and was

the inheritor of much devoted voluntary work undertaken by philanthropic organisations to ameliorate the lot of children

[1] Ref. *Times Educational Supplement*, 3rd June, 1967.
[2] By Elizabeth Irvine, 10th March, 1966.

suffering from poverty or neglect . . . Many voluntary activities were initiated by the school care committee such as the establishment of school treatment centres and the scheme for the supply of milk in schools[1].

The duties of these committees are still those which were laid down in 1907:

in constant contact with heads of schools, to ensure that all children obtain full benefit from the education for which they are best suited by age, aptitude and ability; to ascertain the needs of their families and so, in co-operation with all statutory and voluntary services, endeavour to prevent or alleviate physical and mental distress; to initiate schemes to promote the welfare of school children and to undertake any other duties as they may from time to time be asked to perform[2].

and the service is manned by some 2,350 voluntary workers co-ordinated and given guidance by a small professional staff. The value of their work is recognized by both members and staff of the Education Authority. Referring to 'the important part they play in the London education service' the chairman of the Schools Sub-Committee writes:

care committee workers help in a variety of practical ways to ensure that the full benefits of the various services available are received by those needing them, for example, free dinners, help with clothing, assistance towards the cost of school journeys and holidays for children and mothers . . . Many hard-pressed mothers are able to carry their heavy burdens because they can share them with regular and sympathetic listeners. This, in turn, prevents some of the strain from falling on the older children[3].

The chief organizer is no less enthusiastic. In an article describing their origin and present position she writes:

Social workers are indeed in such short supply that we could never hope to give an improved service by replacing the voluntary workers, only by using both can we maintain and develop our standards[4].

But it is not only for this reason that she values their help.

[1] I.L.E.A. Minutes, 20th July, 1966.
[2] *Ibid.*
[3] Report of School Sub-Committee to the I.L.E.A., 19th January, 1967.
[4] Craft, Raynor & Cohen, *Linking Home and School*, p. 162.

They can often do what school teachers and welfare officers, however devoted, are unable to do because of the nature of their job.

The school care service is accepted by London parents as the link between home and school. The voluntary worker is regarded as a 'friend of the family' and is not considered as one of 'them'[1].

Tributes such as these are an indication of the quality of the volunteers, and such recognition doubtless helps with the recruitment of sufficient numbers of people of the right kind. It is not surprising that men and women who are anxious to serve the community should choose a field where their contribution is appreciated in this way. What is more surprising is that the system which has been so successful in London has not been copied elsewhere.

The reason why the system is still unique to London may partly lie in its origin in the work of philanthropic organizations whose efforts were concentrated there, but a more likely explanation is that it has always been an integral part of the education service in London. It was the authority itself which formed and officially recognized a care committee for each elementary school, and from the start the co-operation of the teachers was secured, and the work of the volunteers was co-ordinated by professional organizing staff. Thus, though the work of the committees is carried out by volunteers, it is not carried out under the auspices of a voluntary body, but by voluntary recruits to a statutory service, who are responsible to the authority through its own officers, and not through any independent agency.

This set-up may in part explain the success of the care committee system in London, and its absence in other places where the same relationship between authority and volunteer has either not been attempted or if attempted has been unsuccessful. The service as it exists and has existed is an example of the way in which well-directed voluntary effort can assist the work of local authorities[2], but it is also a clear case of voluntary workers' helping to bring the needs of those with whom they work to the notice of a wider public. The care

[1] *Ibid.*, p. 159.
[2] This point is emphasized in *New Society*, 2nd Feb., 1967, p. 167.

committees were set up in 1907 as a result of work done and pressure by voluntary workers in 'the philanthropic organizations', and voluntary workers still supply the information on which the education committee takes action. As recently as 1966 they were:

asked to include in their annual reports for the school year 1965–6 information about the number of cases of acute poverty and financial hardship known to them, the main causes of poverty as they found them and the means they used to assist; and to suggest ways in which distress might be further diminished[1].

2 *The youth service*

No hard and fast line can be drawn between work with children before and after they have left school. Play centres, for instance, do not usually exclude those who have left, and many of the activities of the Youth Service include children still at school. The vast ramification of provision for boys and girls made through the youth service is not on the whole restricted to particular age groups, though much of it is specially aimed at the older teenager.

The Youth Service was born in 1939, and powers were written into the 1944 Act[2] which made it an integral part of the national system of education. Though it is nowhere mentioned by name in the Act, two sections lay on local education authorities the duty to provide 'leisure-time occupation . . . for any persons over compulsory school age who are able and willing to profit by the facilities provided for that purpose'[3] and to 'have regard to the expediency of co-operating with any voluntary services or bodies whose objects include the provision of facilities or the organization of activities of a similar character'[4]. The responsibility for providing a youth service was laid on the local authorities, but this responsibility could be discharged through the agency of the voluntary bodies who had long been active in the field. After the passing of the Act they continued and expanded their

---

[1] *Report of Schools Sub-Committee to the I.L.E.A.*, 19th January, 1967.
[2] *Educational Reconstruction, Cmnd.* 6458.
[3] *Op. cit.*, Section 41.
[4] *Ibid.*, Section 53 (as amended by the Education Act 1948).

work with some assistance from local authorities, but the service as a whole failed to provide adequately for the needs of those it was intended to help. This failure led to the appointment of the Albemarle Committee in 1958 to survey the scope of the service and to make recommendations for the future.

The Albemarle Committee[1]

The terms of reference of this committee were:

To review the contribution which the Youth Service of England and Wales can make in assisting young people to play their part in the life of the community, in the light of changing social and industrial conditions and of current trends in other branches of the education service; and to advise according to what priorities best value can be obtained for the money spent[2].

The first chapter of its Report includes an assessment of the service as it then was, summarized in these words:

Overall, thanks to public funds, private generosity, and the timely help of trusts, and thanks even more to the resource and devotion of a great number of voluntary workers and a small band of paid (but often underpaid) ones, provision of some sort has been made for the needs of one in three of the young people between 15 and 21[3].

The Report is not able to estimate the number of these voluntary workers, nor even of the clubs run by voluntary societies unless they are receiving grant-aid[4], but the committee was clearly of the opinion that the main burden was being borne by volunteers, as is stressed in the passage quoted above and again in the categorical statement 'the Service could not exist without them'[5].

How far is it possible to form an idea of the number of people involved? The committee is extremely cautious on this point. 'It has not been possible for us to get exact numbers, but there are probably tens of thousands.' Admittedly it was

---

[1] *The Youth Service in England and Wales*, Cmnd. 929 (1960).
[2] *Op. cit.*, para. 1.
[3] *Ibid.*, para. 33.
[4] 1,222 centres fully maintained by L.E.A., 7,847 youth groups assisted financially by L.E.A. (*op. cit.*, Appendix 4).
[5] *Op. cit.*, para. 286.

difficult to include in an official document figures that could not be verified, but unofficially it may be possible to make an estimate less vague than 'tens of thousands'.

Membership and voluntary workers in voluntary youth organizations

An attempt to do this was made in November, 1966, by sending a letter to all members of The Standing Conference of National Voluntary Youth Organizations (SCNVYO) asking for information about their membership and voluntary workers when the Albermarle Committee was appointed, and at the present time. All twenty-seven member organizations replied to the letter, most of them giving considerable detail. Some were unable to supply all the statistical information asked for owing to lack of records, but sufficient was received to enable a comparison to be made between the position in 1958–9 and 1965–6. Information about overall membership was practically complete, and though no details about voluntary workers were available for nine of the twenty-seven organizations, the facts supplied by the other eighteen are sufficiently representative for a useful picture of the whole to be drawn. This information is set out in Appendix II, Tables I, II and III.

The first important fact revealed by these figures is the comparative stability of the overall membership (Table I). If the totals are split into age groups it appears that membership in the fourteen to twenty age group has not increased at all in relation to population. During a six-year period when the number of boys and girls between the ages of eleven and twenty (inclusive) increased by 11.7 per cent, membership in that age group increased by only 12 per cent (Table I, note 4). Moreover, the increase was in all probability confined to those under fourteen, for during a four-year period when the numbers in the age group fourteen to twenty (the ages with which the youth service is primarily concerned) grew by 15.5 per cent, membership in that age group grew by only 14.8 per cent[1].

[1] The increases in population have been calculated from the tables in the annual abstracts of statistics published by the Central Statistical Office. Increases in membership cannot have the same accuracy since they come from information supplied by the voluntary bodies and are often only approximate. Those for the 11–20 age groups come from the annual

These figures refer only to the part of the youth service for which the voluntary bodies are responsible, and it is possible that the provision made directly by local authorities has increased substantially since the Albemarle Report. There are no official statistics of membership of local authority clubs, but some increase has certainly taken place and a number of purpose-built centres have been opened, but the evidence seems to suggest that the main effort of education committees has been directed to supporting voluntary organizations rather than establishing new clubs of their own. Moreover, some local authority clubs are themselves affiliated to organizations which belong to SCNVYO so that their membership is included in that recorded in the national figures[1]. It is therefore likely that there has been no great increase in the proportion of young people who make use of the service as a whole, and in fact the overall figure of one in three who do so at any one time is generally accepted today as it was at the time of the Albemarle Report[2]. This failure to expand numerically has not however meant that the quality of the service has remained unchanged. More money has been spent on buildings and salaries, and much heart searching and experiment has been going on so that more and better opportunities

[1] Letter to the author from Alan Gibson, Head of the Youth Service Information Centre, 27th July, 1967, and interview with the hon. sec. of the National Association of Youth Service Officers, October, 1967.

[2] A recent study of teenage leisure in Scotland, *Time of One's Own*, by Pearl Jephcott, gives the proportions of the age group in membership of youth organizations as 40 per cent – little change from previous investigations. The proportion is higher among those at school than those at work. Ref. *Times Educational Supplement*, 20th October, 1967, p. 851.

---

reports of SCNVYO since replies to the inquiry did not give the breakdown in a sufficient number of cases. The figure for the latter refers to a shorter period than that for the former (viz. 1960–1964/5 against 1958–1964/5) since SCNVYO did not start publishing statistics until 1960. Population figures with which membership has been compared also refer to a shorter period in the case of the 14–20 group. The figures quoted from SCNVYO reports are for England and Wales only, since their 1960 report does not give U.K. figures. In one case, that of the N.A.Y.C., the figure given has had to be adjusted to exclude the under-14s who had been included in it (see *Annual Report of the N.A.Y.C. for 1965/6*).

are now open to those who make use of the service, and at the same time constant efforts are being made to reach those who do not.

The second striking fact is the increase in the number of voluntary workers. Table II shows that the implementation of the Albemarle Report has not deterred people from giving unpaid service. On the contrary, the number of voluntary workers in SCNVYO has increased by twenty-three per cent since 1958 and there is now a ratio of one to every ten members (Table III). There is thus a total of about 250,000[1] for the 2,500,000 members in these voluntary youth organizations.

This development may be due to the encouragement given to the youth movement as a whole by the emphasis in the Report on the value of its work and the need for expansion. The acceptance of the main recommendations by the government of the day was a shot in the arm for a body of people who had been struggling for many years under great difficulties. At last, they felt, the service to which they devoted themselves was receiving more public recognition and also rather more money. The general feeling of hopefulness for the future was a tremendous stimulus to further effort, and much new and experimental work was undertaken – this was an atmosphere likely to attract more recruits to the service, not only because it was more in the public eye and therefore a more 'popular' form of voluntary work than it had been but also because it offered opportunities for different kinds of activity and therefore was able to involve a different kind of volunteer as well as the 'old faithfuls'[2].

Membership and voluntary workers in L.E.A. clubs

It is difficult to say how far the increase in voluntary work in the voluntary section has been matched in the section for which local education authorities are directly responsible,

---

[1] This figure is very near that given in *Young People To-Day* (p. 45) as 240,000 – though no mention is made of how the figure is arrived at nor whether it applies to the statutory as well as to the voluntary sector or only to the latter.

[2] A glowing account of the effect of the Albemarle Report on youth workers is given in *Young People To-Day*, published by SCNVYO in 1966.

since there are no national figures[1] in this case comparable to those supplied by SCNVYO. There are, however, some figures for Scotland compiled by the Scottish Standing Conference of Voluntary Youth Organizations which give the position in 1966. These are reproduced in Appendix II (Table IV). They show that L.E.A. clubs have many more paid leaders and proportionally fewer volunteers than voluntary clubs; but they show, too, how very small is the proportion of clubs and members for which L.E.A.'s are in fact responsible. Thus even if this section has fewer volunteers now than formerly, and on this there is no evidence since no figures for an earlier date are available for comparison, any decreases here would be more than counterbalanced by the increase in the much larger voluntary section which the SCNVYO figures show has taken place in the United Kingdom as a whole.

The relative size of the statutory and voluntary sections of the youth service revealed by these figures is not peculiar to Scotland. These figures are not dissimilar from those for a number of places in England from which information has been sought[2]. In Bradford (in 1967) there are 500 units, only

[1] Figures for paid leaders are given in the reports of the D.E.S. There are now (1968) approximately 1,500 full-time leaders (in L.E.A. and voluntary clubs together) as against 700 at the time of the Albemarle Report, and a further 4,000 part-timers employed by L.E.A.s as against 4,700-odd at the earlier date. There are also some 2,000 part-timers employed by voluntary bodies at the present time.

[2] These examples have been selected for the following reasons: *Bradford,* because the Youth Officer is the hon. sec. of the National Association of Youth Service Officers and is therefore in a position to have information and views about other places as well as his own which he was good enough to discuss with the author. *Halifax,* because previous studies of voluntary work had been undertaken there by the author (Mary Morris *Social Enterprise* and *Nacoss Occasional Papers No.1 A Study of Halifax*) and because the youth officer kindly agreed to co-operate. *Accrington* and *Bury* because they were the two places which had published documents on the subject which were available at the Youth Service Information Centre, *Like Us — but Younger,* a Report of a Working Party 1966 on the Youth Service in Division 7 Accrington, Church, Oswaldtwistle, Clayton-le-Moors, and *Young People at Leisure.* A Report on Bury (1963) by Cyril S. Smith. *Leicestershire* because it is the County quoted (anonymously) in *Young People To-Day* (SCNVYO 1965) p. 46 and because the County Further Education Advisors and the Secretary of the Leicestershire Standing Conference of Youth Organizers kindly supplied further information.

ten of which are L.E.A. clubs, and there are in all some 2,000 active leaders of whom less than 100 are paid even for one session a week[1]. In Halifax there are (in 1967) just over 120 units, four of which are local authority centres. Here there are three and a half full-time leaders and twenty-one part-time helpers paid by the L.E.A. and 132 voluntary leaders[2]. In Accrington there are fifty-five clubs and groups, three of which are maintained by the L.E.A. and 144 leaders of whom only five are paid. In Bury there are four civic youth clubs and over 90 per cent of the current memberships of youth organizations are in the voluntary sphere. There are seventy-four leaders of whom nine are paid. In Leicestershire there are nine full-time leaders and ten full-time organizers for the whole county and 866 voluntary leaders and fifty-three part-time paid leaders in the voluntary section alone[3].

Partnership between L.E.A.'s and voluntary bodies. Paid workers and volunteers

These examples show how large is the section of youth work for which voluntary bodies are responsible, and how much the whole service, statutory as well as voluntary, depends on volunteers. At the same time, it is important to remember that the active interest of L.E.A.'s is not restricted to the section for which they are directly responsible but extends over

[1] Ref. Youth Officer, Bradford.
[2] Ref. Youth Officer, Halifax, and *Halifax Youth Handbook*, 1967–8.
> (92 uniformed groups
> 8 Youth Clubs
> 21 Church groups)
[3] Ref. *Young People To-Day* (SCNVYO 1966), p. 64, and Youth Officer, Leicestershire.

In 1967 the population of the various places quoted was:

Bradford	296,000
Halifax	96,000
Accrington	39,000
Bury	60,000
Leicestershire	433,000

Unfortunately the figures are not strictly comparable one with another as they have been collected and presented in different ways.

the whole field, so that the distinctions between voluntary and statutory are often difficult to make. This point is frequently emphasized by those involved in the service. The head of the Youth Service Information Centre writes:

Many voluntary organizations are only enabled to operate because of substantial statutory funds and much of the management and leadership of L.E.A. clubs is entirely voluntary. I think it is fair to say that the Youth Service as a whole is less conscious than for some time past of the sharp division between statutory and voluntary[1].

This view is supported by youth officers in the field. The officer at Bradford, who is also the honorary secretary of the National Association, states[2] that building programmes for both types of club are considered together and salaries of leaders in those under voluntary management are grant-aided by local authorities, and there is general unity of purpose and co-operation in seeking to meet the needs of the young. The officer at Halifax writes in similar vein:

There is a good spirit existing between voluntary organisations and L.E.A.'s. . . . Partnership has to be a two-way process, and herein lies the secret of success. I am delighted to be able to say that we seem to have this kind of spirit here[3].

As far as volunteers are concerned it makes little difference whether or not the club in which they are helping is run by the L.E.A. It is true that the figures from Scotland suggest that the presence of paid leaders means fewer volunteers, and therefore in so far as L.E.A. clubs tend to have more paid leaders, they may for that reason prove less attractive to volunteers, but when this happens it is more likely to be the leadership than the management that proves the obstacle.

The question whether, as the Scottish figures suggest, the presence of paid leaders does in fact deter voluntary workers is a difficult one, for the experience of other places points in the opposite direction. This shows that good professional leaders – and an increasing number of the paid youth officers

---

[1] Letter to the author, 27th July, 1967.
[2] Interview, October, 1967.
[3] Letter to the author from the Youth Officer of Halifax, 23rd August, 1967.

are in this category – are developing activities, and stimulating rather than discouraging the recruitment of volunteers by offering opportunities for new and interesting forms of service. In fact the recruitment of volunteers is one of the main functions of some paid workers. Sometimes, too, the leader who is paid for one weekly session will voluntarily give extra time because of his interest in the club and its members. On the whole it seems unlikely that many of the thousands of men and women who give their services freely because of their concern for the work would cease to do so because of the presence of more paid workers, though the lack of hard evidence makes it impossible to give a definite answer on this point.

A question to which a definite affirmative answer can be given is whether the partnership between L.E.A.'s and voluntary bodies is important for successful recruitment. Such partnership can do nothing but good for it eliminates unnecessary competition between those seeking volunteers and makes it easier for helpers to serve in the neighbourhood and in the capacity which suits them best. Above all it presents to the young people it seeks to help and to prospective volunteers a wide variety of opportunities within a united service. A concerted effort by all concerned will be needed to increase its appeal to the young, for if those whom it fails to attract are to be helped, many new recruits will be needed both to strengthen existing services and to pioneer fresh experiments.

The youth service today

An important step in strengthening existing services would be taken if the provision everywhere were brought up to the level of the best. In some areas the present youth service makes an impact on the great majority of boys, though even where it is most successful the number of girls affected is always smaller. In others, less than half the young people concerned are touched in any effective way. Recent research in Bethnal Green shows that ninety per cent of all boys have belonged to at least one youth organization by the time they are sixteen or seventeen, and most of them 'really did belong' – over half for more than two years and only six per cent for less than six months. Here 40 per cent of the 14–18 age group were members at the time of the inquiry[1]. On the other hand, evidence from Bury[2] shows that only 57 per cent of this age group had ever been members (for a minimum of three months), and that the present membership is only 32 per cent, and from Accrington[3] that the figure is as low as 25 per cent. The figures for Bury and Accrington include girls, but even so they are low compared with those for Bethnal Green.

A study of these three reports leads to two important conclusions. First, that it is sometimes absence of suitable provision that is responsible for low membership, and that better opportunities increase the proportion of young people who use the service; and second, that many more do in fact use it than appear to do so from the figures usually quoted, since these are based on membership at one point of time and fail to take past membership into account. Both these points are relevant to a discussion of voluntary work since more helpers are the key to more and better provision. On them will largely depend both the creation of more clubs and centres where these are needed, and the development in those which now exist of new activities designed to retain for a longer period members who leave too soon.

Fresh experiemnts

The success of fresh experiments is even more dependent on new recruits than the expansion and improvement of existing services. The professionals who are involved in 'action research' rely at every stage on the local community and quickly discover that voluntary work is already going on at the grass roots and that much more is needed. Projects such as those sponsored by the N.A.Y.C.[4] and the Y.W.C.A.[5] in an attempt to reach the so-called unattached reveal how often the good neighbour, the employer, the proprietor of dance hall and coffee bar are closely concerned with the well-being of the young people in their midst. Participation by such people, as well

---

[1] Peter Willmott, *Adolescent Boys of East London* (1966), chapter vii.

[2] Smith, *Young People at Leisure*, p. 29.

[3] *Like Us – but Younger*, p. 4.

[4] Mary Morse, *The Unattached* (1965).

[5] G. W. Goetschius and M. J. Tash, *Working with Unattached Youth*.

as by those whose jobs as teacher, minister or social worker give them special responsibility, must form the basis for future work. Without such participation the projects to help the unattached will remain experimental and few in number, and will only meet a fraction of the need.

The experience of these projects shows that some of the unattached neither need nor want provision for such leisure time activities or personal contacts as are available to members of the youth service. Some are well served by commercial provision, while others are satisfied by the opportunities offered through work and education and by what they find for themselves among friends and neighbours. But these projects show, too, how many young people are lost and bewildered, how some lack interests and friends and fall into petty crime through boredom, and how very many lead restricted lives and desperately need things that are now beyond their reach. They need sport, outings, hobbies, and space for their activities; they need, as they show by the way they grasp at proffered friendship, adults to whom they can talk and from whom they can seek advice. These things can only be achieved with the help of older people, and much of that help must be given voluntarily. Voluntary help is necessary not only because there will never be enough paid people to meet the need but also because the volunteer has a special contribution to make by virtue of the unofficial and disinterested nature of his work.

Tasks for the volunteer

There are three main tasks which demand urgent attention from those concerned in work for young people: first, to press for more provision for sport and outdoor activities as well as for better building and more trained staff; second, to increase the number of clubs and centres and to raise their standards; and, third, to give personal friendship and advice to the growing number of individuals who seek it. These tasks are not new, and there have always been youth workers who tried to tackle them, but a far greater effort is needed if they are to be successfully accomplished.

The massive developments which are needed both inside and outside the youth service will only come if more government money is available, and this will only be granted in response to public pressure. This pressure will be most effective if it comes from people who are closely involved and see at first hand how restricted are the lives of the majority of young people compared with those of the privileged few. Volunteers who are working with the under-privileged have the knowledge to make the case for equal opportunities for all young people, and they must see that they use this knowledge to the full.

The second task is to continue and expand the work of the existing clubs and centres. Thousands of volunteers have long been engaged in the day-to-day work of the youth service, and they are there in even greater numbers today. It is largely thanks to them that the service, as at present organized, meets the needs of as many young people, for at least a part of their adolescence, as it does. But while it is wrong to maintain that all boys and girls between the ages of fourteen and twenty should belong to a youth club, and especially wrong to maintain that they should belong for the whole period of their 'youth', it is right to claim that there are many who now remain outside who would enjoy the companionship and activities once they were drawn in, and that some who now leave early could with advantage stay longer if more and better provision were made. Such expansion can only take place if the present leaders and members receive the help of more volunteers – and, moreover, of volunteers of the right kind. People with special skills which they can share with the members, and with sympathy for young people and their aspirations, and people who are prepared to undertake some training are the kind of recruits that are needed.

The third task is to give personal friendship and advice, and this will make great demands on the skill and time of volunteers. The whole need for this time-consuming service cannot easily be met by paid workers, and, besides, volunteers are often more acceptable to the young than professionals because they are less associated with officialdom. The demand for help of this kind, whether it be called 'counselling' or simply 'help and advice', has always existed, but the expressed demand for it is growing, and the need for it is becoming more widely recognized and more attempts to meet it are now being made. This new recognition may be partly due to a general spreading of public interest in social problems, but it must also be due to a genuine increase in demand for which modern life itself is responsible. The practical business of living is more complicated than it used to be, and more information and advice are needed about education, work and training. Few parents are sufficiently well informed to be able to supply the necessary advice about careers. At the same time moral standards are being questioned, and people of all ages are less likely to accept rules of conduct without argument. Children are less ready to adopt the views of their elders as to what is right and wrong, and need more help in thinking out a philosophy of life that makes sense to them. Parents are adopting a more permissive attitude, and though the majority of young people still rely on the guidance of their own parents, they also look beyond the family for advice on the problems of work and education and for help in adjusting to the outside world. The family, too, tends to be narrower than it was in earlier times. The break up of neighbourhoods and the separation of generations means that there are no grandparents and uncles and aunts near at hand. The fragmentation of families has left a gap for volunteers to fill in the lives of the elderly: there is a similar gap in the lives of young people deprived of the extended family.

These facts of modern life may be the cause of the greater demand for personal help and advice which is being voiced by young people today, and of the growing recognition that this demand must be met. What matters, however, is not the cause but the urgency of the demand, and the fact that it can only be met with the help of volunteers.

3 *Service by youth*[1]

No less important than the work of adults in the youth service

[1] For further information about service by youth both overseas and at home see Margaret Campbell, *Lend a Hand! An Introduction to Social Welfare Work for Young People* (1965), and Nora and Alec Dickson, *Count Us In*, a Community Service Handbook (1967). *The British Volunteer Programme*, in association with the N.C.S.S. at 26, Bedford Square, W.C.1, issues statistics giving the number of volunteers sent by the four societies within its framework (Catholic Institute for International Relations, I.V.S., U.N.A., and V.S.O.) and the countries to which they go.

is the part played by young people themselves in voluntary service both at home and overseas, and in both fields striking developments are taking place.

Service overseas

There are several organizations which recruit and allocate young people to jobs in the developing countries. Conditions of service vary to some extent, but in most cases recruits are between the ages of eighteen and twenty-one and are paid travelling expenses, maintenance and pocket money. They are expected to give about a year's full-time service, usually teaching in school or helping at clinics. Overall numbers are small, but there are often more volunteers than vacancies.

Voluntary Service Overseas (V.S.O.) accepts people, usually for twelve months, between the ages of eighteen and twenty-four and can therefore include graduates as well as school leavers and apprentices. International Voluntary Service (I.V.S.) is able to accept volunteers for shorter periods as it can provide opportunities for short-time service in work camps lasting anything from two weeks to three months. The minimum age is eighteen and there is no maximum. Its long-term service is for at least a year, and for this it recruits qualified people of twenty-one or over to work as doctors, nurses, teachers, social workers and agriculturalists in all parts of the world.

The United Nations Association (U.N.A.) also arranges both short- and long-term assignments, and volunteers for work abroad must be eighteen years of age. The long-term schemes, which are for a year or more, are only open to those with a qualification similar to those required by I.V.S., but this condition does not apply in the case of short-term jobs, which may last from two weeks to two months. In U.N.A. schemes the volunteers pay their own travelling expenses, but they, too, are expected to work hard.

'Service Overseas' is a scheme for graduates or those with a professional or technical qualification and is a joint enterprise between the voluntary societies and the overseas governments. In this case the host country pays a small salary or board and lodging plus pocket money and the return passage. It may be objected that the receipt of pocket money or even of board and lodging is incompatible with volunteer status, but service overseas cannot be compared with work in this country since the volunteer is not able to live at home while he is serving. Moreover, he is working full-time which few people can afford to do without wages or at least maintenance. They can only do it, with the best will in the world, if they have private means or if they are supported by parents or spouse.

Service at home

The numbers involved in these exciting tasks overseas are comparatively small. Many more are engaged in voluntary work at home, for which until recently there has been less publicity. This work is usually short term or part time, or both. It might take the form of an intensive week-end of house cleaning or decorating, or of an hour a week of friendly visiting. But though it is often limited and sporadic, its extent and the enthusiasm of the young volunteers is impressive. An article in *New Society*[1] described how more and more young people from all walks of life were coming forward and how varied were the tasks undertaken. The field of recruitment now includes 'not only school-leavers putting in a few months before going on to college and university, but also industrial apprentices, police cadets, clerks, secretaries and factory workers'. These volunteers 'are engaged in hospitals, in approved schools, in Borstals, in schools teaching immigrants English; they are also engaged in more day-to-day tasks, in visiting old people and redecorating their flats . . . Yet others may carry coal, deliver papers, and run messages for old people.'

Much of this expansion has taken place through comparatively new organizations, Community Service Volunteers (C.S.V.), Task Force, the International Service Department of U.N.A., Volunteer Emergency Service and International Voluntary Service (this dates from the thirties). Most of these are nation wide and are attracting attention both from the public and from prospective volunteers, but there are in

---

[1] 14th October, 1965.

addition large numbers of independent local groups, many of them of long standing[1]. Some of these are organized through schools, youth clubs, churches, Councils of Social Service and O.P.W. committees, and through branches of national bodies like the B.R.C.S., St. John and the W.R.V.S. Some are not officially organized at all, but consist of a few friends who offer help in their neighbourhood.

Service by the young is not a new phenomenon – what is new, at least on its present scale, is the harnessing of so many volunteers to new kinds of tasks. The number and variety of schemes are growing fast and careful planning will be needed if they are to work well. Machinery of some kind is essential both at the receiving end – at the hospital, school, or social service committee – and among the volunteers themselves through their school, club, church or society, to fit them successfully into the institution they are to serve. Unfortunately neither they, nor the general public, always realize how difficult an operation this can be. The experience of places with successful schemes shows that it is vital to recognize the difficulties and to take practical steps to meet them. The organizer at Fulbourn Hospital, herself a firm believer in the value of voluntary work, writes:

In a period when there is a remarkable upsurge of interest in voluntary help, particularly among young people, I do not think it is generally realized how difficult it is for institutions or societies of any kind to accept any great quantity of voluntary help. I believe that the project at Fulbourn proves that voluntary help can be accepted, provided that there is one person responsible for its organization[2].

Other hospitals have since followed this pattern, and Councils

[1] Asked in the House of Commons how many separate voluntary societies at national and local level and how many schools in various categories were organizing programmes of practical community service by young people, Mr. Denis Howell (Under Secretary at the D.E.S.) replied, 'In addition to a number of bodies concerned almost solely with this topic, there are many local youth organizations as well as schools which include practical service of this kind among their activities. No record is kept of their numbers.' *Times Educational Supplement*, 28th April, 1967.

[2] *Report from organizers of voluntary services to Nuffield Provincial Hospital Trust*, (Cyclo) (1965), and see above pp. 86–8. See also Jan Rocha, *Organizers of Voluntary Services in Hospitals*.

of Social Service and O.P.W. Committees, too, are beginning to appoint special officers to recruit and allocate volunteers.

The Nottingham Council of Social Service, for example, in applying for financial help for its scheme for service by youth to the elderly writes:

If this enthusiasm and goodwill towards the elderly is to be harnessed effectively it is considered that careful preparation is required and that the involvement should be continually reviewed – not only in general terms but also by regular consultation with those giving and those receiving the service,

and explains how the development that has already taken place has been due to the presence of a full-time person (in this case a volunteer who was ready to give her services during the months between school and college). The presence of a full-time worker, says the C.S.S.

suggests that there are important advantages in having a central figure responsible for involving young people in work with the elderly[1].

The need for organization applies to all volunteers, but it applies especially to the young, both because they may become discouraged more easily than their more hardened elders, and because they are more mobile and therefore less likely to be reliable over a period. It is unfortunate therefore that some community service societies seem to reject organization, though fortunate that this rejection is often only temporary. Some of the leaders of the newer bodies feel very strongly that 'the young do not wish to join anything – they simply want to be given the opportunity of doing something useful'. The Director of Task Force is quoted in the article in *New Society* as saying:

If I want to visit an old lady, why do I have to call myself a Task Force Volunteer? Young people don't want to join anything . . they don't want to be classed. In Task Force they join nothing . . . We are not an organization. If we were we wouldn't exist.

The founder of V.S.O. says: 'We don't need co-ordination – we need stimulation' and the general secretary of I.V.S.

---

[1] *Nottingham O.P.W. Committee, Divisional Officer's Report*, 1966–7, (Appendix 2).

rejects any idea of an 'imposed pattern'. 'If it comes from above, then it is someone else's fire and enthusiasm and it'll all die out. If it comes at all it must come naturally'. These statements were made in 1965 and by 1967 Task Force had become an organization of massive proportions with fifty full-time paid staff and a budget of £75,000[1]. The need for 'friendly visiting' when there are 40,000 old people living alone in every London borough and the success of the campaign in recruiting 11,000 young visitors in three years has made organization inevitable. The fifty paid staff have justified their appointment if they have efficiently recruited and allocated an average of two hundred young people each. Clearly an exercise on this scale would be impossible without organization and without substantial funds. Other community service societies, too, have found it necessary to increase staff and improve machinery as their work expands. For enthusiasm on the part of the young, important though it is, is not enough to ensure satisfaction at the receiving end. There is sometimes a tendency among the leaders of these community service movements to pay more attention to the needs and demands of the young who wish, or at least who they think ought to wish, to give service, than to the benefits that may accrue to the recipients. The needs of giver and receiver can be reconciled, but the receiving end needs constant watching, especially in view of the fact that the young themselves are so anxious to avoid the label 'do-gooder' that they are sometimes more concerned with themselves and their place in the community than with welfare problems that are being met inadequately.

It is true that this attitude on the part of some of the young has not prevented many of these welfare problems being tackled with energy and enthusiasm. It is true, too, that some of the new societies have succeeded where others have failed in rousing the desire to serve in a new type of volunteer; but it is not always true that the voluntary action has been of the right kind. The desire to serve is important for the success of any scheme, but efficiency, reliability and acceptability are important, too. These three qualities are essential in the case of voluntary service of a personal kind, such as

[1] See the *Guardian*, 28th October, 1967.

visiting the elderly or the handicapped and befriending immigrants or deprived children. They matter less in projects such as collecting litter or conserving the countryside, where less personal disappointment will result if the project breaks down. Impersonal projects are more suitable in cases where continuity and quality of service cannot be guaranteed, and personal service should only be encouraged when there is someone responsible for seeing that it is properly done. It would certainly be a pity to discourage a type of service which young people are keen and able to undertake and which is often so much appreciated; but it is essential that it should be rendered reliably and well, or disappointment on the part of those who receive it will take the place of satisfaction. The pleasure that old people undoubtedly often feel in visits from the young, and the practical help they receive from them will turn to pain and a sense of loss if the visitor fails to return or the promised shopping is not done or the needed coal brought in. The delight of the young immigrant or the lonely child at finding a friend will fade if the friend lets him down. The value of work of this kind can be so great to those who receive it that there is an absolute obligation on those who give it to give it regularly and well. This obligation cannot be discharged without efficient organization.

A national plan?

The increase in the number of community service societies and of separate projects for service by youth has led the Department of Education and Science to work out a national plan to co-ordinate existing work, to stimulate further efforts and to find outlets for useful service.

This has aroused some hostility from the societies concerned for they fear that any scheme that works from the top down will damp the enthusiasm of the young[1].

It is true that control from the centre is bound to have some

---

[1] Their attitude is discussed in the *Guardian* for 28th October, 1967, in an article, *Service without a Smile*, by Jonathan Steele. See also *Times Educational Supplement*, 10th November, 1967 – 'The bitterest criticism of all is that the projected plan is completely undemocratic, that what should be a "grass roots" movement will be stultified by a paternalist structure.'

effect on local groups, but control from a co-ordinating body will not necessarily differ from control by a separate society, at least as far as the individual volunteer is concerned. The existing societies might lose some of their independence under a national plan, but the young people themselves might be unaffected by the change.

If the national plan involved no more than the co-ordination of existing work and its continuance and expansion along present lines, there would be little reason to fear the consequences, and it could be welcomed as a means of giving better service to more people. It would be able to provide information about opportunities for voluntary work by publicizing what was being done in various places, and it could stimulate local effort. It might also provide machinery for retaining the interest of young people when they move from one place to another. Unfortunately, however, it would involve dangers and difficulties for both givers and receivers of voluntary service.

The dangers lie not in co-ordination but in the size of any scheme run on a nation-wide basis, and in the sponsorship by institutions, statutory or voluntary, whose concern is with the givers rather than the receivers of the service.

Any plan for voluntary service must have two aims: first and most important, the satisfaction of those who receive the service, and second, the preservation of a voluntary element for those who give it. It is doubtful how far any scheme for the whole nation sponsored by the D.E.S. could achieve these aims. Its size would almost inevitably involve standardization, and this would have an adverse effect on local initiative and achievement. Local people have knowledge of local needs, and ideas as to the ways of meeting them which are most likely to be successful. They can benefit from information about what is being done elsewhere, and from advice drawn from the experience of others and also from financial help, but their decisions should be made on the basis of local needs and not as part of a national pattern. Local control is essential to the success of local projects, and though it could be retained under a national plan, this would not be easy in a plan which embraced the whole youth of the nation. A plan sponsored by the D.E.S. might do just this, and would have the additional danger that its main concern would be the young themselves and not those who might benefit from their service. If the work is primarily conceived as 'good for the young', as part of the youth service, or even of the school curriculum, or as an alternative to national service, the satisfaction of those for whom it is done will take second place. This emphasis is already present in the attitude of some of the community service societies, when the value of a scheme as a desirable outlet for the energies of the young is stressed more strongly than the fact that it is meeting a social need. This emphasis would be stronger still in schemes under a national plan sponsored by the D.E.S., since it is after all the department responsible to Parliament for the education and welfare of the young. This emphasis is wrong in any scheme, and especially wrong in a national plan. However great the benefit of voluntary work to those who undertake it, the benefit to those on whose behalf it is undertaken must have priority. This means that those government departments, voluntary bodies and individuals who know the needs for voluntary service, must play a central part in the conception and execution of a national plan[1]. Only so will a plan for voluntary service achieve its first aim – the satisfaction of those to whom the service is rendered.

The second aim, the preservation of the voluntary element, is also in danger in any plan on a nation-wide scale too closely linked to educational authority. In this connection the warnings and misgivings of the community service societies that a national plan might destroy the spontaneity of the young have some relevance. Though, as has been suggested, control by a co-ordinating body would not necessarily of itself affect the young more than control by separate societies, control by a national body with the purpose and the power to make a voluntary service part of the programme for the youth of the nation would be a different matter.

If voluntary service became the rule rather than the exception the element of compulsion present in all group projects would be greatly increased. While there is some such element in

[1] People who are primarily concerned with the welfare of the elderly, for example, understandably have doubts of the value to them of work undertaken as an exercise for young volunteers.

all projects organized through institutions, since some conformity is always expected from group members, and some
pressure, gentle or otherwise, is put on those who do not
participate, the compulsion becomes more serious as the
projects become more numerous and more official. If the
point were reached when all children had to join in as part of
their school life, and all youth club members were committed
to group projects, the non-conformist would be under such pressure to volunteer that his service would cease to be voluntary,
and even the conformist would lose enthusiasm if he felt his
service was taken for granted. Once this happened the motive
for undertaking voluntary work might change from a genuine
desire to help to a grudging acceptance of the inevitable.

How far a change of motive would affect the quality of the
work depends on the nature of the service. A practical job
like shopping or gardening could perhaps be satisfactorily
carried out as part of a school curriculum by children who
had no choice in the matter, but it is difficult to see how
personal service like friendly visiting can be worthwhile to
the receiver unless it is freely given. The relevance of motive
to the value of work is not peculiar in the case of service by
youth: what gives it its special importance in this case is the
problem inherent in a national plan which embraces the
whole youth of the nation. If all young people are obliged to
do unpaid work, their services cannot be said to be freely
given. This will affect the value of the work not only to the
receiver, but to the giver of the service. It will affect the receiver
because service given as a duty will generally be less valued
than true voluntary service. It will affect the giver because an
obligation to undertake tasks simply by reason of age when the
rest of the population is free to accept or reject them will
produce a reaction consistent with lack of choice. If the voluntary element is to be retained for this age group some way
must be found of reconciling the provision of opportunities
for service with the freedom of the individual boy or girl to
accept or reject those opportunities. A plan which imposes an
obligation will defeat its own ends if its purpose is to enable
the young to give disinterested service.

It is certainly not easy to strike a balance between the
control needed to ensure satisfaction to the recipients and the

freedom which is essential to true voluntary service, especially as even the smallest project usually involves at least four parties. It involves the recipient, the institution or society through which he is contacted or put in touch, the organization which undertakes recruitment and allocation, and finally the volunteer. The personal service of individual to individual is what matters, but except in the case of spontaneous neighbourly help, it is institutions that make this service possible. Too little machinery means that many people who need help and friendship will remain neglected while many who are eager to serve will be unsatisfied: too much, that unnecessary and even unwanted services may be organized in order to find jobs for young people, while the young themselves may lose enthusiasm for projects which they have not chosen to undertake.

The task of a national plan is to help to bring giver and receiver together simply and efficiently; and to do this on as wide a scale as is consistent with meeting real needs on the one hand and retaining the voluntary element on the other.

The scheme announced in Parliament on 14th November, 1967, by the Under-Secretary for Education and Science[1] was on a smaller scale than had been anticipated. A charitable trust – the Young Volunteer Force Foundation – is to be set up, and the government will make £100,000 available in the next three years. It is worth noting how this compares with the sum of £75,000 which is Task Force's *annual* budget for London alone. The aim of the scheme is to give young people more opportunities of giving voluntary service and its emphasis is on the benefit to be derived by the young people themselves. It plans to offer assistance to local and hospital authorities and to voluntary bodies, and if these institutions whose first concern is the welfare of those who are to receive the service are properly consulted the scheme may result in some useful work being done. In any case its small scale will not give rise to the dangers that would be inherent in a national plan involving all young people. There are certainly enough jobs waiting to be done to keep the numbers likely to be involved through the Young Volunteer Force occupied, and the

---

[1] See the *Guardian*, 15th November, 1967; *Observer*, 19th November, 1967, and *Times Educational Supplement*, 17th November, 1967.

participation at local level of people concerned with the receivers of the service may ensure that their work is well done. From the point of view of the young people, the limited nature of the scheme should make it possible to retain a voluntary element though it is doubtful how far it will attract the 'unattached' whom the Minister particularly had in mind.

The scheme may well make a modest contribution to the welfare of some of those who need more help from the community than they are getting now. But it cannot go very far towards meeting the real needs of the whole group of elderly, sick, and handicapped who need this help. Nor is it likely to do much towards solving those problems of modern youth which are uppermost in the minds of its promoters, except perhaps to give an extra boost to the youth service.

CHAPTER IV

Prisoners and Ex-Prisoners

The prevention of crime and the promotion of constructive methods of treatment of offenders have long been the concern of social reformers who have sought both to change the law and improve prison conditions, and also to bring personal help to prisoners and ex-prisoners. The reforms that have taken place in the penal system have been largely due to the persistence of men and women who were deeply concerned at the severity and even injustice of much of the law, and at the harshness of conditions in prison. Pressure from such people has persuaded successive governments to reduce the number of offences punishable by death until at last capital punishment has been suspended. It is more than half a century since this reform became part of the official programme of the Howard League[1] and it had been advocated by a minority of League members long before that time. Progress in this and in other ways has always been slow because the reformers, both in and out of Parliament, have been ahead of public opinion, and every step forward has been preceded by years of patient preparation. But gradually, ever since the movement for reform took shape at the end of the eighteenth century, the penal code has become more humane, prison conditions have been improved and more constructive work has been undertaken to rehabilitate offenders and when possible to keep them out of prison.

---

[1] The Howard League for Penal Reform was formed in 1921 by the amalgamation of the Howard Association (founded 1866) and the Penal Reform League (founded 1907). Its objects are: 'The prevention of crime and the promotion of constructive methods of treatment for delinquents'. A plebiscite held in 1921 resulted in a large majority in favour of abolition which thereafter became the acknowledged policy of the League. (See Gordon Rose, *The Struggle for Penal Reform*, chapter 15.)

Early voluntary work

The success of the work of rehabilitation now depends largely on the probation service, which owes its own existence to the pioneering work of volunteers and the voluntary societies which they formed. Among these was the National Police Court Mission which was formed in 1876 by the Church of England Temperance Society 'to arrest the downward career' of those who 'got into trouble'[1]. It appointed missionaries to the courts and set up homes and work centres for discharged prisoners. The work was carried out by paid staff, but it had been launched by volunteers and was built up with their help. The knowledge acquired by those who were involved in this work encouraged them to help to lay the foundations for more enlightened treatment of offenders, and led some of them to take an active part in the movement for reform.

Prison visiting

The reformers to whose efforts changes in the penal system have been due were more than members of pressure groups, active though they were in this capacity. They were social workers, too, and spent time and energy in equipping themselves as penal reformers by getting to know the problems at first hand. They did this through personal contacts, not only with men and women facing trial in the courts and with discharged prisoners, but with those who were serving sentences, and with prison officers. Gaining access to the prisons as magistrates or through the churches, they spoke of conditions they had themselves seen, and were able to form their own ideas of the changes needed in the interests both of the prisoners and prison staffs and of society as a whole. They saw that the prisons were not succeeding in reforming their inmates and this, they held, should be their main purpose, for the sake of the community as well as for the prisoners themselves. They believed that the prison system should aim at achieving this reformation by rehabilitation rather than by punishment.

As prison visitors they were not only gaining ammunition for the battle for reform, they were bringing companionship

---

[1] See National Police Court Mission, *Annual Report*, 1963-64, p. 1.

and comfort to men and women who were cut off from ordinary human contacts. Fortunately the work of visiting was not left to the small group of active reformers but was undertaken also by other people of good will who were anxious to help in a personal way though they did not feel able, or necessarily impelled, to join in active pressure for reform. Visits from such people usually seem to be welcomed by those who receive them. They only take place at the request of the prisoner, and may therefore be assumed to meet a felt need. They provide some relief from monotony and a contact with the outside world. At their best they form the basis of valuable relationships which are often continued outside, while at the least they offer temporary companionship. The history of penal reform provides a good example of personal service and pressure for reform going hand in hand, and the changes that are now taking place and those that are still needed will depend for their success on the continuing efforts of volunteers active in both directions.

As far as personal service is concerned there is clearly much that can and should be done by volunteers. The part they play in the care of prisoners and ex-prisoners has changed considerably in recent years, and the new pattern has not yet been fully worked out. Some work is still being carried on along familiar lines, and at the same time new methods are being tried and experimental schemes launched.

The greater part of this work is being carried on outside the various penal institutions, since opportunities for voluntary service inside are still limited, being mainly restricted to visiting and to occasional recreational or educational activities. It may seem a small thing to help to provide an entertainment or to join in a discussion group, but such service is apparently appreciated. A former Governor of Holloway writes of a concert party: 'The performers receive no fees or expenses and their readiness to give up their Sunday afternoons is very much appreciated by the women: it may, in a small way, help to reduce the sense of rejection felt by prisoners'[1]. The part played by visitors, whether singly or in groups, is much more important than the provision of entertainment since it is both more personal and more sustained. It is valuable

[1] Joanna Kelley, *When the Gates Shut*, p. 88.

not only at the time of imprisonment but afterwards since it often leads to constructive after-care. The main task of the visitor to the prison is to give companionship. This is no easy task, but the experience at Holloway at least shows that it is often carried out successfully. 'There is generally a very happy relationship between visitors and those they visit, and the women enjoy and look forward to their visits'[1]. There are (in 1967) twenty-four such visitors in Holloway who come about once a week to visit prisoners in their cells and sometimes take part in group discussions and even take the prisoners out when the time for their release is near.

This favourable view of visiting is not, however, shared by all writers on the subject. The authors of a recent study of Pentonville[2] are far from enthusiastic about the scheme at that prison. At the time of their inquiry there were about twenty visitors who varied in age and outlook but were mainly of the same socio-economic status, being middle class. Some adopted what the authors felt was an excessively evangelical attitude, and some were resented by those they visited. The attitude of prisoners to visitors and vice versa natually varied from case to case. Some prisoners complained that once they had been allocated a visitor 'it was difficult to get rid of him' while some visitors felt that their prisoners were out to 'con them'. Yet in spite of these criticisms the authors felt that visitors could make a valuable contribution to prison welfare, and urged them in a special lecture entitled *Friend, Counsellor or Therapist*[3] to re-appraise their position. The lecturer stressed that visitors should maintain contact with trained social workers, and that their main function was really 'just listening'. Listening was clearly an important part of the work of the successful visitors at Holloway, and on the value of this there seems to be general agreement. How much more visitors can and should contribute is a matter of opinion, and different people working in and writing about different prisons have different views.

The views of the visitors themselves also vary from person to person, and their attitude to the job naturally affects the way in

---

[1] *Op. cit.*, p. 142.

[2] Terence and Pauline Morris, *Pentonville* (1963).

[3] Printed as Appendix B in *Pentonville*.

which they carry it out. They are, however, bound to adhere to certain rules since they are officially appointed and recognized by the Home Office. Some may wish to impart their religious views but this is now discouraged by their National Association which expressly instructs them to avoid religious as well as political argument, and stresses that their role is simply to offer friendship to the prisoners and to co-operate with the prison staff in working for their welfare[1].

Voluntary visiting has been officially established for nearly half a century. The first male visitors were appointed in 1922, and female visitors had been active in the women's prisons for some time previously. There are now (1967) some seven hundred visitors in all whose ages range from twenty-five to seventy. They come from various walks of life, though the majority everywhere, as at Pentonville, are middle class. Originally their work was restricted to providing companionship and discussing personal problems, and sometimes to introducing crafts and hobbies – the early 'lady visitors' taught the girls needlework – for men and women while they were in prison, and they were expressly discouraged from continuing the relationship outside. Recently their functions have been enlarged to include work with prisoners' families during the period of sentence and with the prisoners themselves after their discharge. Now that they can continue afterwards the relationship formed in prison they can help in easing the transfer to life outside by offering continuing friendship and practical help with jobs and accommodation. Work of this kind is an important feature of successful after-care.

The development of after-care

This is still true now that after-care has become the statutory responsibility of the Probation and After-Care Department of the Home Office. It was formerly in the hands of the Discharged Prisoners' Aid Societies, which sprang up at the beginning of the last century as part of the surge of philanthropic effort which marked the period. Attached to the city and county jails they quickly formed a network of local groups

[1] See J. H. M. Sykes, *The History, Aims and Activities of the National Association of Prison Visitors* (Notes for Prison Visitors).

concerned to meet the immediate needs of men on their release and to help them to find work and lodgings. The societies were independently run and were financed from private funds until 1862 when the Discharged Prisoners' Aid Act started a partnership between State and private benevolence which continued and developed until 1963[1], when the decision was taken by the Government to transfer the functions of the voluntary bodies to an expanded and re-organized probation and after-care service[2].

This change only took place after several official inquiries and reports. It was due to a variety of causes, but fundamentally to the recognition by those in authority, and indeed by public opinion, that after-care was an essential part of rehabilitation and as such a responsibility of the penal system which should not be left to local voluntary effort. The societies had been locally based, and although they formed a national association they had retained their independence and separate control. Moreover, though they covered the whole country after a fashion, their organization did not fit in with the new prison system. They were also finding it increasingly difficult to raise voluntary money and were becoming more and more dependent on government grants. At the same time the material needs of prisoners which they had helped to meet were now supplied from public funds.

The dissolution of the National Association of Discharged Prisoners' Aid Societies (NADPAS) and of its constituent local bodies must have caused pain and disappointment to many people who had given long and devoted service. They had helped, both materially and personally, many thousands of unfortunate people during a time when the State's responsibility ceased at the prison gates, and had striven to resettle them in an outside world which was much more hostile than it is today. They had shown concern for fellow-men whom society as a whole not only neglected but actively shunned, and they pioneered and showed the way to a more enlightened and

---

[1] For the historical background see *The Organisation of After-Care*, Report of the Advisory Council on the Treatment of Offenders (ACTO), H.M.S.O., 1963, Appendix B.

[2] *Report on the Work of the Probation and after-Care Departmnt*, 1962–5, Cmnd. 3107, paras. 91 and 92.

constructive attitude to rehabilitation. It is not surprising that some of these volunteers did not whole-heartedly welcome the change.

At the same time there were many in the voluntary movement who recognized and advocated the need for reform, and whose pride in past achievements was combined with satisfaction at the new opportunities for voluntary effort which the future offered. These forward-looking people from the former Aid Societies, with others whose social conscience also takes the form of concern for offenders, have realized that there are many ways in which their help is needed under the new set-up, and that this help is welcomed and encouraged by those in authority.

Already, before the formal dissolution of the NADPAS, such people had been giving thought to different ways of helping discharged prisoners, and a new voluntary body to co-ordinate voluntary effort, the National Association for the Care and Resettlement of Offenders (NACRO), has been formed. This body, which held its inaugural meeting in September, 1966, aims not only 'to provide a meeting point and central voice for every kind of voluntary effort concerned in any way with the prevention of crime and the resettlement of offenders[1], but will emphasize crime prevention and promote research'[2].

Voluntary workers in the new set-up

The main functions of voluntary workers in the new set-up, under which after-care is part of the probation and after-care service, are three – membership of committees and working parties; providing amenities, including hostels; and helping probation officers with after-care[3]. These functions are in

[1] *New Society*, 31st March, 1966 (p. 17).

[2] *New Society*, 15th September, 1966, comments: 'It is interesting that, just as the prisoners' aid societies hand the responsibility for aid-on-discharge to the statutory services, volunteers are more concerned with the problem than before. The establishment of NACRO shows that extending state welfare provisions does not sap individual initiative, and bodes well for partnership between the probation service and the community.' (p. 409).

[3] See *Cmnd.* 3107, Foreword by Rt. Hon. Roy Jenkins, M.P., former Secretary of State for the Home Department.

addition to those of the Justices of the Peace, who as is well known, are unpaid servants of the public. The Justices are in a different position from that of most other voluntary workers since they are appointed by the Lord Chancellor and form an essential part of the judicial system. Though their statutory duties include an element of service to prisoners, especially now that rehabilitation is an important consideration in many of the sentences they impose, their first duty is to administer the law. At the same time they perform some of the same tasks as other voluntary workers since they act as managers of Borstals and approved schools and often take a personal interest in prisoners and ex-prisoners, in addition to carrying out their duties on the bench.

1 *Membership of committees and working parties*

This involves many hundreds of people in voluntary service. 'Probation committees, case committees and managing committees of approved probation hostels and homes are all composed of people who give their time to these voluntary public duties'[1]. These duties often involve more than occasional attendance at meetings, for the conscientious member takes a personal interest in those who live and work in the institutions for which his committee is responsible. Managers of approved schools have an especially important part to play since the majority of these schools are still under the control of local committees. These vary considerably in their composition and therefore in their influence on the school. According to a recent study[2] they are mainly self-appointing and self-perpetuating so 'the result may be that excellent local people with much relevant experience are appointed to the committees, again it may be that local bigwigs or active but not suitable voluntary workers are selected'[3]. They tend to be old, well-to-do and often inefficient, and few of them are teachers or social workers. These criticisms of the present management of approved schools may well be justified, but this does not mean that the

---

[1] *Ibid.*

[2] Gordon Rose, *Schools for Young Offenders* (1967).

[3] *Op. cit.*, p. 113.

system itself is wrong. There are many men and women who would make suitable managers and who would be able to improve the work of the schools by appointing the right staff and taking an interest in their work, and by offering friendship and support both to them and to the children in their care. There is likely to be more intervention by the Home Office in the affairs of approved schools, and more of their number may be transferred from voluntary committees to local authorities[1], but the management is to remain in the hands of voluntary workers. Some of these will be elected members of local authorities, others co-opted from the general public. The transfer of responsibility should provide an opportunity for bringing in a greater number of suitably qualified people.

2 *Provision of amenities*

The second main function of voluntary work is to provide amenities, including hostels. Suitable accommodation is the most pressing need for many offenders. This was recognized by the working party on the *Place of Voluntary Service in After-Care*, set-up by the Home Secretary in 1965. In the introduction to their first report the members say: 'We have concentrated as a first priority on the resident needs of offenders because we consider them of paramount importance'[2], and go on to stress the value of hostels as an alternative to prison as well as for after-care. They consider that the establishment of hostels is one of the most fruitful fields for voluntary bodies and for volunteers, and stress the need for specialized provision for different groups of ex-prisoners – for the young, the aged, for alcoholics, for the mentally ill – as well as for more multi-purpose hostels.

Some hostels promoted and run by voluntary bodies are already in existence and more are being planned[3]. They are

---

[1] This trend is likely to continue at an increased rate as a result of the Court Lees affair in 1967 when an approved school was closed by the Home Secretary because excessive corporal punishment had been administered to the boys. It was removed from the control of a voluntary body and re-opened under a different name under local authority control.

[2] *Residential Provision for Homeless Discharged Offenders*, H.M.S.O., 1966.

[3] These are listed in the *Manual and Directory* published by N.A.C.R.O.

proving their value, but they are still few in number, and more are urgently needed. Places such as Norman House, where homeless offenders live in a family group, provide a great deal more than food and shelter. They provide an element of stability and make it possible for rootless men to settle and to find employment. Moreover, they offer opportunities for companionship and recreation which some men who have been shut away in prison have lost the capacity to find for themselves. Men who are less dependent in these respects are still often unable to find accommodation without help. Bed-sitter hostels and friendly landladies would meet their requirement, but again voluntary effort is needed if landladies are to be enrolled and bed-sitters provided.

The success of pioneer projects shows how much the provision of suitable accommodation can help resettlement. But the number of prisoners who benefit from these projects is still painfully small and much more must be done to meet the need. The size of the problem is stressed by the working party. They note that only twenty hostels involving 242 places had so far been approved for grant by the Home Office, whereas they estimate that there are at least 5,000 potential clients per year[1]. If the present policy of leaving the initiative to the voluntary bodies works too slowly most of the accommodation needed will have to be financed and indeed directly provided by the State. The Home Office has sponsored the Bridgehead Housing Association 'to assist the community in providing residential help for offenders'. This will certainly help the setting up of hostels, both financially and in overcoming the local opposition that is always encountered by those who seek to provide accommodation for social misfits, but it still leaves the initiative and some financial responsibility in the hands of voluntary committees. The Association is administered by the Church of England Council for Social Aid (which incorporates the old National Police Court Mission) and the Church is now actively engaged in persuading its members to form the necessary local committees. Non-church

---

[1] *Residential Provision for Homeless Discharged Offenders*, para. 14. The figure of 5,000 is 10 per cent of the number of discharges from penal institutions each year. The other 90 per cent, which the working party feels is too high a figure, are assumed to have homes to which they can go.

people are joining in and other voluntary groups are also becoming interested. But it is doubtful whether voluntary effort, even backed by government money, can meet the full need in a reasonable time, and it may be necessary for the State to provide at least some of the required accommodation without the help of voluntary bodies. Whether or not the various hostels are State-provided as well as State-financed their success as a means of rehabilitation will depend on voluntary help, for if offenders are to be resettled in the community, the community itself must help with the resettlement. This means, in practical terms, that volunteers must come forward to help with the management if not with the provision and financing of the hostels, and must help, too, with the personal needs of their residents. Here, surely, is a wide field of work for people of good will, who are concerned with the welfare of offenders. Many thousands of volunteers will be needed if enough of the right kind of accommodation is to be provided, and if those who come to live in it are to receive the help and friendship they need.

Accommodation is the first priority for the discharged prisoner who has no home of his own, but he needs more than a roof over his head. Both he, and his more fortunate fellows who have families to receive them, are dependent on the support of others for rehabilitation. This support can sometimes be given through clubs where ex-prisoners can meet people who take an interest in their problems, discuss their difficulties and advise on jobs and re-adjustment to life outside. There are a few clubs of this kind sponsored by churches, settlements and other voluntary groups where volunteers are playing an important part in helping offenders to find their feet and go straight. They are especially valuable during the first weeks of freedom when men need extra support to prevent relapse into crime. They provide a social outlet for those who live in bed-sitters or lodgings or in the kind of hostel where there is little community life; and even for those who have homes they give valuable help in adjusting to jobs, to families and to neighbours. Many more such clubs are needed, and though some will have paid leaders, all will need voluntary helpers if the members are to receive the personal attention they will be seeking.

3 *Personal service*

The third function of volunteers in connection with after-care is to give personal service as 'associates' and in other ways. The transfer of responsibility from the voluntary societies to the Probation and After-Care Department of the Home Office was not intended to mean the end of voluntary work in this field. In fact the contrary is the case, and it is specifically stated by the Home Secretary[1] that volunteers are being recruited to help probation officers with their work, while the *Report on the Work of the Department for* 1962–5 states that 'a start has been made on the long-term task of developing voluntary effort to full advantage throughout the country'[2]. The Home Office clearly considers that voluntary bodies and volunteers can make a valuable contribution since it has circularized probation committees suggesting that they should start experimental schemes. This circular[3] stresses that voluntary help is a supplement to the professional service and not a substitute for it. It makes the point, however, that 'as a private individual the volunteer may be able to establish a good relation with an offender who would shun all contacts with officials'. It expresses the view that long-term relationships will probably be few in number, and draws attention to the many other ways in which volunteers can help: 'simple acts of practical help may do much towards breaking down an offender's sense of isolation and rejection', and adds that volunteers can also give material help and can assist the families. On the subject of recruitment it suggests that probation committees should make use of interested voluntary bodies and of personal contacts, and specifically suggests that suitable volunteers might be found among prison visitors. The policy of discouraging visitors from maintaining contact after a prisoner's discharge has been discontinued, so this obstacle has been removed, and the visitors' interest in forming personal relationships makes them suitable recruits to the after-care service. The new conception of after-care as beginning at the

---

[1] In the Foreword to the *Report on the Work of Probation and After-Care Department,* 1962-5.

[2] *Op. cit.,* para. 93.

[3] No. 238/1965, *After-Care. Use of Volunteers.*

time of sentence means that voluntary work inside and outside prison is now being handled by the same people. Thus former prison visitors can now extend their work to include after-care and former members of D.P.A.S.'s can start theirs during the period of sentence. Church people, too, are being encouraged by the Church of England Council for Social Aid to participate in this work, and some are being recruited.

The suggestions in the circular are discussed and amplified in the second report of the working party on *The Place of Voltary Service in After-Care*. This emphasizes the distinction between the accredited associate, 'who provides support for a considerable period by a personal relationship', and the ordinary volunteer, who performs those simpler acts of practical help to which the circular refers[1]. The former have an especially responsible task and are appointed by the probation committees and responsible to the principal probation officers.

The success of the scheme for accredited associates will clearly depend on the attitude of the probation officer responsible. The Home Secretary has given a lead, but probation officers and their committees can follow with greater or less enthusiasm. An example of a successful scheme comes from one large city where the co-operation of some of the people who were previously working as prison visitors and with the D.P.A. has been secured, and though the responsibility for recruitment and training rests with the principal probation officer, considerable latitude is left to individual workers. These accredited associates are so far few in number – less than a score – but they are dedicated workers who devote a great deal of time to exacting personal work with individual offenders. Numbers here and elsewhere are expected to grow, but to grow slowly. The long-term relationship in which an associate gives personal support to a very small number of ex-prisoners, perhaps only to one, is only at present sought by a small proportion of offenders, and the demand is not expected to grow quickly. This should make it possible to find enough suitable people to undertake this specialized and exacting work. It is not possible to forecast exactly how many will be needed as this will depend on the number of prisoners

---

[1] *The Place of Voluntary Service in After-Care*, paras. 17 and 18.

who seek this kind of help, but it may be no more than twenty to thirty for each of the eighty-four probation committees.

Many more volunteers will, however, be needed for other kinds of work with prisoners and their families, and many are already undertaking a variety of tasks. Some of these are listed in the second report of the working party. They include prison visiting, group work during sentence with prisoners and with wives and families, work with families during sentence, and support and advice to offenders and families after discharge. Visits and group activities during sentence will not necessarily lead prisoners to seek prolonged after-care. Many who appreciate contacts with the outside world while they are inside will not wish to keep up the relationship after their release. This does not mean that voluntary work within the prisons is unnecessary. It has great value both in bringing companionship to lonely people and in helping to fit them to face the outside world later. Moreover, even men who do not seek a continuing personal relationship with an associate need some support after release, both in adjusting to the community socially and through employment, and in all kinds of practical ways. Voluntary workers can organize clubs and meetings and perform practical tasks such as supplying furniture and clothing. In ways such as these help can be given not only to the offender himself but to his family, which is often in desperate straits both during his time in prison and afterwards.

It will be seen that though some of these tasks require special skills and can only be undertaken by volunteers who are suited by training and by temperament, others can be tackled by people with no special qualifications or exceptional gifts. In the words of the working party:

Many of these services are aspects of befriending and may be restated in a variety of psychological terms, the two outstanding effects being the reduction of anxiety and the improvement of interpersonal relationships; both these basic effects can be often attained through the simplest services and by unsophisticated people[1].

Thus there is room in voluntary work with prisoners and their families not only for the person who is able to visit regularly during sentence and to follow this up after discharge by

[1] *Op. cit.*, para. 47.

helping with accommodation, employment and social contacts, but also for people who take part in group activities in prison and who show an interest in the lonely wife. This interest can take the form of neighbourly friendship and the offer to care for children while she visits her husband or enjoys an occasional outing, or it can lead to the promotion of clubs and social gatherings. Prisoners' wives value greatly anything that breaks down their isolation, and gain strength from meeting one another in sympathetic surroundings.

Voluntary bodies and voluntary workers today

While the associate must always retain direct contact with the probation officer, the volunteer who undertakes less exacting tasks can and does still operate through the voluntary bodies as he has done in the past. Some of these bodies, like the D.P.A.'s and the Police Court Missions which date from the last century, have now ceased to exist, but many of their supporters have continued their work for prisoners through other channels. Today the work is being done partly by organizations, like the London settlements, which have been in existence for some time and have recently extended their activities to include prison welfare, and partly by societies and groups newly formed for this one purpose.

Most general social service bodies which undertake case work have some dealings with prisoners' families, but one is particularly concerned with their special difficulties. This is Family Service Units[1], which was started in 1947 'to provide an intensive case-work service for "problem families"' and though it is not concerned with prisoners' families only, such families form a high proportion of its cases. The W.R.V.S.[2], though not a case work agency, now also includes prison welfare among its many activities. Its members visit women prisoners and Borstal boys, help with after-care and take an interest in the families. The Prisoners' Wives Service[3], formed as recently as 1964, is also associated with the probation

---

[1] For more information about F.S.U., see above, p. 28.

[2] A summary of the work W.R.V.S. undertakes in prison welfare is given in their *Bulletin* (June, 1968), p. 25.

[3] See *Observer*, 15th October, 1967.

service in visiting and befriending the wives of prisoners in the London area. Many religious groups, too, make a special point of helping prisoners and their families. There are special advantages when nation-wide organizations, as both the Churches and the W.R.V.S. are in their different ways, undertake this kind of work, since links can be maintained through them when offenders are in prison some distance from their homes. W.R.V.S. undertakes to inform families in any part of the country of the arrest of relatives, and will undertake emergency help when this is needed.

Of particular interest in prison welfare is the work being done by societies and groups, newly formed for the purpose, such as the New Bridge (1956), the Blackfriars Scheme (1950) and the Circle Trust (1961). The idea behind the New Bridge Scheme is 'that ordinary members of the public should play their part in re-integrating in society men and women discharged from prison'[1]. There are about 100 voluntary workers, half of whom are in London and half in the provinces. In addition there are 200 subscribing members. Workers and members are of both sexes and all ages over twenty-one and come from different social classes, though the majority are middle-class business people.

The voluntary workers cover every aspect of the problems which a prisoner will face both while he is in prison and when he is released. They visit in prison and write to the men there. If they are required to do so, they visit the prisoner's family. They meet him on release, deal with problems of work, accommodation and personal home matters[2].

The Blackfriars Scheme is one of the activities of the settlement of that name. It has 130 voluntary workers, about half of whom are active at any one time. Two thirds of these are men, and all are over twenty-one, and again the majority are middle class. Their work resembles that of the New Bridge volunteers, and their leaflet *Gaol Delivery* states that the key to the successful working of the scheme is 'personal friendship', and appeals for volunteers with 'friendship to spare'. This scheme is closely integrated with the Inner London Probation

[1] *New Bridge*, leaflet, 1967.
[2] Letter from the secretary to the author, 14th December, 1967.

and After-Care Service which has now assumed financial responsibility for it. Two other settlements, Bishop Creighton House in Fulham and Toynbee Hall in Stepney, have joined Blackfriars and these three form the bases for the work of volunteers in London, each covering a third of the geographical area[1].

The Circle Trust concentrates its efforts on the provision of clubs for discharged prisoners and groups for wives and families. The Circle Clubs in Camberwell and Pentonville provide meeting places and personal friendship both for men who need long-term support and for casual callers, and the regular use which is made of them shows that they meet a felt need. There is some full-time trained staff, but considerable use is made of voluntary helpers. These number twenty-two women and sixteen men whose ages range from twenty-five to fifty. Once again they are mainly professional people, though in this case there are four who are artisans. They assist with serving meals, which are an important part of club life, and act as companions and friends to the ex-prisoner members. The Trust also runs three groups for wives; one at Pentonville, one in South London and the third in Ipswich. In these three groups twenty-two women and two men are giving a regular service[2] talking to wives and helping with their problems and playing with the children.

These are some of the societies through which people (other than associates) who want to help prisoners and their families can do so. The volunteers are still comparatively few in number and many more will be needed if all prisoners, ex-prisoners and families are to have adequate opportunities for securing the support they need.

Actual numbers of those helping this section of the community are difficult to estimate. In addition to the J.P.'s, who number about 16,000, there are members of committees and working parties, prison visitors, promoters and managers of residential accommodation and clubs, and groups attached to the eighty-four probation committees. There are also the volunteers who are actively involved with the specialized

---

[1] Leaflet, *The Blackfriars Scheme and how it works* (1967).

[2] This information was supplied to the author by the Secretary of the Circle Trust in December, 1967.

societies, and those who are undertaking less regular and exacting but still valuable work.

More volunteers will be needed, and it is fortunate that there are people to whom this type of work appeals, for it can be extremely demanding both in time and in personal commitment. Even the lesser tasks which can be carried out by people whom the working party describes as 'unsophisticated' require patience and resilience in the face of discouragement; but these, too, are doubly satisfying – they involve neighbourly service and they help to combat crime. The working party states that:

Endless opportunities confront the voluntary societies in After-Care. Similarly the potential and importance of the individual volunteers are undoubted[1].

There is certainly plenty to be done, and much that can be done by voluntary effort, but it is to be hoped that the number of people who can usefully be absorbed into this kind of work will remain small, at least in relation to such work as old people's welfare or the youth service. It is the aim of the after-care service with which the volunteers are working to reduce the number of offenders, whereas it is not the aim of those who work with the aged or the young to reduce the numbers of those sections of the community. People who are engaged in voluntary work with offenders should certainly be sufficiently numerous to give every possible assistance in the work of after-care, but it is to be hoped that the number needed will automatically decline, since it would be pessimistic indeed to assume that the number of offenders and therefore of people needing help of this kind will always remain as high as it is now.

[1] *The Place of Voluntary Service in After-Care*, para. 4.

CHAPTER V

Information and Advice

Voluntary agencies with the express purpose of providing information and advice are comparative newcomers to social service. The charitable organizations which were formed in the eighteenth, nineteenth and early twentieth centuries existed primarily to relieve poverty, sickness and distress by giving material help. In some cases this help was accompanied by personal support, but the element of advice was part and parcel of the kind of charitable work which was undertaken by one section of the community for the other, by the fortunate and well-to-do for the poor and unfortunate. The new type of agency is different in two important respects – first, it offers information and advice unconnected with material help of any kind, and second, it is intended for everyone, without distinction of wealth or social status. It provides a service of which everyone who wishes can make use, rather than help whose bestowal depends on the decision of some philanthropic society.

There are now three main agencies of this new type which operate on a nation-wide basis, the Citizens' Advice Bureaux, the Marriage Guidance and Advice Councils, and the Samaritans. All are voluntary bodies and all rely largely on voluntary workers. The first aims to supply information and advice to all comers on every conceivable topic, the other two are concerned with more specialized problems: to help those with marriage difficulties, and those 'tempted to suicide or despair'.

Citizen's Advice Bureaux

These were established at the outset of the second world war by the National Council of Social Service. They had been planned well beforehand as an emergency service of free and unbiased information 'for the citizen by the citizen'. 'For the citizen' meant everyone, because everyone was involved in the war and was faced by the same problems and complications of call-up, evacuation and rationing. 'By the citizen' meant volunteers, for though the initiative and guidance came from the professional staff of the promoting national and local organizations, the day-to-day work was from the first in the hands of unpaid workers. Bureaux were linked with local Councils of Social Service and similar bodies where these existed; in other places *ad hoc* committees were set up to sponsor them, and close links were everywhere established with local authorities and government departments. Two hundred bureaux were set up on the day war was declared, and the number grew to 1,000 during the next few years. Once set up they had to be supplied with a regular flow of information. This tremendous task was undertaken by the C.A.B. Committee of the N.C.S.S.[1], which circulated regular notes and instructions. Bureaux workers had to learn how to assimilate the information and transmit it to those who sought their help. They needed not only to be reliable in their attendance and helpful in their approach to inquirers, they needed above all to be well informed and up-to-date. They had to study all the material they received from head-quarters and in addition to be familiar with the local scene, and with the special problems of their own areas. That they succeeded in doing this is shown by the fact that the bureaux quickly won the confidence of the public.

It soon became clear that what had been established to meet the emergency of war would be needed, too, in the period of reconstruction. The main problems of everyday living are not always the same in peace as in war, but they are problems none the less, and problems which the bureaux are helping to solve.

The questions which loomed large in the immediate post-war period and which are still urgent today cover every aspect of new legislation in the Welfare State, and include

---

[1] In 1946 the National Standing Conference of Citizens' Advice Bureaux was set up as an associated group of the N.C.S.S. and the C.A.B. department became the National C.A.B. Council.

difficulties over housing, hire purchase, consumer protection, and personal matters of all kinds. The N.C.S.S. realized the importance of C.A.B. work in peace as in war and its C.A.B. Council has continued and expanded the work of collecting and disseminating information, of maintaining contacts with government departments, and of promoting training.

The volunteer who undertakes to serve in a C.A.B. is not choosing an easy job, nor one that can be tackled without training. He must, as must all voluntary workers, be reliable. He must, as must everyone whose work involves personal contacts, know or learn how to approach in a sympathetic way those who seek his help – to gain their trust and to respect their confidence. To do this well demands personal qualities as well as training, but training can help the new worker to develop the right attitude. In addition to the right attitude he must have knowledge to impart the information which it is the job of the C.A.B. to give. For this he needs a good general education and some simple training such as is increasingly being supplied by national and local committees. He must, moreover, take active steps to keep his knowledge up-to-date.

In spite of these demands, recruitment of suitable volunteers is not usually a problem for C.A.B. committees. True, the number needed is small in comparison with those engaged for example in old people's welfare or in youth work; true, too, there is now a proportion of paid staff, but it is all the same impressive that so many people are ready and indeed anxious to undertake this demanding work, and to fall in readily with conditions such as regular weekly service and preliminary and refresher training courses.

There are now nearly 500 bureaux in the United Kingdom open at least part of every day except Saturday and Sunday. Many are open all of every day and some have evening sessions. About three-quarters of the workers are unpaid, and the quarter who receive some remuneration are mostly part-time. The National C.A.B. Council does not keep statistics of voluntary workers, but they estimate that each bureau has at least ten who give an average of one and a half sessions per week, one session being the minimum requirement. This estimate means that there are now some 5,000 voluntary workers actively engaged on this very exacting work[1].

These workers are in the main women – some 75 per cent – and in the main middle-aged or elderly. The men are for the most part retired and professional people, the women either temporarily retired from professions such as teaching, nursing and social work, or housewives whose experience consists of bringing up a family and running a home. The very young are not likely to be attracted by C.A.B. work nor would they always be acceptable to those seeking help since many of the problems require handling by people of maturity and experience. Moreover, as it is mostly morning and afternoon work, it cannot be undertaken by men and women in full-time employment whatever their age. But as a comparatively small number are likely to be needed even if the national target of nine hundred bureaux (one for every centre of 30,000 population or more) is reached, there should be no difficulty in recruiting these from men and women who are not in gainful employment. Moreover, those bureaux which arrange sessions in the evenings and on Saturday mornings for the convenience of inquirers who cannot come during ordinary working hours can use for these sessions volunteers who are themselves in full-time work. Such volunteers, like the paid workers, can be from any age group, but the majority of those who conduct the normal sessions will probably continue to be middle-aged or elderly.

The National C.A.B. Council does not anticipate difficulties about paid and unpaid people working side by side. The tendency, in the larger bureaux at least, to have one or more paid staff does not seem to deter volunteers and tends to improve organization. The pattern now seems to be that there is a paid, usually part-time, organizer with voluntary workers in the bureau itself. The small number of full-time staff are trained social workers when these are available; those who are part-time tend to have the same kind of qualifications and experience as most of the volunteers. The organizers

---

[1] This may be an underestimate. The chairman of the National Citizens' Advice Bureaux Council, Sir Harold Banwell, in an article in *Social Service Quarterly* (Spring, 1967), suggests that those engaged in all capacities probably number nearly 8,000. This figure includes specialist advisers, who, like the majority of workers in the bureaux, give their services voluntarily, and also paid staff, who apparently make up a quarter of the whole.

of the C.A.B. service both at national and local level are coming to adopt the view, which is also gaining ground in other voluntary work[1], that a key person is needed to keep the machine going, and that the key person usually has to be paid[1].

Marriage Guidance

The original Marriage Guidance Council was formed in 1938. Its early activities mainly consisted of discussions among interested people in London and elsewhere, and it was not until 1945 that it embarked on the task of giving active help with marriage problems by selecting and training lay people to act as counsellors. The fact that the number of broken marriages increased greatly during and after the war was doubtless responsible for the urgency with which the M.G.C. set about this task. The movement had the support of people like probation officers, doctors, parsons, teachers and social workers, whose work brought them up against marital problems. They realized how urgently help was needed if marriage breakdowns were to be avoided and personal tragedies for husbands, wives and children were to be overcome.

The National Marriage Guidance Council (N.M.G.C.) has three main aims: to provide a skilled and confidential service for those who have experienced difficulties in their marriages, to send education counsellors to youth clubs and schools to run discussion groups with young people, and to publish booklets on topics concerned with courtship, marriage and family life. Local Councils recruit marriage and education counsellors, distribute publications and offer marriage guidance to the public. They receive help from the paid officials and tutors of the National Council, but all counsellors work voluntarily; so also do consultants (professional men and women to whom counsellors may refer special problems), committee members, fund raisers and many of the speakers.

---

[1] For example, in work with the elderly and in hospitals. See above, pp. 57–8 and 87.

[2] For more details about the history of the C.A.B. see Margaret E. Brasnett, *The Story of the Citizens' Advice Bureaux* (1964), and for an account of the service by a team of investigators from the U.S.A. see Alfred J. Kahn, *et al.*, *Neighbourhood Information Centres* (1966).

It is the counsellors who are the key workers in the service, and there are now some 1,400 of them working in 116 local Councils[1]. Great attention has always been paid to their selection and training. Candidates must attend a two-day selection conference before they are even selected for training, and only forty-five per cent of those who attend are in fact accepted. The training itself consists of a course of reading followed by four 48-hour residential periods of lectures and discussions, followed by further reading, by in-service training and by refresher courses. The nature of the training means that future counsellors must have a fairly high level of general education, and most of them belong to the middle- or upper-class.

The rejection rate is probably higher and the training more demanding than in any other voluntary organization, and it is encouraging that so many people are prepared to offer their services for this difficult work, and to be ready both to face a fifty-fifty chance of rejection and to commit themselves to a course of serious study. Yet the time devoted to preparation and the expertise required are small indeed compared with those involved in courses leading to a professional qualification. It is not surprising, therefore, that it is sometimes questioned whether work of this kind should be left to 'well-meaning unpaid amateurs'. Can such people acquire sufficient competence through the training they receive, and what measure of success do they have?

The success of marriage guidance, whether undertaken by the N.M.G.C. and its Catholic counterpart, the Catholic Marriage Advisory Council (C.M.A.C.) which also uses volunteers, or by the Family Discussion Bureau which is staffed by professionals, is difficult to estimate. No follow-up work is done, and moreover success in this context is hard to define. The Family Discussion Bureau would like to keep an eye on the families it has tried to help if it had the necessary resources, but makes the point that even so it would be difficult to estimate the lasting value of its work. The secretary of the N.M.G.C. 'has the impression that about a third of the clients are really helped, about a third not. As for

---

[1] These figures are taken from the Report of the Study Group of the N.M.G.C. for the British National Conference of Social Welfare, 1967, as is the wording of the 'aims'.

the others no one ever knows'[1]. His Council takes comfort[2] from the fact that the numbers who come to see their counsellors increase every year, though it admits that they only succeed in seeing both parties in a third of the cases. Estimates of improvement are therefore often based on the reports of one spouse only. This is a drawback, but it does not alter the fact that help given to one spouse is better than no help at all. The increase in numbers is at least a sign that some more troubled people are being given hope and an opportunity to discuss their problems, and it may mean much more than this. At best it means that more couples are being helped to find their way to married happiness.

In spite of the absence of hard evidence it seems clear that something of value is being provided by the marriage guidance service as at present organized. This does not mean, however, that it is organized in the best possible way, nor that it might not do more good if more of its work were in the hands of trained social workers. There would be advantages in this, but it is a matter of opinion whether they would outweigh those of the present system. If it were possible to organize a nation-wide scheme staffed by professionals whose skills were available to all comers the quality of guidance might be better and more uniform than it is now, and it might be more acceptable to those people who prefer to consult official rather than unofficial sources even on such personal matters as marriage problems. On the other hand there are definite advantages in the present system. First, the obvious one that the cost of providing a comprehensive service without voluntary help would be high both in money and in manpower, and since it would to some extent duplicate what is already provided by probation officers the taxpayer might be unwilling to foot the bill, and the trained manpower, even if it were available, might well be put to better use.

The second advantage is the unofficial and unspecialized status of the volunteer. His unofficial status is often the very thing that makes him acceptable, for though some people prefer to consult authorities which are official, many take the opposite view and seek the volunteer just because he is not

---

[1] Quoted in the *Guardian*, 4th May, 1967.
[2] See the *Guardian*, 26th January, 1968.

official. Those who prefer to seek advice from official sources can consult the probation service, and indeed some two-thirds of all matrimonial problems for which help is sought pass through the hands of its officers. They are trained social workers with the statutory duty of attempting reconciliation. They often establish valuable personal contacts with the husbands and wives in their care, but they are inevitably associated in the public mind with the courts. The Marriage Guidance Councillor, on the other hand, is known to be completely independent. The counsellor, too, gains from the fact that he is unspecialized, and this, like his unofficial status, puts him in a rather different position from that of the professional. Though not himself a specialist he can call on lawyers, doctors and parsons, when the kind of help is needed which they are qualified to give. Specialists such as these have much to offer but are often unable to find a complete solution to marriage problems; and the fact that an increasing number of people are turning to M.G.C. counsellors shows that these, too, have a contribution to make. The specialist is concerned with a special problem – of law, of health or of religion – while the counsellor is concerned with the marriage as a whole and with helping the partners to understand and face their situation and reach their own decision about their future. He hopes, of course, that those who are estranged will be reconciled, and that their health and spiritual welfare will improve, but his job is to help them find their own way out of their difficulties.

The voluntary worker may have to refer to others those who need specialized help, but he will often himself be able to comfort and to reassure. In this he will be doing for those who seek his help what many families and friends are doing in their own circles. He is a friend in need for those who have none at hand, or who do not wish to confide in relatives and neighbours, and his training and detachment gives his advice an extra quality over and above that given by families and friends. Like them, he gives something of value simply by listening, and this he can always do. Even when he does not succeed in helping people to solve their problems – and some problems are beyond solution – he does at least offer to share another's burden. He has time to listen, and a good listener is often what those in trouble most need and cannot always find in their home circle. This part of the work of marriage guidance rightly belongs to the volunteer, and for this there will still be room whatever expansion takes place in the number of paid workers. Unlike the paid worker the volunteer does not have to account for the use of his time, and in marriage guidance as in every other person-to-person social work he can give his time freely to those who need it. In doing this he does more than supplement the work of the hard-pressed professionals: he fills a gap that can be filled in no other way. The freedom of unpaid workers to give time is the third advantage of the present system of marriage guidance[1].

The Samaritans

The Samaritans came into existence more recently than either the C.A.B. or the N.M.G.C., but they have grown at an astonishing rate and now have branches all over the world. The organization came into being not as a result of meetings, discussions and conferences, as was the case with marriage guidance, but on the initiative of one man – a London clergyman[2] – who invited people contemplating suicide to telephone him at a given number. This was in 1953 and was a personal response to his realization that there were three suicides a day in Greater London, and that something should be done to make emergency help available. He had received several hundred letters as a result of an article in the press on 'an enlightened Christian philosophy of sex' which led him to believe that non-medical counselling such as he was able to offer had a contribution to make in the prevention of suicide, since only one in eight of his correspondents appeared to be cases for psychiatric treatment – a proportion which is still roughly the proportion of those coming to the Samaritans who are thought to need such specialized help.

Press publicity was obtained for the emergency telephone and quickly brought calls for help on the one hand and volunteers on the other. These were mainly unqualified

---

[1] A description of the remedial work of the N.M.G.C. is given by J. H. Wallis in *Someone To Turn To* (1961).

[2] This was Chad Varah, whose book, *The Samaritans* (1965), includes an account of the origin and development of the movement.

'ordinary' people, though the service also enlisted the support of psychiatrists, psychologists, social workers and parsons[1]. The 'ordinary' people soon found useful jobs to do in welcoming and talking to those who were waiting for interview, and the value of their work resulted in the original concept of the non-medical but still professional counselling service being replaced by that of a *befriending* service by lay volunteers, who were selected and supervised by counsellors. These lay people not only set the counsellor free for work which only he could do, but themselves performed tasks of which he for his part was incapable. For their task is to *befriend*, to give time and thought to the person in trouble in the same way as they would to any other friend in need. Clearly nobody can do this for more than one or two people at any one time since it demands much time and energy. The befriender does not seek to give professional help: the value of what he gives is personal, and depends not on knowledge and skills but on his human qualities and his concern for the person he is befriending. He is supported in his work by the Samaritan organization in somewhat the same way as the associate is supported by the probation service in his relationship with an offender[2]. This pattern of lay volunteers' providing the day-to-day contacts with those who need help against a background of professional support is one of the ways in which voluntary service is being increasingly used. The volunteer of this type is asked to give not material help, not special skills, but some of his time, and what is still more valuable, some of himself. How valuable this often is, is shown by the case histories of many of those who call on the Samaritans. While some need help of a kind the befriender cannot give, and these are referred to more qualified people, and some less serious cases only want temporary reassurance, the majority appear to need the kind of support over a period which the voluntary Samaritan is able to give[3].

[1] The contributors of articles to Chad Varah's book include no less than seven psychiatrists who are honorary consultants to various branches of Samaritans. This gives some indication of the extent to which qualified professional people give voluntary service to the movement.

[2] The value of support of this kind is discussed above, pp. 139–142.

[3] *The Annual Report of the Telephone Samaritans in Manchester* (quoted in the *Guardian* for 8th July, 1967) gives the reasons for calling for help in the previous twelve months in order of frequency – depression, anxiety and

Though the Samaritan is chosen not for any particular abilities but for the human qualities which make him a good friend, he has to learn how best to help people who may be seriously disturbed. This he does through preparation classes and case conferences, and from his own experience and that of others. He must learn from the first to understand when the person he is befriending needs the kind of help which he himself cannot give, though the dangers of an inexperienced person trying to tackle cases beyond his powers seem usually to be avoided by the foresight of the skilled people who allocate the cases.

The movement spread from London first to Edinburgh and Liverpool and then to other places in the United Kingdom and in other Commonwealth countries. At the same time work of a similar kind was being started in continental Europe and in America. By 1965 there were sixty-seven branches in the United Kingdom and those who worked in and for them numbered several thousand[1]. Even small branches need ten or a dozen volunteers to keep the telephone manned, as well as counsellors and befrienders, and to these must be added those who act as advisers and consultants.

This is a growing movement, and one which will go on growing, because it helps to meet two fundamental needs – the need for immediate response in emergency, and the need for sustained personal befriending. It is a movement in which volunteers have a leading part to play and which makes great demands on its members; but fortunately there seems to be no shortage of people of goodwill whose human qualities make them suitable candidates who welcome the opportunity to serve in a field where professional skills are not required. The explanation for the existence of these people is expressed by the founder of the movement in these words:

[1] See list in Chad Varah, *op. cit.*, p. 224 et seq., and for his estimate of numbers, see *ibid.*, p. 9.

---

mental illness (361), marital relationships (324), emotional relationships (229), financial problems (208), loneliness (193), down to drug addiction (36) and the theological problems (15). Ten per cent of the callers were would-be suicides. This list gives some idea of the relative importance of the various problems.

In our day, the State has more and more taken over the responsibility for the welfare of its citizens, and this is a right and necessary development; but it has left many men and women of goodwill with a feeling of frustration because there is so little that they can do for someone other than themselves which can compare with what professionally trained people can accomplish. To such people, the Samaritans and other organisations which utilise the services of untrained volunteers come as a godsend. To be able to make all the difference in the world to another human being is to find one's real self[1].

The desire to help others is certainly an important factor in the readiness of people to give service in this and other fields. For some volunteers it may be the only or at least the predominant factor, though the fact that serving others is 'to find oneself' makes it a not altogether altruistic occupation. If the desire to help is wholly absent, little work of value will be done by either paid or unpaid workers; but most people's motives are usually mixed and the presence of other factors alongside the desire to help others does not necessarily detract from the value of the service either to those who receive or to those who render it. An attempt will be made later[2] to consider this complicated question of the motives which prompt people to undertake voluntary work, and how far these affect its value.

[1] Chad Varah, *op. cit.*, p. 30.
[2] See Chapter VIII below.

CHAPTER VI

Race Relations

The presence in Britain of a substantial number of coloured people is a new phenomenon. As recently as 1950 there were only 100,000 in the whole country, and, apart from a few students and professional people, they were concentrated in the dockland areas, and were for the most part single men. Now, in 1968, there are over a million; they are no longer concentrated in a few areas and have become a mixed population of men, women and children. This new situation has created problems whose solution will largely depend on the attitudes of ordinary men and women in their capacity of good neighbours and voluntary workers.

In many parts of the country there are now large groups of immigrants from the West Indies, from India and from Pakistan who are settled members of the community with the same hopes and needs as their fellow-citizens. Many are buying houses and plan to make this country their permanent home. They want regular well-paid employment and good accommodation and social services. In these respects their needs are similar to those of other people, and their contacts with voluntary workers as mothers, children, sick or handicapped persons should be the same as those of anyone else. But they have other needs as well. These other needs are due to three main factors: first, they are newcomers, second, the difference in their culture, way of life and language, and third, the colour of their skins. The first two factors time will remove, and children born and educated in this country will speak the language and adopt the habits of children of British-born parents, but the difference in colour will remain at least until after many generations of intermarriage. Continued effort on the part of both white and black will be needed before contacts with voluntary workers are entirely unaffected by the colour of the people concerned.

The first generation immigrant is affected by all three factors, and suffers not only because of his colour but also because he is a newcomer and because life in his new home is strange and unfamiliar. The most valuable help that can be given him by members of the host community is ordinary neighbourliness, and where this exists organized voluntary work is much less necessary. If all newcomers were welcomed whatever the colour of their skin, the coloured immigrant might have no special needs apart from language difficulties and ignorance of local customs, but because of widespread prejudice against 'foreigners', especially coloured ones, and against strangers of any kind the essential neighbourly help is often lacking. Efforts must therefore be made by voluntary as well as by statutory authorities to fill the gap left by the absence of good neighbours, and at the same time to do everything possible to enlist the goodwill and support of the neighbourhood, since on this satisfactory relations must ultimately depend.

There are thus two main tasks for those who want to help to improve race relations: first, to educate the host community, and second, to give to immigrants the kind of help of which, as immigrants, they are in special need – help with language, with adaptation to new surroundings, with problems arising from discrimination in employment, housing or any other field. The accomplishment of these tasks is beyond the powers of voluntary bodies and volunteers alone: anti-discrimination laws and active statutory bodies are essential. Yet government action alone will not achieve racial harmony. This depends at every stage and at every level on active participation by voluntary workers. From the members of influential organizations which press for a better deal for immigrants and handle their problems at national level, to the ordinary citizen who lives or works beside a coloured person, all have a part to play, and so, too, have the immigrants. Indeed, the achievement of racial harmony will depend in no small measure on the efforts they themselves make. Those who are settled here can do a great deal to help new arrivals to adjust to life in this country.

*Organizations concerned with race relations and
the welfare of immigrants*

The Race Relations Board, established in 1966 by the Race Relations Act of 1965, set up local conciliation committees to consider complaints of discrimination and to attempt conciliation. Its powers have been limited by the limited field to which the Act applies, but this will be extended now that the bill of 1968 has become law. The National Committee for Commonwealth Immigrants (N.C.C.I.) was appointed by the Prime Minister, also in 1965, to advise the government on matters relating to the integration of commonwealth immigrants. This has now become (by statute) the Community Relations Commission.

The N.C.C.I. co-ordinates the work of the local liaison committees of which there are now (1968) over fifty. These have originated in a variety of ways and some were in existence long before the N.C.C.I. itself was set up. They were formed on the initiative of groups of internationally minded citizens, and were sometimes sponsored by Councils of Social Service or Councils of Churches. They aimed at drawing together the voluntary bodies which were interested in international affairs and in the welfare of immigrants and the local authority departments concerned with the needs of these newcomers; and attempted, with varying degrees of success, to include representatives of the different immigrant groups.

At national level many of the local liaison committees are linked with immigrant groups in the Joint Council for the Welfare of Immigrants. This is a voluntary body set up in September, 1967, by a small group of organizations which were handling cases at ports of entry to help immigrants on their arrival in the United Kingdom and to co-ordinate the work of organizations and individuals concerned with their welfare. It numbers over 150 organizations and includes both national and local bodies. Nearly two-thirds of its members are societies for a single national group, the most numerous being those composed of West Indians, Indians and Pakistanis. The other third of the membership is made up of local inter-racial bodies, such as the liaison committees, and of national organizations concerned with race relations, civil rights and international affairs. Its main concern at the moment is to help new arrivals, and it has recently appointed a welfare officer to assist in this work. Both at headquarters and in the field the bulk of the work is in the hands of volunteers.

The various local co-ordinating committees were and are the most important channel through which voluntary workers give their services. It is difficult to estimate how many people are involved and how much they do, but every active committee can certainly call on several hundred. Committee members themselves may not do more than attend meetings, and do not always do that, but they are instrumental in bringing in groups of helpers from the various organizations which they represent. A women's society may agree to run a playgroup or a club for immigrant wives, a teachers' organization may undertake informal language instruction, a youth group may make a special effort to include coloured youngsters or may undertake a specific task such as house decoration or repairs, a housing association may help with accommodation. In this way many individuals will be drawn into giving voluntary service. At the same time the committee members and their personal contacts will be involved to a greater or lesser extent, depending on their individual enthusiasm and energy in spreading knowledge of the racial situation in the locality and in helping to educate the host community.

In London, where the largest numbers of immigrants are concentrated, the Council of Social Service has been especially active. Through its Immigrants' Advisory Committee, it seeks to maintain contact with all the voluntary organizations concerned with race relations and spreads information about their work so that successful experiments can be copied. One such is the Cambridge House Literacy Scheme. This was started in 1963 as an internal affair by means of which illiterate members of the settlement youth club were taught to read and write. In 1965 an advertisement was issued reading as follows: 'Volunteers required to make illiterates literate. Mainly immigrants and teenagers on probation. One tutor, one pupil, one evening a week'. It produced over 300 replies, and the scheme was widened to include people whose problem was not illiteracy but ignorance of English. By 1967 it was split in two and the Language Scheme specially designed to meet the needs of immigrants was set up. Teaching is on a one-to-one basis and therefore requires a large number of volunteers if all those seeking to learn English are to be helped. Results have been most encouraging, largely, no doubt, because great care has been taken in matching tutor and pupil, and some forty non-English-speaking immigrants have learnt the language of their new home and have, in addition, acquired a personal friend in the process[1]. Work of the same kind is going on in some other places, sometimes arranged by a voluntary body, sometimes on an unorganized neighbour-to-neighbour basis. Clearly there is room for many more such schemes, and the experience of Cambridge House shows that there are people anxious to participate as tutors when the necessary arrangements can be made.

The London Council of Social Service itself is directly responsible for a wide range of services to immigrants. It provides interpreters at airports, hospitals and social service agencies, offers advice and information; encourages the formation of mixed play groups and the integration of children and young people into existing clubs. All these activities depend on the use of volunteers both from the host community and from the immigrants themselves.

The value of activities of this kind goes beyond the value of the actual services rendered for they form a meeting ground for voluntary workers of all races and help to break down the barrier that will always exist so long as one race is in the position of 'doing good' to another, and the voluntary work of that other takes the form of self-help rather than community service. One-sided service by the host community is certainly better than nothing, and it is a step towards bringing the newcomers more closely into the life of their new home, but it is no permanent substitute for a situation where members of different races help each other as well as helping their own people.

Self-help among immigrants

There is a strong element of neighbourly help among many immigrant groups, and this is a valuable part of the life of the whole community. The interdependence of families coming

[1] For further details see *The Cambridge House Literacy Scheme*, a report by Anthony Hurst (November, 1967), 131, Camberwell Road, London, S.E.5.

from the same parts of countries overseas creates an element of stability which makes life more tolerable in an alien and often unfriendly place. In some ways this resembles the kinship and neighbourhood networks of the older parts of British towns and villages, but it is strikingly different from the pattern in the newer communities where established links have been broken and left gaps so that needs which were previously met by neighbours are now dependent on the help of voluntary bodies and of volunteers who do not necessarily live in the same locality. The strong family loyalty shown, for example, by the worker from India and Pakistan, even to his most distant relatives, supplements the more formal organization of social services by both statutory and voluntary bodies; and the workers' organizations assist in finding jobs for fellow-nationals and contribute to their support during unemployment and sickness. The obligation to offer houseroom and food to members of the extended family, and even of the native village, takes the place for the immigrant of the duty felt by some members of more sophisticated societies to help a stranger through a voluntary body or as a good neighbour – a duty felt not because of any special kinship tie but simply because he is a fellow-man who needs help. This difference in attitude accounts to some extent for the difference in the way in which the host community and the immigrants meet their social problems – it accounts, too, for the difficulties which the two groups find in understanding one another. It partly explains the extent of self-help among the immigrants, and their comparative reluctance to participate in the more sophisticated ways of meeting social needs adopted in the host community – a reluctance which is often enhanced by difficulties of communication. The host community, for its part, finds it difficult to understand the implications of the difference in attitude, and tends to underestimate both the extent and value of the self-help among the newcomers and the obstacles which prevent them from co-operating in joint efforts in ways to which they are unaccustomed.

Volunteers in the host community

Work in the field of race relations is a formidable challenge to the volunteer. He must try to put himself in the place of the immigrant in order to undertand in a personal way what it feels like to be a stranger of a different colour in a strange land, and must learn something of the way these strangers live. He must educate himself in this way so that he can educate others in the host community. At the same time he must act as interpreter – and not only in language – of the attitude of the established residents to the newcomers. For newcomers also must be educated. They must learn not only to speak the language and to adapt to urban life in a developed country, but also to understand the reasons for the prejudices of their hosts. Only by understanding can they make real contact with those among their hosts who genuinely wish to co-operate with them. In the achievement of this understanding the better-educated members of the immigrant communities have a vital part to play as voluntary workers among their fellow-nationals. Joint action involves action by both sides, and its success depends on mutual understanding, but this does not alter the fact that the host community has a special responsibility to take the first steps.

How far is this responsibility being discharged? Members of national and local committees, of churches and of voluntary organizations together with other people of goodwill, are doing something to improve race relations in this country, but their efforts are inadequate and much more help will be needed. Many more volunteers must be drawn in, and they must come from every section of society. At present the majority are middle class, and as most of the immigrants are workers there is a double gulf of class and race between those who give and those who receive help. The middle-class volunteer must therefore try not only to give personal help himself, but to encourage people from other social groups to do likewise. The behaviour of those who are in daily contact with immigrants at home and at work is more important for racial harmony than that of middle-class well-wishers who usually only associate naturally with people of any race if they belong to their own social group. The close association of people of different classes tends to be artificial even if there is no difference of race, and becomes more artificial still when difference of race is added to that of class. Some people find the class barrier the more difficult of the two to break down, and the professional classes at least are more at ease with their opposite numbers of another race than with fellow-nationals of a different educational level. This fact may not be encouraging for those who hope for a classless society, but it gives modest ground for hope that racial harmony may not be impossible to achieve. But it will not be achieved without the help of many more volunteers from all sections of the community.

The first task for those who are already active is to persuade others of the importance of this form of voluntary work, and thus to build up a body of opinion which is opposed to discrimination in any form and which takes neighbourly service to people of other races for granted. Acts of Parliament and government-sponsored committees are essential if the battle against racial discrimination is to be won, but they must be supplemented by voluntary action to a far greater extent than has so far happened. Only so can the responsibility of the host community to the newcomers be met.

The second task for voluntary action is to undertake practical work on behalf of and in co-operation with immigrants. This work is of two kinds; first, that which concerns needs which are shared by everyone, irrespective of race, and second, that which concerns the special needs of immigrants. People of all races have needs in early childhood, in sickness, in poverty or in loneliness, and the services provided from both statutory and voluntary sources to meet needs such as these should be available to all alike. Immigrants and their families have additional needs of a different kind. They need help, first of all, with language, and this applies to many West Indians and Europeans as well as to Indians and Pakistanis; they need information; they need help in meeting discrimination, especially if they are coloured, and they need help in adjusting to different customs and attitudes and in learning to share the activities of their new neighbours.

Language difficulties are, of course, a special problem for the first generation immigrant of any age. Schools and colleges are working hard to overcome these difficulties, but much more informal help such as that given by the Cambridge House Literacy Scheme is needed, particularly in the case of adults. Teaching on a one-to-one basis with voluntary tutors can enable non-English-speaking people to reach the stage where they can face and profit from a class. This is specially so in the case of women who are often too shy to venture to a public place for group instruction and are sometimes even prevented from doing so by their national customs; but it applies, too, with men, and even with children, though these sometimes have the benefit of special instruction in school. Even a few sessions with a private tutor may be enough to break down the barrier of a strange language, and enable men and women to tackle jobs from which they were cut off by ignorance of English, and children to catch up with their locally-born schoolfellows. The capacity to speak and to understand also helps the immigrant to overcome the hostility which he is liable to meet when he applies for employment, for accommodation, or for personal service of any kind. A knowledge of English is probably the single most important gift that can be given to the immigrant, and it is a gift that many potential volunteers are in a position to bestow.

For those who cannot speak English, the importance of readily available interpreters is obvious, and here again the volunteer has a vital part to play. Much is being done by the immigrants themselves – the National Federation of Pakistani Associations, for example, has thirty-seven branches, all of which can be quickly contacted from London and will supply voluntary interpreters at short notice for anyone in need, whether or not he is a fellow-national; and the Indian Workers' Association (Southall) assists immigrants from all over the country, especially in relation to problems arising at Heathrow Airport. Such service is additional to the day-by-day help at work and at leisure given by those who speak English to those who do not. Without the help, freely given, by organizations and individuals among the immigrants, difficulties of communication would be far greater than they are, especially since comparatively few of the native Englishmen who volunteer to help in the work of race relations can speak the required languages.

Knowledge of English is the necessary first step for the immigrant towards finding work of the kind for which he is qualified by ability, and towards settling happily in his new home. But it is only the first step. Other things are desperately needed if successful integration is to be achieved.

Particularly valuable are pre-school playgroups where children of different races can mix in a natural way. These are needed by a large proportion of all children under school age, especially those who live in crowded conditions and in high flats, but they are needed most of all by coloured children who live in the same unsatisfactory conditions. These children have needs additional to those which they share with their white neighbours, because their surroundings are unfamiliar and their family life is different. West Indian children seem to be especially deprived: their housing conditions are usually very bad, they have no opportunities for play, and are separated from mothers and other kin for long periods. Some never learn to play or even communicate before they reach school age, unless they get the chance of mixing with other children in a pre-school playgroup. All the advantages of playgroups for the ordinary child and its mother are magnified in the case of the coloured immigrant.

Little public money has been made available for the playgroups, and their formation and running depends largely on voluntary effort[1]. The growth in their number is a tribute to the energy and unpaid work of enthusiasts, many of them themselves mothers of young children. Unfortunately, however, they are most numerous in the areas where the need is least acute, rather than where immigrants are concentrated. Wherever a group can include one or more coloured children, it is making a real contribution to racial harmony.

Playgroups are one way – and one of the most important since they provide help for those who are especially vulnerable – of helping to integrate immigrants into the community, and here voluntary action on a large scale is needed. Once children reach school age the part played by statutory provision obviously becomes much greater and the school becomes the most powerful influence in their lives. But even at this stage special help is needed for immigrants. They, even more than other children, need provision for their leisure – after school,

---

[1] The Association of Multi-Racial Playgroups has been formed by the Advisory Centre for Education, the Indian Workers' Association and the Race Relations Committee of the Society of Friends to start multi-racial playgroups in what the Plowden Report calls 'educational priority areas'. See *Where?*, July, 1968.

at week-ends and in holidays – because they tend to live in especially overcrowded conditions, and because their family life is often different from that of their schoolfellows. Because of this difference, and because of their shyness, it will often be necessary to make special efforts to persuade them to join in out of school activities and to take advantage of the opportunities for recreation which are available. Everyone who is connected with play centres or youth clubs, whether as leader or member has a special responsibility to draw in and support those who are held back by shyness or ignorance, or who fear that they may be penalized because of their foreignness or their colour.

Children undoubtedly have some difficulties because of foreignness and colour even while they are at school, and have considerably more when they try to find jobs. Voluntary workers may not have much direct influence in the field of employment, but they can help indirectly by seeking to influence employers and by supporting coloured youngsters in their applications. The acceptance of a coloured applicant can often be made possible by the intercession of a volunteer who knows him personally, and every time a youngster succeeds in getting a job in spite of his colour and carries it out as well as his white colleagues, another step towards racial harmony has been taken. Help of this kind in individual cases will reinforce anti-discrimination laws and give young coloured people a better chance of getting the work for which they are fitted by ability and qualification.

The same thing is true with older workers: personal help in the early stages can often determine whether or not the newcomer settles well into suitable work. A great deal of help in finding employment is given by fellow-nationals, but what they can do is often limited to low-grade jobs, and the help of more members of the host community is needed if discrimination in jobs is to be overcome.

For the adult worker a satisfactory job is the first need, but it is clearly not the only one. He needs somewhere to live, and he needs to share in the life of the neighbourhood. Housing is probably the most intractable problem facing the immigrant, especially when he has to live in overcrowded cities. Here again members of his own community are the most likely to help, though something is also being done by other well-wishers, by means of assistance with the problems of house purchase and occasionally by the formation of housing associations to meet his special needs. Here, as in the field of employment, a satisfactory situation can only be achieved if help is given on a person-to-person basis to back up the anti-discrimination laws.

Leisure-time activities present special problems because the immigrant often wishes both to preserve his own culture and traditions and to acquire those of his hosts. Like most other people he will usually be happiest with people of his own kind, and will choose to spend his leisure with relatives and friends from home. Yet if he is satisfied with these limited social contacts his integration into the host community will not take place, and true racial harmony will be difficult to achieve. Hosts, as well as newcomers, will suffer if different sections of the community remain too separate, and the hosts must take the main responsibility for bridging the gap. Friendly day-by-day contact with neighbours at home, at work and in the street is the basis for integration, but it can be assisted by organizations designed to bring the different groups together. Clubs are important, especially for women who are full-time housewives, and it may be necessary to have separate clubs for different nationalities if those who most need social contacts are to be persuaded to venture outside their homes. But clubs which start by catering for separate groups should strive to widen their membership so that people of all races can share in social intercourse. This is valuable for all parties since each will gain from learning at first hand about the way of life of other peoples. Newcomers are reluctant to lose their own culture when they adopt the customs of their new home, and they need not do so if understanding between the races can be built up on personal knowledge and friendship. In this way integration can be achieved, and society as a whole will benefit from the variety of cultures. Attendance at a special club may be a stepping-stone to joining one with a general membership, and through club life the individual may come to feel a part of his neighbourhood and to share in more of its activities. Though the lead must usually be taken by local people the aim should be to invite active co-operation from the newcomers, so that the club becomes a joint enterprise.

These are some of the ways in which individuals of goodwill can help to create racial harmony. Though what is being done is still on a small scale, its value shows what can be achieved by voluntary effort, and how this effort can best be directed. Every word or action that helps even one person to get the job or the home he needs, or which makes him feel less of a stranger in a strange land, makes a positive contribution. While the fact that so little is being done is certainly discouraging, there is ground for hope in the fact that little though it is, its effects are so great. If there were more voluntary workers taking positive action along the lines already being followed and in other ways, clearly much more could be achieved. More volunteers are essential if more practical schemes are to be promoted and, what is more important, if public opinion is to be educated to stamp out discrimination and to treat the newcomers as neighbours. This is their human right, for human rights begin at home, as the late Eleanor Roosevelt said in 1958:

Where, after all, do universal human rights begin? In small places close to home – so close and so small that they cannot be seen on any map of the world. Yet they are the world of the individual person; the neighbourhood he lives in; the school or college he attends; the factory, farm or office where he works. Such are the places where every man, woman and child seeks equal justice, equal opportunity, equal dignity without discrimination. Unless these rights have meaning there, they have little meaning anywhere. Without concerted citizen action to uphold them close to home, we shall look in vain for progress in the larger world[1].

Citizen action is action by voluntary workers, and nowhere is this action more needed than in the field of race relations. Twenty years ago there were few opportunities for service of this kind at home since there were few coloured people here. Now that times have changed there are opportunities on every side crying out to be met. The urgent need now is for volunteers from every walk of life to seize these opportunities wherever they arise, and especially, as Mrs. Roosevelt said, 'in small places, close to home'.

[1] Quoted at the beginning of *Human Rights*. A study guide for the International Year for Human Rights, 1968.

CHAPTER VII

Neighbourly Help

The preceding chapters have been concerned with work undertaken through a voluntary body or at the request of a statutory authority, and the volunteers described have been for the most part associated with an organization through which they have given their service. It has been possible to find out something about volunteers of this kind from the various agencies, and from an examination of what these agencies have achieved in the different fields of social action. But voluntary work in social service is not confined to action of an organized kind – it is being carried out in every town and village, and often in every street, by the giving of spontaneous neighbourly help. Work of this kind is unrecorded since it has no connection with any organization, and information about its nature and extent can only be obtained by direct inquiry of the people concerned.

An inquiry of this kind was undertaken in Bradford in 1967 by means of a survey which is described in Appendix III. This set out to discover how many people were doing voluntary social work of any kind, who those people were and what kind of things they were doing.

The most striking fact revealed by the survey was that four times as many people were giving regular neighbourly help as were workers in the social service agencies. This fact is of great importance for the future of voluntary work as a whole, since the proportion of such work which is carried out by unorganized volunteers must profoundly affect the overall contribution to social welfare which can be made by voluntary service.

The question at issue is not whether the total volume of voluntary work should be increased, since the obvious existence of unmet needs clearly makes this necessary, but how the desired increase can best be achieved.

More voluntary work will be needed whether or not the present pattern of service persists under changing conditions, but the form it takes will depend on the ways in which the life of the community develops. If, as is often assumed, help on a neighbour-to-neighbour basis is decreasing and if this decrease is inevitable, then more action by voluntary bodies will be needed if the same level of service is to be maintained, and still more if the level is to be raised. If, on the other hand, neighbourliness is not declining, or if, though it is declining, this process can be arrested or reversed, then the present balance between organized and unorganized voluntary service can be maintained even when the total volume is increased. What happens in the future will partly depend on the natural evolution of community life in the changing conditions of today, but it will depend, too, on planning policy and on social action. The development of the kind of community in which neighbourliness will flourish can be profoundly affected by the attitude of the planners to the needs and desires of its future inhabitants and by the efforts of professional and voluntary social workers to stimulate neighbourly feeling and action.

Problems of new communities

The view that neighbourliness is decreasing is widely held at the present time, and there is considerable evidence to support it. Anyone who has talked to people who have been uprooted from an overcrowded city centre and transplanted to a housing estate knows how lonely the new life can be. Old neighbours have been lost and new ones have not been found. Anyone who has wandered round the empty streets can testify to the feeling of isolation that seems to permeate the air. Most of the houses are empty during the day – all the adults except the elderly and the young mothers are out at work, and the children are away at school. The only sign of life in a whole street may be a solitary woman pushing a pram or an old man standing by his gate. Not only are factories, workshops, offices and even schools at some distance from the homes but there are often no obvious meeting places at all – no churches, pubs, halls or corner shops. In the evenings when the children come home there may be more life in the streets for a while, but the older ones are eager to get out as quickly as possible from a place where there is so little going on. This is the kind of district where neighbourliness is of slow growth.

In high blocks of flats, too, there is often a complete lack of community life, and people who have left the companionship of a street may feel terribly isolated in a box among scores of other boxes. Even when friendships develop between those who live on the same floor or corridor there are serious difficulties to be overcome for flat dwellers, especially for toddlers and old people. Supervised play space near at hand is essential unless small children are to be confined all day, and this, though better than nothing, is a poor substitute for a garden or even a street where their own mother can keep an eye on them. Even children who are old enough to go out on their own need space for their activities and cannot always manage the lifts when they return from play at ground level. Old people also find life difficult in tall blocks. They may get used to the lifts, but unless they are housed in groups of like-minded people they are often lonely, and they miss the life of the street with its daily comings and goings. Problems such as these are evident to anyone who visits a large block of flats or has even the slightest contact with its residents.

Such impressions of life on new estates or in high flats could be gained by any casual visitors, but planning policy cannot be justified on the basis of mere impressions. There is, however, ample evidence of a reality behind the impressions. This evidence comes from social workers of all kinds, from those concerned with individuals and families, and from those involved in group work and community organization, and from professional and volunteers alike. It comes, too, from studies of community life in various settings and in different parts of the country.

The work of the Institute of Community Studies[1] shows that the break-up of old neighbourhoods and the resettling of people away from kin and friends in housing estates and in new towns results in a loss of social cohesion which means that many of the needs which were previously met by relatives and friends either go by default or have to be met by organiza-

---

[1] Michael Young and Peter Willmott, *Family and Kinship in East London* (1957).

tions, be they statutory or voluntary. Hilda Jennings' account of redevelopment in Bristol[1] and Rosser and Harris's comparative study of Swansea[2] lead to the same conclusion. Studies of the effects on families[3] of moving into blocks of flats show how difficult people find it to adjust themselves and to realize 'the full potential of their new surroundings'[4]. Some who were visited a year after the move had not really settled down – there was tension over children playing at ground level and over shared facilities, stairways, noise, storage for prams and cycles. Improved accommodation and modern kitchens and bathrooms did not of themselves always result in social rehabilitation, and education for new housing was found to be necessary[5].

The findings of these and other studies are supported by social workers all over the country and by references in the annual reports and at the conferences of organizations concerned with social service. The social needs of people who have been uprooted are greater than those of people who have stayed put, and community spirit, on which ability to help each other depends, takes a long time to grow. Not only are societies for mutual aid and for the happy use of leisure slow to form, but neighbours are shy of making personal contacts and of giving and receiving help in an informal way.

Fortunately, however, communities do not stand still. They grow and develop, and as the strangeness wears off people begin to feel at home in the new environment. They start to make friends and to take an interest in and to feel responsible for their neighbourhood and for the people in it. Children meet at school and at play, and through them their parents get to know each other better. Adults meet on the way to work and in the shops – where these exist – as well as in the street and over the garden fence. Though contacts with neighbours are more difficult than they were in more familiar surroundings they do gradually take place. The same studies which described the sense of desolation which attacked the

---

[1] Hilda Jennings, *Societies in the Making* (1962).
[2] C. Rosser and C. Harris, *The Family and Social Change* (1965).
[3] *Community Organisation*, N.C.S.S. (1962).
[4] *Ibid.*, p. 28.
[5] *Ibid.*, p. 57.

people of Bethnal Green when they first moved out of London, report some change of attitude a few years later[1], while a study of Dagenham shows that a group of Londoners had succeeded in forming a stable and satisfying community in the forty years since they left the East End[2].

Forty years, however, is a long time, and the absence of a satisfying community life and of neighbourly help for at least the early part of that period is a serious deprivation for the people concerned. Planning should be able to reduce the period, and social action should be able to stimulate community feeling and provide alternatives for neighbourly help during the initial period when this is lacking.

Old and new communities in Britain and the United States

There are other forces at work, too, which are likely to reduce the period needed for the evolution of a community if what is happening in the U.S.A. is any guide to likely developments here. Increased prosperity, better education and greater mobility are some of the factors which are changing people's lives. Increased prosperity and extended education lead to the adoption of middle-class attitudes and these make people more prepared to accept a new environment. At the same time greater mobility, which is made necessary by the distance between home and work and by industrial change, is made tolerable by the motor-car. People who move by choice for promotion at work or for a more attractive house accept the need to settle and make friends more quickly than those who are forced to move by redevelopment. This is illustrated by studies of new communities both in the U.S.A. and in Britain.

The picture of a completely new town for commuters from Philadelphia drawn in *The Levittowners*[3] is very different from that of Bethnal Green in *Family and Kinship in East London* or of Bristol in *Societies in the Making* but bears some resemblance to that of the suburb described in *Family and Class in a London*

[1] Young and Willmott, *op. cit.*, Chapter IX.
[2] Peter Willmott, *The Evolution of a Community* (1963). 'In part, Dagenham is the East End reborn', p. 109.
[3] By Herbert J. Gans (1967).

Suburb[1], while a comparative study[2] of new estates in England and the U.S.A. shows that there are definite similarities in the way in which community life is devoloping in the two countries in spite of differences due to national characteristics. In both countries the great majority of new arrivals were satisfied with their home and neighbourhood, but there was considerably more loneliness in England. Less conscious effort was being made here than in the U.S. to welcome incomers, and there were fewer organizations which provided opportunities for meeting and for making friends.

It is evident from these and other studies that much depends on layout and that the planner of the new community is one of the most important agents in creating a socially satisfactory neighbourhood. In some cases in the U.S.A. planned communities have been able to grow with a spirit of neighbourliness growing with them from the start. This has not happened to the same extent in this country, though here, too, there are encouraging developments. Some of the new towns and more recent housing estates are evolving into satisfactory communities much more quickly than those which were built in the inter-war years, and loneliness does not seem to be a permanent problem for the great majority of those who settle in them[3]. It is clear that the right kind of layout based on planning for social needs can make a tremendous difference to the quality of life of the new residents in this country as well as in the U.S.A.

It is much less clear, however, what it is that makes a layout 'right' and what are the ingredients in planning for social needs which makes such planning a success. Much more knowledge is needed by those responsible for making and carrying out policy of the real needs and desires of those for whom the plans are being made. It is now government policy 'to bring people into planning' and an advisory commitee, the Skeffington Committee, has been set up by the Ministry of

---

[1] By Willmott and Young (1960).

[2] H. E. Bracey, *Neighbours on New Estates and Subdivisions in England and U.S.A.* (1968).

[3] Out of 3,000 families who had moved to Stevenage by 1955 only 96 had returned to London and only a third of these had moved back because they could not settle. See *Loneliness*, N.C.S.S. (1957).

Town and Country Planning to recommend how best this can be done. It is to be hoped that public participation will involve consultation not only with elected representatives and with leading members of interested organizations but also with the actual people who will be living in the new accommodation[1]. Representatives, whether elected by the public at large or chosen by voluntary bodies, are often out of touch with those they represent, and even when they take steps to try and find out the wishes of the people for whom the plans are being made, they are all too likely to take decisions on the basis of what they themselves think other people ought to want. It is often only after the first families have moved into new homes that mistakes like the siting of an infant school on the wrong side of a main road, the absence of a corner shop or the lack of play space in high flats are recognized. Any mother could have told the planners what to do and what to avoid. These are obvious examples, and examples on which the opinions of consumers could be easily discovered, and where needs and desires coincide. It is admittedly more difficult in the large number of cases where personal preferences affect the issue, or where needs and desires do not coincide, and also in cases where people think they will want something which they find later on that they do not want after all. Yet in such cases, too, the people who are going to live in a place have a better idea than the planners of what they want in the way of homes and environment, and more effort should be made by direct inquiry by means of meetings and discussions and by market research to discover the views of the consumer. Such information will sometimes, as in the case of a dangerous crossing or the siting of a shop, give an obvious answer to a planning question; more often perhaps it will bring out the fact that people do not all want the same things and that where possible variety in the size and design of houses or flats and in the provision of gardens and open space should be the aim.

Needs and desires differ with individuals and also with social groups. They differ, too, from north to south in Britain, and from Britain to America. The success of some of the new

---

[1] A strong case for participation of this kind is made in an article by Bernard Crick and Geoffrey Green in *New Society*, 5th September, 1968.

towns in the United States does not mean that communities of the same kind would be equally successful here. It merely means that research into what kind of homes people want is a necessary pre-condition of success in both countries. American data cannot of course be used as a basis for building new communities in this country, but it can teach the planners here the value of collecting data of their own.

Communities in the two countries develop along different lines because of different conditions and different national characteristics. These differences make it unlikely that the kind of life which appeals to *The Levittowners* will satisfy people here. One important difference is that those who move to new communities in the U.S.A. are not as a rule leaving districts which are old in the same sense as the central areas of British cities, so the change to new places is not so dramatic as the move to housing estates or new towns in this country. Few of the Americans who move have been settled long in their previous homes, many are recent immigrants who hardly knew their last neighbours and could leave such comparative strangers without a pang. The break for them had come when they left their original homes, and from then onwards frequent mobility became a way of life. The British, on the other hand, were part of close-knit societies of relatives and friends often living in the same street and even the same house as parents and grandparents. Leaving a society of this kind is a wrench, and mobility is a new experience for people with this background.

Another difference between the two countries is their attitude to conformity. The desire to conform is strong in America, partly no doubt because many of them are first- or second-generation immigrants who naturally want to be assimilated as quickly as possible, and hope to achieve this by conformity to the way of life of the majority. This involves such things as membership of car pools for the journey to work and to school, frequent attendances at coffee parties and informal gatherings, and constant pressure on the individual to behave and even to think as much like everyone else as possible, The social inter-action resulting from the desire to conform helps to create what appears to be a satisfying community life, but many sociologists – and Americans among them – feel that it is being created at too great a cost – at the cost of creating at the same time 'a tyranny of the majority'[1].

The desire to conform is less strong in England[2] and people who have been used to being part of an extended family are slow to accept the substitute support of strangers who just happen to be living near. They are often shy of new contacts and disinclined for intimacy with unknown neighbours. It is, moreover, doubtful how far the superficial intimacy that springs up so quickly in some of the new towns and districts in the U.S.A. would be adequate to meet the social needs which are met by the kinship network in the older parts of British towns and villages, and therefore whether community life on the American pattern would be a satisfactory alternative to what has been left behind for those in this country who have moved to new surroundings.

Social action in new communities

Social action in new communities must develop in two directions at the same time. On the one hand the work of the organizations already in the field must be stepped up, and where their scope and effectiveness are inadequate new ones must be formed. This applies both to group work and community organization and also to personal service where help from neighbours is inadequate. On the other hand, and at the same time, efforts must be made to stimulate and extend this neighbourly work.

Voluntary work which is being carried out through organizations has been described in previous chapters, and suggestions made about its expansion and improvement, but the unorganized work of the good neighbour cannot be described in the same way. Its nature and extent cannot be easily gauged, and it is difficult to suggest where it most needs expansion and how planning and social action can best assist its development.

[1] William H. Whyte, *Organisation Man*, Penguin special, p. 364 (first published in 1956).

[2] It seems, however, from Willmott and Young's *Family and Class in a London Suburb* that this may be in part a class difference The middle class are less dependent than the working class on kin and near neighbours and are more inclined to make new friends and to conform to a suburban pattern of life.

Attempts are, however, being made by those concerned with community work to answer these difficult questions, and there have been a number of conferences[1] and study groups[2] in which people have come together to learn from one another's successes and failures and to point the way for future action. Prior to these discussions the subject had been considered in J. H. Nicholson's *New Communities in Britain*[3]. This is a review of the achievements and problems of housing estates and new towns and contains a number of recommendations which bear both on the structure of the new communities and on their social development.

The literature on the subject stresses the importance for social development of the work of organizations, both statutory and voluntary, carried out by their paid workers and by volunteers working with and through them. It recognizes the special value of such voluntary bodies as Community Associations and Councils of Social Service, but considers that paid development officers and neighbourhood workers are essential if new estates and towns are to become real communities.

The activities of statutory and voluntary bodies and of professional workers are certainly necessary in the building of communities, but they are not the only kind of social action needed. They must be supported by individuals and by informal groups within the neighbourhood itself. Mutual aid must be stimulated and encouraged by joint action among neighbours and by the example of individual enthusiasts. This applies not only in new communities but also in the older areas in both town and country. One of the results of rehousing is a

---

[1] See *Communities and Social Change*, Report of the Fifth British National Conference on Social Welfare, N.C.S.S. (1964), and *Social Aspects of Urban Development*, The United Kingdom Report for the Thirteenth International Conference on Social Work, N.C.S.S. (1966).

[2] *Community Organisation, An Introduction* (1962), and *Community Organisation, Work in Progress* (1965), reports published by the N.C.S.S. of seminars arranged by the Standing Conference of Councils of Social Service. See also *Working with Communities*, ed. by Raymond Clarke, based on a conference sponsored by the Society of Neighbourhood Workers in 1963.

[3] N.C.S.S. (1961), see also Roger Wilson, *Difficult Housing Estates*, Tavistock pamphlet no. 5 (1963), and *The First Hundred Families*, H.M.S.O. (1965), and *The Needs of the New Communities*, H.M.S.O. (1967).

need for more neighbourly help in the old areas. Any up-rooting of population is bound to have effects both on those who move and on those who are left behind, and the break-up of families and neighbourhoods affects both groups. This is especially marked in the case of families where the young couples miss their parents and the older generation miss their children and grandchildren. Ideally, not only those who move but also those who stay should be the concern of the planners, and the concern, too, of those who try to meet social needs. More neighbourly help is needed to relieve the loneliness of the depleted areas no less than to combat the unfamiliarity of districts which are newly settled. One of the ways in which such help can be increased is through good-neighbour groups, which are growing in number in both old and new areas.

There is, unfortunately, only sketchy information about this development in print, but what has been published can be amplified from unpublished material, and from reports of what is going on in various parts of the country which make it clear that there is much more activity of this kind than has been recorded centrally. Such information as is available, sketchy though it is, is worthy of attention because, though the picture it shows is incomplete, it succeeds in showing the kind of work that volunteers are doing on a neighbourly basis and provides some striking examples of successful schemes.

Good-neighbour schemes

The information that is available was collected by the Central Churches Group. It did not restrict its inquiries to groups sponsored and supported by the churches but co-operated with local Councils of Social Service, Citizens' Advice Bureaux and Rural Community Councils. In the summer of 1965 a questionnaire was sent to all these organizations and to all Councils of Churches – some 1,100 in all. Although less than 200 were returned and only 130 described schemes of the good-neighbour type in operation or in process of formation, the exercise was not without value for a number of reasons: it revealed a wide variety of activity and showed that wherever and whenever a group of this kind came into being there was work waiting to be done; it showed that there were different ways in which a satisfactory group could operate and that uniformity was unnecessary and indeed undesirable; it showed that there were common pitfalls into which groups might fall, whatever their origin and set-up. It also provided a number of examples of successful schemes which were subsequently described in the first edition of *The Caring Community*[1]. These differed from one another in organization and in scope, but were alike in their aim of caring for people in their own homes, and in their method of breaking down the problem into units of manageable size, for each of which a volunteer warden or liaison officer was responsible. These schemes are reminiscent of the Housewives' Service of the W.R.V.S.[2], which did so much to help ordinary people in times of stress during the last war. When they succeed they owe their success to factors which they share with this Housewives' Service – the felt need for the service offered, the small unit, and the personality of the leader. Their success is, however, made vastly more difficult because they lack a vital factor which contributed more than anything else to the success of the Housewives' Service – the sense of urgency and common purpose of a nation at war. The needs which the good-neighbour groups seek to meet are urgent enough, but they do not have the same immediate appeal as the reality of enemy action, nor indeed the appeal of famine relief which is so successful as a fund raiser. Cases of 'elderly people living alone or with relatives who have to be out for the whole or part of the day; housebound invalids and patients recently discharged from hospital or attending out-patients' departments; families with young children where there is no relative or near neighbour to help during periods of illness or other domestic crisis'[3], certainly need help, but they do not need it so dramatically as evacuees, air-raid victims, or starving children.

This lack of a sense of urgency is one of the reasons why the formation of good-neighbour groups is not more widespread. Another reason is the nature of the work, which is quiet and

---

[1] Published for the Central Churches Group by the N.C.S.S. (1966).
[2] See Charles Graves, *Women in Green* (1948).
[3] *The Caring Community*, N.C.S.S. (1966), p. 25.

informal and shuns publicity. This is illustrated by comments such as these: 'Individuals are loath to report work they have done'[1] – 'much is frequently done which . . . is very often known only to the helpers and the person being helped'[2]. Lack of publicity means not only that the example of successful schemes is not available to encourage the formation of others. but also that many of those which are in operation have not made known their existence to the central body and so could not be included in the evaluation of projects which it undertook. This evaluation is contained in the 1968 edition of *The Caring Community*. Sufficient information was available from the ninety-two projects included for a number of points to be stressed, and this, together with the general advice given in the booklet, is likely to be extremely helpful to people contemplating the formation of good-neighbour groups. Already 1,500 copies have been supplied in response to requests for information. This demand for information is one of the reasons why it must not be assumed that the projects included in the evaluation form the sum total of what is being done and planned in this field, and indeed if they did it would have to be admitted that the contribution of good-neighbour groups to the overall well-being of those in need of neighbourly help is very small. It is certainly larger than the evidence on which the evaluation was based, because although no one knows the actual number of groups in the whole country, there is fortunately some information available from other sources. There is information about the general situation from reports of the People Next Door campaign[3] and of the British National Conference on Social Welfare and about what is going on in particular places from local data.

The People Next Door (P.N.D.) campaign, though primarily an ecumenical exercise, was intended to cover not only church-goers of all denominations but neighbours outside the Church and people of other races both at home and overseas. It took the form of study groups held throughout the country in the spring of 1967, and although Church-sponsored it

[1] *Ibid.*, p. 19.

[2] *Ibid.*, p. 22.

[3] See *Agenda for the Churches*. A Report on the People Next Door Programme (1967).

raised questions 'more about the problems of living than about categories of belief'. The campaign itself was for study rather than action, but it showed the determination of many groups of Church people to give service of the good-neighbour type not only side by side with members of other denominations but with non-church-goers also.

The British National Conference of 1967 on 'Welfare State and Welfare Society' was naturally concerned with the various aspects of community care. Reference had been made to a number of good-neighbour schemes in the study groups held in preparation for the Conference, and the summary of the reports dealing with community care mentions in a general way that such care 'required a good-neighbour service'.

More detailed information can be found in surveys and reports of what is being done in particular places. Two examples, one from a county and one from a city, give some idea of the ways in which this kind of work can develop. The Surrey Council of Social Service carried out, in 1964, a survey of voluntary service in the county. No report has been published, but a study of the completed questionnaire reveals the following facts. Of the forty-seven organizations which replied, thirty-one were church groups, eight old people's welfare committees, two women's institutes and the other six miscellaneous.

They were asked *first*, whether they operated any scheme to organize or co-ordinate voluntary welfare work and *second*, whether it was open to all members of the community to offer and to receive the services of such a scheme. To the first question thirty-nine organizations answered 'yes', three 'no' and five gave other answers. Twenty-nine of the organizations accepted offers of help from any member of the community, eleven were restricted to church members, and in the remaining cases another organization was mentioned or the reply was unclear. In thirty-two cases service was offered to all members of the community, in five it was restricted to old people and in the other cases it was restricted to some other category, such as the sick or the handicapped, or no reply was given to this part of the question. The service most often rendered was visiting the sick and the elderly but many others were mentioned – welcoming newcomers, clubs for mothers, transport and emergency service. This last is one of the most important tasks that can be tackled by a good-neighbour group, and the impression gained from these forty-seven questionnaires is that even in those cases where this service is not mentioned something of the kind was usually in existence since most of the communities concerned were small enough – usually only one parish – for most people to know whom to contact at short notice. In the numerous cases where the vicar was the organizer of the scheme his whereabouts were always known, and he was in a position to contact the volunteer most suitable for the need in question. Moreover, many of the schemes were organized on an area basis, with street wardens who were known to all who lived near them and could be approached in a few minutes. The service provided by these groups in Surrey is uneven, and depends, like all social work, professional or voluntary, on good organization and leadership, but it is clear from these questionnaires that a great deal of valuable work is going on. A follow-up conference was held in May, 1968, to report progress, which was attended by about a hundred people and received reports of the launching of a number of new schemes.

Information of what is happening in a city, Nottingham, also comes from its Council of Social Service. There are now (1968) nineteen groups that can roughly be classified as neighbourhood groups. They are described as networks rather than organizations and people move in and out as they feel the need to participate in something which they feel makes a direct impact on their own lives. They owe their origin to different individuals and groups and take a variety of forms. All, however, start as a response to a felt need, the most common being concerned with old people. They rarely restrict their activities to one problem, and usually combine personal neighbourly work with the co-ordination of voluntary societies and with acting as pressure groups for the general improvement of their neighbourhood. The success of the Nottingham groups seems to bear a direct relation to the breadth of their base, but it undoubtedly also depends on the quality of their leadership both inside the community which they serve and outside. The existence of an active C.S.S., with staff specially concerned with community work of this kind, is an important factor in stimulating the work of volunteers and, moreover, in helping to link the local community more closely to the elected members and officers of the statutory authority.

Neighbourhood work may be exceptionally well developed in both Surrey and Nottingham but it is not unreasonable to suppose that the patterns shown to exist there may be repeated to a greater or lesser extent in other places.

Good-neighbour groups can make an important contribution to the stimulation of neighbourliness by involving more people in giving active help to those in need. It is important, however, that they should be as widely based as possible. As far as can be discovered from the available evidence the majority of them appear at present to be definitely linked to a church or churches, and though this has some obvious advantages, such as the focal point of the church, the presence and availability of a full-time professional worker in the person of the minister, and access to a ready-made, albeit often small, band of willing helpers in the church members, advantages are probably outweighed by disadvantages. For the position of the churches today is such that anything led by them is likely to leave many sources of help untapped. The evidence from the Central Churches Group, which is itself most anxious to widen the appeal of good-neighbour schemes and seems to have re-written its *Caring Community* with a view to attracting more non-Church people, and from the Surrey survey, shows that though good-neighbour groups usually *serve* everyone they tend at the present time to draw mainly on church members for their helpers. Considering how small a proportion of the population are members this is unnecessarily restricting. There are other means, through Settlements, Councils of Social Service, Rural Community Councils, Community Associations and societies of flat-dwellers[1] by which people can join in service of this kind without leaving it all to the churches.

Development by such means is needed on a far bigger scale than appears to be taking place if neighbourliness is to be strengthened under present conditions. Such development is

---

[1] See *Community Organisation in Great Britain*, ed. Peter Kuenstler (1961), and R. A. B. Leaper, *Community Work;* see also above, pp. 179–181.

even more important for the future of voluntary work as a whole than the expansion of organizations. It is more important because neighbourly help is the most widespread form of voluntary work and also because it is often the best way of meeting people's needs.

Part II

The Volunteer and the Community

CHAPTER VIII

Voluntary Work and the Volunteer

It was suggested at the beginning of this book that one of the reasons why voluntary work is important is that it provides opportunities for service, and thus meets a personal need on the part of many individuals. It is now time to ask what is the evidence for the existence of this need, and to examine its extent and importance. If it can be shown to exist on any scale, two further questions follow: what are the motives which lead people to satisfy this need through voluntary work, and how far can a knowledge of these motives help with the recruitment of volunteers?

How many volunteers?

It is comparatively easy to find evidence for the existence of the need to serve, since this lies in the simple fact that people recognize it in themselves and in others and seek and find ways in which it can be satisfied. It is not so easy to define the extent and importance of the need, for these cannot be judged simply by the number of those who undertake voluntary work. The numbers which can be counted do not tell the whole story. They exclude some who would like to serve, but who, for some reason or other, have not yet managed to do so, and at the same time include others who are reluctant volunteers. They exclude potential workers who have not found or been offered the kind of opportunity which meets their need, and include actual workers who have been persuaded or pressurized into action against their real inclinations.

Though numbers do not tell the whole story, they can give some indication of the extent of voluntary activity and of the proportion of the population which is involved. Various estimates can be made, but none can be other than approximate, since definitions vary, since no nation-wide inquiry has been held, and since the volunteer population is constantly changing and shifting. It would be possible to take a rough count of those who give unpaid service in local government and hospital management, on the bench, on advisory committees and commissions, in trade unions and professional and business associations, and of those who are active in and through the thousands of voluntary bodies at national and local level. At a guess these must number at least two million (four per cent of the adult population at any[1] one time), and many more if all who had served at any time during their lives were to be included.

This estimate takes no account of those who are engaged in voluntary service of an unorganized kind, and it is safe to say that these are far more numerous than those who serve through statutory and voluntary bodies. As the Bradford survey[2] showed, four times as many people are giving regular neighbourly help as are voluntary workers in social service agencies – no less than 32 per cent of the adult population was so engaged at the time of the survey. If this pattern is typical of the country as a whole, and if it is accepted that voluntary work is not for all of its practitioners necessarily an affair of a lifetime, it follows that a large proportion of the population, probably as much as half, undertake some work of this kind during their adult lives.

The extent of the involvement of children and young people is even more difficult to estimate accurately than that of adults since community service often forms part of the programme of youth organizations, and even of the curriculum of schools, and must therefore rely on conscripted as well as on voluntary labour. The 'good deed every day' is part of the duty of scouts and guides, and community service is compulsory in some youth clubs. Tasks of this kind are not always freely undertaken, so it is difficult to distinguish between what is and what is not genuine voluntary work. It is clear, however, that much of the unpaid work which is being done by children and

---

[1] The population of the United Kingdom of persons over twenty-one was approximately 37 million in June, 1966 (see *Abstract of Statistics* 1967, Tables 6 and 9). Four per cent is probably a conservative estimate since the Bradford survey revealed nearly twice as high a percentage.

[2] Appendix III.

young people is work for which they have volunteered spontaneously, and the enthusiasm with which it is carried out, and the ingenuity in thinking up new activities which is displayed, shows how strongly those concerned feel the desire to serve.

Exact numbers, whether for adults or children, cannot be given, not only because there are so many different ideas in the public mind as to what constitutes voluntary work, but also because many who give unpaid service do not think of themselves as voluntary workers. The public's view of voluntary work may or may not include such things as the activities of pressure groups and of political and industrial movements on the one hand, and of membership of societies from which the worker benefits personally on the other – committee work in cultural societies or social clubs for example. The unpaid organizer of a reform movement may think of himself not as a voluntary worker but as a pioneer or missionary, the housewife who cooks for a housebound neighbour may not class herself as a volunteer but as a friend. These examples from many that could be found illustrate the difficulties of definition, and therefore of counting accurately the number of people involved. Fortunately, however, it is not necessary to know actual numbers in order to ask and attempt to answer the really important question about people's motives for becoming involved in this work.

For this it is sufficient to know that the number is very large indeed. Motives matter because so many people are involved, and because so much work is being done by voluntary labour. They matter, too, because much more could be done if more help were available, and because an understanding of motives is one of the keys to successful recruitment.

Motivation

There has been little study of the motives which lead people to undertake voluntary work, and it is certainly not an easy subject, since those concerned are themselves unclear about their motives and often find it difficult to explain them either to themselves or to others. If asked, even in a confidential questionnaire in which they remain anonymous, they cannot always answer; if asked personally and publicly they sometimes claim to be incredibly high-minded, and sometimes lean over backwards to undervalue their motives.

The discussion which follows is based not on scientific research but on forty years' experience of working with volunteers of all kinds in different parts of the country, though mainly in the midlands and north, and of continuing discussions both with individual volunteers and with people responsible for recruiting them and allocating them to jobs.

The first point to be made is one on which there will be general agreement, and that is that motives are usually mixed. This is not peculiar to voluntary service, but is common to all human endeavour: few people choose a job or a career or even a spouse for one reason only, and it is not surprising therefore that they have more than one motive for giving voluntary service. The second point is that the kind of reason which causes a person to undertake a particular task at a particular time is rarely the same as that which keeps him involved. Both are essential, but they are often different, as the match which lights a fire is different from the fuel which keeps it burning. One of the commonest starting-points for voluntary action is the dislike of saying 'no' to someone who asks for help, yet this of itself is rarely sufficient motive for the sustained action to which such a start often leads.

The main motives which prompt people to take part in voluntary work can be grouped under three headings: *first*, a genuine desire to help other people, to relieve suffering and increase happiness for individual human beings; *second*, an urge to further a cause, to improve conditions and to right wrongs; and *third*, a wish to satisfy a personal need to participate in activities outside the spheres of home and work.

Each of these groups is made up of a variety of desires and aims. The first is made up of goodwill, and of an instinctive dislike of seeing suffering and desire to relieve it at least when it is near at hand. It is a natural instinct to want to feed the starving and comfort the sorrowing who are on the doorstep. The strength of this instinct is recognized by those who seek to enlist support for causes further afield by bringing 'home' the need for help of the starving in far-off lands and of the lonely who are out of sight by showing pictures of maimed and hungry children with captions like 'If this child came to play at your house you'd soon do something to help'[1] or of solitary old ladies without the home and family which are enjoyed by others.

The first group of motives also includes the call of duty whose strength may depend on religious conviction, on parental example, or perhaps on an inborn love of justice. Certainly people can be moved to action by the desire for social justice and for greater equality. Some who are fortunate feel an urge to help the less fortunate, to provide for the children of others advantages their own children have enjoyed. Some again feel a need to propitiate fate, or to give service freely as a thank-offering for blessings received. Those who are happily married or whose children turn out well, who have robust health and avoid accidents, who enjoy their work or are comfortably off, often feel that these blessings are due more to good luck than good management, and therefore feel impelled to try to help those whose luck has been less good than their own. Some of these people have the kind of conscience which actually prevents them from enjoying their blessings unless they can try in some way to help others to enjoy the same good fortune.

The desire to help is also present in the second group of motives which includes the urge to further a cause, to improve conditions and to right wrongs, but the voluntary work to which this urge gives rise is of a less personal kind than that which is inspired by a desire to help individual people. It may take the form of striving for world peace or racial harmony or be limited to the preservation of a village green or historic windmill. Participation in pressure groups and active membership of movements for reform of all kinds derives from a desire to improve conditions and achieve progress whether the object is a particular group or the nation as a whole, or even the world at large. This does not mean that voluntary service of this kind is prompted solely by love of one's neighbour whether at home or abroad, and clearly self-interest, whether of person, class or nation, is often a powerful ingredient in the motivation of some who are working for a cause. The well-to-do advocates of health reform in nineteenth-century

---

[1] Oxfam advertisement in the *Observer*, 14th April, 1968, and in other papers.

England were influenced by the fear of infection spreading from poor to rich, the supporters of overseas aid today are concerned to increase national trade as well as to help developing countries, the preservers of the countryside are seeking rural pleasure for themselves as well as for others. But motives such as these can and do exist alongside a disinterested love of justice and a desire for the welfare of others. Not only are different motives present at one and the same time in any one reformer, but movements for reform are made up of people whose motives differ one from another.

In addition to the desire to help individuals and the urge to work for a cause is the wish, sometimes more readily acknowledged than others, to satisfy a personal need. This satisfaction may be sought simply in the work itself, and sufficient reward for the time and energy expended may be found in the happiness given to others or in the furtherance of the cause. But personal satisfaction may also be sought and found in other ways. Some volunteers seek to be well-known and important in their neighbourhood or in a wider sphere; they want to be influential and to be credited with public spirit. Some want to make use of special skills and talents which may not be fully exploited in their paid jobs, others want to enlarge their knowledge and experience, to learn at first hand 'how the other half lives' and to gain insight into the 'human condition'. Others again look to voluntary work as a way of getting out of themselves: if they are lonely or unhappy they hope to drown their sorrows and forget their loneliness in such activity. Desire for social contacts is not confined to the lonely or depressed – many who would never dream of classing themselves in these categories long for a larger circle of friends and more interesting personal relationships than they actually enjoy. They may be attracted to voluntary work because people they know are already involved, and they anticipate doing with them and with new friends things that they will find interesting and amusing. Even if they lack this positive approach of expecting great satisfaction from voluntary work, they often fear they may be missing something if they stand aside. They are inclined to accept the chance offer of a voluntary job partly because there seems no special reason for saying 'no', and partly because they see that other people seem to be enjoying it and feel that they themselves might do so, too.

The chance of a job being offered of a kind a person feels he can tackle, at a time when he is not too busy or is at a loose end, is often the starting-point for a life-time's devoted work. This is fortunate, since evidence from the voluntary bodies shows that the best way to recruit helpers is by personal contact. Far more people are started on their course of voluntary service by the persuasion of a friend or acquaintance than by a burning missionary zeal for a particular task or cause. The value of their work to themselves and to its recipients is not necessarily less great, for once they have become involved they usually find that what they are doing meets and satisfies a pressing need in themselves, of whose existence they were not previously fully aware.

This personal need can for most people find satisfaction in the here and now, but for some of the most devoted workers the need is for reward and recognition not in this world but in the next. Such people were more common in previous generations when there was more general faith in an after-life, but they still exist, and have their modern counterparts in those reformers for whom the achievement of their aims is its own reward.

The various desires and aims which together make up these three main groups of motive – to help individuals, to work for a cause and to meet a personal need – are all human characteristics, and as such are likely to be shared to a greater or lesser extent by most human beings. There must be very few people who are not stirred by some of these feelings at some time in their lives, but it does not follow that all will be led to undertake voluntary work. Some are slow to take action on behalf of others, and reluctant to get involved. Their paths may not be crossed by someone obviously needing help, and their imagination may not have been moved by an appeal. Their inaction is by no means necessarily due to unworthy motives – they may simply have less opportunity, less imagination, or be less able to overcome shyness or diffidence, or they may find sufficient outlet in their ordinary work or in the family circle. Among all these different kinds of people who are not at present doing voluntary work there must be many who could be drawn into activities which would benefit both themselves and the recipients.

The reluctant volunteer

The total number of voluntary workers at any one time not only excludes some who would really like to serve, but also includes others who have become involved against their true inclinations. Voluntary work which is undertaken unwillingly seems a contradiction in terms, but work which is voluntary only in the sense that it is unpaid certainly exists, though it differs from that which is freely given. Reluctance on the part of the volunteer is bound to affect the quality of his work and may diminish its value both to himself and to others.

The value to the volunteer varies according to the reasons which led him to undertake unpaid work which he did not really want to do. These reasons are often complex, and vary from person to person. The main reason may simply be the inability to say 'no', but this may be complicated by fear of being penalized or missing promotion at work, or of losing popularity with neighbours. People who accept jobs through fears of this kind must be subject to personal conflict which nullifies the satisfaction to be found in service freely given. Those who are not subject to such fears but simply drift into voluntary work because they cannot say 'no' are more fortunate. They will probably either drop out before the conflict becomes serious, or will discover that the work does after all meet a need in themselves of which they had been unaware.

The value to the recipient of the services of a reluctant volunteer depends largely on the type of service involved. Sometimes efficiency can be more important than goodwill. As was suggested in the case of service by youth,[1] good organization can make acceptable help of a practical kind whatever the attitude of mind of those who actually give it. In the case of personal service, however, those who do the work must have a genuine desire to serve if their help is to be of real value. Service of this kind which is given reluctantly can be of little value to the recipient.

Value to the recipient is after all the vital test of the value of any voluntary work. His needs must always have priority over those of the volunteer. This may sound obvious, but there is a danger that the recognition that voluntary work has value

---

[1] See above, pp. 121–2.

for those who do it may lead to the recruitment of people for the good of their own souls and for their personal satisfaction rather than for the welfare of others, and that jobs will be found which either do not need doing or would be better done in other ways.

This is a real danger, but it should not be met by attempting to restrict voluntary work as such. It should be met by positive action, by encouraging volunteers to undertake tasks not being done by paid labour which need doing now, and by planning future action to meet the kinds of need which will always be better met by voluntary than by statutory help.

The extent and variety of these tasks has been described in previous chapters, and suggestions have been made as to how the quantity and the quality of voluntary work might be improved in the various fields of social welfare, The future of voluntary work as a whole, in the light of the overall needs and resources of the community, will be considered in the final chapter.

It is fortunate that there are many men and women ready and anxious to perform these tasks and to meet these future needs. Some, it is true, question the value of much of the voluntary work that is going on, and these critics even include people who are themselves giving unpaid service. This fact strengthens rather than weakens the argument that service of this kind fulfils a basic human need. The unemployed man in the depression who dreaded that the activities of social service clubs would deprive people of paid jobs devoted himself without payment to providing recreation and occupation for his mates; the magistrate or town councillor who disapproves of voluntary workers in the social services is himself working without pay on the bench or in committee; the professional worker who looks askance at voluntary helpers is often giving hours of extra time for which he never dreams of being paid. These and many other examples of people who themselves give unpaid service in spite of their doubts and criticisms show how powerful is the attraction of voluntary work.

It is true that what the critics are condemning is not voluntary action as such, but only certain kinds of voluntary work done by certain people; but the conflict for them between what is and what is not of value is a real one. The pull of voluntary work which is felt by everyone who freely undertakes it is felt most strongly by those who have to overcome this conflict.

Recruitment and allocation of volunteers

The existence of this pull is an obvious help in the recruitment of voluntary workers. The personal need to do some voluntary work which is felt by many people is the best possible basis on which to build an appeal to them to undertake particular jobs at particular times. In seeking helpers the first essential is to decide what kind of people, by age, sex, character, education and qualifications, are most suited for the job in hand. The second is to find out which among possible recruits who satisfy these conditions are most likely to want to do that particular job, and what it is about it that most appeals to them. Starting with the assumption that they feel the need to do voluntary work of some kind, what motives are likely to induce them to accept this particular job? Do they want public recognition or gratitude, or is the satisfaction of the work likely to be its own reward? Are they anxious to use special skills or talents, or are they ready to do anything which they can be persuaded is useful? Do they seek to enlarge their experience of life, or are they primarily concerned with pleasant social contacts? These are some of the questions which are relevant to recruitment, and the answers to them will determine the kind of appeal that will be most likely to succeed. For it is necessary to understand the motives of the volunteer if he is to be persuaded both that the job in question needs doing, and that he is the right person to do it.

Timing is also important for successful recruitment. People who are in general right for a particular job, both because they are the kind of people who would do it well, and because it is the kind of work which would give them satisfaction, may not be accessible at a particular time. There are right and wrong times to approach even those who appear most suitable and most likely to respond. Obvious examples of likely volunteers are housewives whose children are growing up and leaving home, newly retired men and women, and people of all ages who have recently moved house and have few social outlets in their new environment – these are all people who may be expected to have time on their hands. People with time to spare are not, of course, the only ones who are likely to help. Indeed, it is often easier for those already involved in voluntary work to undertake something extra than for those who have not been initiated to take the first plunge, and extra effort may be needed if these new volunteers are to be drawn in. As was suggested earlier, there are some who would really like to give voluntary service but who have had no obvious opportunity and have been too shy to seek one out. Many of these become the most hard-working and devoted workers if they can be taken at the psychological moment and helped to gain confidence in the initial stages. They represent a source of unused talent and devotion which should be tapped by those responsible for recruitment.

The proper allocation of volunteers and their support and supervision are no less important than recruitment. Those who allocate recruits must have some understanding of their personalities and motives as well as of their qualifications if they are to place them to the best advantage. They must understand their personalities if they are to place them where their good qualities will have most scope and where their failings will do least harm. Volunteers present the same problems as paid workers and the same care is needed in allocating them. Both kinds of workers have good and bad qualities of different kinds in varying degrees which make them suitable or unsuitable for particular occupations. Both include some who are good with people and bad administrators, and others who are good organizers and bad at social contacts. Some work is suitable for those who talk too much, and some for those who cannot make conversation. Sometimes special skills and qualifications are required which on other occasions would be out of place. These are obvious points, but they and others like them are often overlooked when volunteers are being placed, and the work suffers as a result.

Insufficient attention is also paid to the motives of volunteers, yet these are no less important than personality to successful allocation and to satisfactory work. The quality of a man's work depends on its fulfilling a personal need in himself and providing opportunities of the kind for which he had hoped.

Though he sometimes discovers satisfactions different from those to which he had looked forward, and though the reasons which make him continue to give service are not always the same as those that led him to volunteer, his motives at every stage include the desire for personal satisfaction, and unless the work to which he is allocated can provide this satisfaction he is unlikely to do it well.

It is therefore important that those who seek to recruit and to retain voluntary workers should have some understanding of their motives as well as of their personalities and qualifications. Such understanding will be needed if sufficient numbers of people are to be successfully recruited and allocated. It will be needed, too, if a high standard of voluntary work is to be reached and maintained.

CHAPTER IX

Voluntary Work and the Community

The value of voluntary work to the community is not limited to the meeting of specific needs: it makes a further two-fold contribution since it affects both the practice and the policy of social work as a whole.

The practice of social work

Voluntary workers are actively engaged in every branch of social work and in every capacity – as managers and employers, as members of committees, councils and governing bodies, as workers responsible to statutory and to voluntary organizations, as colleagues, auxiliaries and humble helpers of professionals and as independent 'good neighbours'. They may perform tasks of the same kind as those for which other people are paid, and there is often no hard and fast line between the kinds of service carried out by paid and voluntary labour; they may be reponsible to the same employing body and to the same officer; they may even accept the same rules with regard to standards of work. Yet there remains the essential difference that they are not dependent for their livelihood on the good will of those in authority over them.

The volunteer, like his professional colleague or superior, owes allegiance to the organization, statutory or voluntary, for which he is working as well as to the people he is trying to help. For him, as for the paid worker, the first duty is to these people and not to the organization, but for him it is easier to put this first duty first. It takes less courage to expose bad conditions and to criticize the shortcomings of administration and of individual officers, if all you risk is dismissal from an unpaid job. This may be unpleasant, but it is not nearly so serious as dismissal from a paid post which may be followed by unemployment and even by victimization. Resignation from the job, whether paid or voluntary, may be necessary before criticism can be freely made, and this is clearly a different proposition for the two types of worker. A nurse who exposes ill-treatment of patients, a teacher who protests at excessive punishment, a youth leader who criticizes the policy of his education committee runs risks of a quite different order from those of the management committee member or friendly visitor in the case of the hospital, of the governor or 'friend' in the case of the school, and of the voluntary helper in the case of youth work.

Those voluntary workers who are in positions of authority – in local government and on management committees of hospitals, approved schools and other institutions – have an obvious duty to learn at first hand about conditions in the institutions for which they are responsible, and to be ever ready to listen to reports from their employees, paid and unpaid. But it is often voluntary workers not in positions of authority who are most knowledgeable and have the most valuable contribution to make. The hospital volunteer who gives regular help in a ward is a better judge of the relations of patients and staff than the committee member who visits twice a year; the 'friend' of an approved school who invites the boys to his home may gain more insight into their problems than the average member of its governing body; the housewife who helps in the canteen at a youth club and observes the reactions and behaviour of the young people, week by week, may know more about the quality of the leadership than the member of the education committee who makes an official visit.

In these and other cases the voluntary worker is in a strong position to check the way the social services are working, and to help to maintain standards. But this is only a small part of the contribution he can make, since the cases where criticisms should be made are few in comparison with the total volume of work which he is able to observe. For every case where publicity is needed so that a serious wrong can be put right, there are many more where it is needed simply so that the barriers between those who need social help and society as a whole can be broken down. Voluntary workers are a vital link between those in receipt of welfare and the public in whose name that welfare is provided. This link is needed in spite of the fact that most members of the public are at some time or other at the receiving end of welfare – as children, as young people, as sick, handicapped or aged. Being at the receiving end of a social service does not of itself involve insight into the way the service is working over a period, since conditions change and, moreover, memories are short.

It is notoriously easy for adults to forget what it felt like to be young, and difficult for them to be reminded by their own children. The voluntary worker who is constantly in touch with young people other than his own children has special opportunities of learning what they feel like, and of understanding the ways in which they choose to spend their time. He can, therefore, draw attention to the need for more provision for their activities, and to a certain extent at least interpret them to the adult community. It is true that professional youth leaders have the same opportunities, but they are too few in number to be able to break down the barriers between the generations without the support of their unpaid colleagues.

The ex-patient and his relatives may not actually forget what it felt like to be in hospital, but their recollections will be personal ones. Their knowledge of hospital life will depend on what they or their families experienced, and their views will depend on the treatment that they themselves received. The hospital volunteer will be able to witness the day-to-day life of many patients, and to see the effects of such things as short staffing and visiting regulations. He will be able to draw the attention of the public to what could be done by ordinary people to increase the comfort and happiness of patients and staff where conditions are difficult, and to help to ensure that restrictions on visiting are in fact relaxed in the way advocated by the Ministry of Health.

In the everyday life of the community no less than in the institution the volunteer has an important part to play. The good neighbour who baby-sits for the isolated mother, who takes the handicapped person for an outing, who visits the lonely and housebound, who welcomes newcomers whatever the colour of their skins, is helping to create a community of people who understand and seek to meet the needs of their fellow-citizens. Understanding is in most cases all that is needed, and the barrier to understanding is ignorance. Every person who performs voluntary service, whether through an organization or simply as a good neighbour, acquires knowledge which helps to break down this ignorance and build up this understanding. The more people who are personally involved the greater will be the knowledge of the general public, for every one who undertakes even the humblest task is not only learning himself but sharing his knowledge with his family and friends. The friendly visitor who sees for himself what it is like to be lonely will realize what help can be given by voluntary action, and will pass on his knowledge to others. The volunteer who ventures into the hospital will discover what the non-professional can do for the welfare of patients and staff, and will help to break down the fear of the institution that is still strong in the public mind. The more people there are who go freely in and out of hospitals and other institutions the more will the public know about what goes on inside, and the more interest will be shown in both residents and staff. The youth worker who sees for himself the effects of the strains and stresses of modern life on boys and girls will gain some understanding of what makes them behave in the way they do, and will share this understanding with his friends. Every increase in the number of adults who gain this understanding from personal contacts with the young will help to bridge the so-called gap between the generations.

In these instances, as in all cases where voluntary workers are actually in touch with individuals and groups, the knowledge and understanding which can be gained not only by those concerned but by their families and friends is different in kind from what is gained from broadcasting and from the press. To learn at first hand, even from a single visit, how a lonely pensioner spends his day is a more moving experience than reading a dozen articles or seeing a TV programme. It is real, and not a picture on the screen or a paragraph in a paper. It is a human problem with which another human being has made personal contact, and with which he personally can help. Every experience of this kind has results far wider than those which touch the actual people concerned, for it forms part of a growing knowledge about the problems of different groups and individuals and the ways in which their problems are being met by statutory and voluntary bodies and by individual volunteers.

The spreading of this knowledge of the working of the Welfare State is a vital part of the contribution made by voluntary workers to the well-being of society, for a wider understanding of what its problems are and of how they are being met is essential if its shortcomings are to be remedied and the general level of practice raised.

Social policy

It is not only in the practical working of the Welfare State, at any given time, that the voluntary worker has an influential part to play. His voice is heard in the framing of policy, and today, as in the past, it can be a powerful voice for reform.

There is often no hard and fast line between practice and policy, since weakness in practice may itself point to the need for a new policy, and it is sometimes only when a policy is seen working that it can be judged good or bad. This means that those who meet social problems at first hand may be led either to try to improve practice or to change policy. The friendly visitor who finds a pensioner living in poverty and squalor may feel that what is needed is help in the home, meals on wheels and regular visiting. These things, for the person in question and for others like him, depend on existing statutory and voluntary services being mobilized, and if this can be done no change in policy may be needed. If, on the other hand, money and personnel are not available to meet the needs, a change of policy involving greater expenditure on home helps and mobile meals will be called for, and for this the friendly visitor can raise his voice. He may also feel that even with the help of these services the pensioner will still remain in poverty, and that the right solution is to raise the rate of pension. If he feels this strongly enough he will work for change of policy as well as for improvement in practice. The youth worker who feels that the youth service is un-satisfactory may feel that the improvements he seeks, such as better premises, more skilled leadership or increased voluntary help, could be achieved without changing the policy of his authority, and that all that is needed is that the policy should be better carried out in practice; he may, however, feel that what is wrong is the whole approach to young people, and that provision of a different kind should be made for them. In this case he will attempt to influence public thinking in the new direction so that a change of policy will ensue.

Such volunteers, and others like them, who are working in the community or in institutions are in a position to see how social policy is working in practice and where change is desirable. Their first-hand knowledge will enable them to inform the public about the problems and difficulties of the existing situation and about the nature and likely repercussions of changes that may be under consideration, and their independent position will make them free to express forcibly any views they may have formed about necessary reforms.

The outcome of the controversy that is now going on about institutions versus community care in many fields of social provision will certainly be greatly influenced by the views of voluntary workers. For they, no less than those who are paid to make the social services work, are in a position to study the situation. The more people that there are in this position, and who are ready to use the personal knowledge they can acquire to stimulate thought on the subject, the more likely will be a satisfactory outcome to the controversy. Community care can only work if sufficient numbers of people both believe in it and are prepared to play a personal part. Really to believe in it means understanding what it involves, and what a commitment to making it work will mean to the people committed. It is not enough to hold the view that it is better for the sick, the aged, the mentally and physically handicapped to be cared for at home than in an institution, and leave it to the home to cope. Not only may this place intolerable burdens on the family, for there are no shifts limited to eight hours for the mother who cares for a subnormal child, or the daughter who nurses an incontinent parent, but it may also be most unsuitable for the person cared for. To be shut up in an institution is certainly distressing, but it is distressing, too, to be shut up at home in the care of overstrained relatives. Even the most devoted families may crack under the burden imposed by a severely handicapped member, and in extreme cases can only retain their affection for the invalid if he can receive some institutional care so that the rest of the family can have a life of its own. Help from the community would often make it possible for patients now in institutions to be cared for at home without unduly straining the family. This is especially desirable for the younger handicapped for whom institutional life is particularly sad and who can in many cases be helped to gain sufficient independence to live at home with only a minimum of support from their families. There are certainly disabled people of all ages now living in institutions who could return home if they themselves and their families received more help from the community. Both they, and those whose families are already struggling to keep them at home, depend for their future well-being on greatly increased community care. This means not only the expenditure of more public money but real community involvement, and community involvement depends on there being large numbers of people who understand the problems at issue. Voluntary workers are the key to this understanding, and it is they who must make community care work in practice. Decisions about the respective roles of the institution and the community have to be made nationally so that the necessary accommodation in hospital, school or hostel can be planned, but what happens in practice will depend on the response in the country as a whole. The way each local community is in practice willing and able to care for those of its members who need special help will determine whether the decisions made nationally can be carried out, and will influence the future pattern of institutional care.

Community care is only one of the fields in which participation by voluntary workers is influencing policy. Their voice is heard wherever they are actively involved. This is increasingly the case in education. Concern about children and young people may be less disinterested than concern about the sick, the aged and the handicapped, since most of those involved are or have been parents, and thus have a more direct interest in education than the healthy and the young or middle-aged have in the sick and the elderly. But voluntary activity does not lose its value when it is partly inspired by personal interest, Pressure from groups of parents brings reforms which benefit other children as well as their own, since public support will only be gained for reforms which are seen to be generally beneficial. Parental interest is one of the strongest forces in the formation of educational policy today, and it should be welcomed in the interests of all children.

Active concern for a cause by individuals and groups is an essential ingredient in social progress in a democracy. This has been so throughout history and is still so today. The connection of the ordinary citizen with the government and local authorities who are running the country is remote. He can vote for his parliamentary candidate and local councillor according to his views as to whether, on balance, the party they represent will do most good or perhaps least harm to the country or locality as a whole and to himself personally. If this were the sum total of democratic action the power of the individual would be small indeed, but fortunately this is far from the case. The individual makes up for the minute influence he exerts as a voter by active participation in the working of society by membership of groups and organizations which seek to improve conditions and to change policy, and by humble day-to-day work as a good neighbour. This is democracy in action. The voluntary body that tackles a job which the State has neglected, and paves the way for State provision, the pressure group that alerts the public mind to an evil that needs uprooting, the society that informs its members of the nature of problems and their remedies – all these are performing an essential function in a democratic society by helping to bring change where change is needed. They are made up of voluntary workers who, like those others who are helping to make the Welfare State work in practice by giving neighbourly service, are contributing to the well-being of society.

This contribution is vital. It is not enough to criticize politicians, national or local, and their paid officials, necessary though this often is. Criticism alone will not produce reform either in policy or in practice. It must be accompanied by positive action to convert public opinion to the need for change, and by personal effort to improve conditions and to give help where help is needed.

Action of this kind is being taken in every field of social

need by groups of citizens with concern for a cause. They are working to discover facts, to inform public opinion and to campaign for reform. The number and variety of these pressure groups makes it impossible to compile a complete list but a mention of some of those which are most active at the present time, and of some of the reforms which have recently reached the statute book, will serve as a reminder of the importance of this form of voluntary activity.

The abolition of capital punishment, abortion law reform, changes in the law respecting homosexuality and in the law of divorce have all come about as the result of the determined efforts of people with concern for a cause. The Child Poverty Action Group, Shelter, the Disablement Income Group, the Campaign against Racial Discrimination are examples of pressure groups which are protesting against present conditions, and are at the same time aiming both to give personal help to other people in particular categories of need, and to campaign on their behalf for government action. The causes for which these groups are working, a decent standard of living for every family, houses for the homeless, pensions for the severely handicapped, the elimination of racial discrimination, are all causes with which every citizen should be concerned. Most people are in fact concerned about them in a vaguely benevolent way, but concern will only lead to action because of the personal effort of members of these and other groups who are prepared to devote time, energy and money in their support.

The personal effort devoted to such action is one kind of voluntary work which has a value over and above the direct benefits it confers. In the case of Shelter, for example, the personal benefit to the families which it manages itself to rehouse will be only a small part of its contribution to the problem of the homeless if its campaign succeeds in stepping up the government housing programme; in the case of C.A.R.D., the help given to individual sufferers from discrimination is only incidental to spreading the gospel of toleration and justice.

The success of voluntary workers in achieving reforms is to a large extent dependent on the actual work they are performing in the social services. On the quality of this work will depend both the value of their criticisms of social provision and their ability to impart a right understanding of the needs of society. For the effectiveness of what they are themselves doing in their chosen field of social action is bound to affect their influence for reform, and on their day-to-day work in the field the further contribution to society of their influence on practice and policy will be judged.

This work, with its achievements, its shortcomings and its future possibilities, has been described in some detail so that a judgment can be made on the basis of the facts. The picture that emerges is of voluntary action in every field of social life, and of volunteers engaged in an almost endless variety of tasks and on a very wide scale. Yet there are serious gaps in social provision, and large areas of need which are still not being met by either statutory or voluntary means. Though it is clear from the evidence of what is being done by unpaid workers that society could not function without them, it is clear, too, that that work is limited in extent and sometimes poor in quality. Shortage of money and of trained personnel will certainly mean that voluntary workers will continue to be used in the day-to-day working of the social services if even the present standards are to be maintained. It is most important, therefore, that they should direct their efforts where they can be most effective, not only in maintaining the existing services but by raising standards and by filling gaps. They can do this both by giving personal service and by exposing short-comings and pressing for reform, and they can use their first-hand knowledge of social needs to form a public opinion that will support the increased expenditure that will be necessary to meet them.

The concluding chapter will discuss what these needs are and what resources, both statutory and voluntary, are likely to be available to meet them, and will consider how voluntary effort can best be mobilized to play its part in the process.

CHAPTER X

The Future of Voluntary Work

The future of voluntary work in the social services will depend on the extent of statutory provision, but it will depend, too, on the thinking and planning of voluntary bodies and of social workers and researchers, and on the way in which ordinary people continue to help one another as neighbours and to play an active part in meeting social needs. The extent of statutory provision will affect the type of work to be done by volunteers, and the attitude of those responsible for the statutory services towards voluntary work will have an important bearing on the recruitment of volunteers for participation in the social services. At the same time, the way in which those services are seen by the public to succeed in meeting social needs will determine the future pattern of that other kind of voluntary action which is designed both to change policy where change is needed and to raise standards where practice rather than policy is at fault.

The expansion of welfare services by central and local government should mean not only that overall provision will be increased but that some tasks which are now being carried out by unpaid labour will be transferred to the salaried staff of statutory authorities. This should be welcomed by the voluntary bodies and by all 'good neighbours' since it should set them free to concentrate on tasks for which they are specially suited, instead of having to fill gaps which could be better filled by paid workers. There will always be such tasks since it is inconceivable that the State could ever meet all social needs without voluntary assistance – indeed, the very concept of community care which is central to present social policy involves the active participation of ordinary members of the community. The question at issue is not whether volunteers will have work to do in the future but what that work should be.

At the present time it is clear that there are large tracts of social need which are not being covered either by statutory or voluntary workers – need among the elderly, the young, the handicapped, the sick, the lonely. This is partly due to inadequate financial resources and to shortage of trained personnel, but it is also due to lack of knowledge of what and where the needs are, to indecision on the part of policy makers as to how they can best be met, and to insufficient thought on anyone's part – both on the statutory and on the voluntary side – as to the right division between statutory and voluntary bodies and between paid and unpaid workers, and of the implications of changing patterns of neighbourly help.

Concerted effort by all concerned will be needed in order to discover what needs to be done in the main fields – health, welfare, education, housing – and to make overall plans as to how much can be done by statutory bodies and their paid workers, and how much must be left undone unless voluntary workers play a part alongside the staff of statutory authorities, in and through the voluntary bodies, and on their own as good neighbours. Plans must be made by government departments and by local authorities. Voluntary bodies engaged in welfare work, social workers, writers and researchers, and ordinary interested individuals must all contribute their views and be taken into consultation. All these groups and individuals must carry out their own inquiries and draw on their own experience so as to make suggestions and recommendations to the authorities concerned, and to plan how they themselves can best help.

Inquiries must be carried out at national level if there is to be an overall review of the social services, but they will have to be made on the basis of information received from local sources, since estimates of nation-wide need made centrally do not always take account of local differences. For example, the need for hospital beds of various kinds varies in different parts of the country and depends on factors which are not everywhere the same. It depends on the incidence of certain diseases, on the proportion of vulnerable age groups in the local population, and even on local habits and attitudes regarding the care of the sick. Thus, the provision of beds for such cases as maternity, respiratory diseases or geriatrics cannot be made on the basis of the same number per thousand of the population throughout the country.

An overall review involves co-operation not only between national and local authorities but between different departments at both national and local level. If separate plans are made by different departments there is a danger that the various kinds of social need will be considered in water-tight compartments on the basis of the Ministry or Local Authority Committee concerned. This danger has become less serious at local level with the reforms that have already been made in line with the recommendations of the Maud[1] and Mallaby[2] Committees, and should be less serious still if those of the Seebohm Committee[3] and of the Ministry of Health Green Paper[4] are adopted. At national level the danger may be avoided if the review of the social services being undertaken by the government results in closer co-ordination of the Ministries and departments responsible for the various services.

Plans made by statutory authorities at both national and local level must also take account of the views of potential volunteers, if these are to perform the tasks that may be allotted to them. Voluntary workers will be more likely to co-operate in carrying out the plan if the voluntary bodies are taken into consultation and the general public given an opportunity to consider the proposals and to express their views. Consultation at an early stage should make for easier co-operation later. For this reason it is unfortunate that the initiative of the Ministry of Health in calling representatives of the voluntary bodies into consultation at the launching of the ten-year plan was not followed at local level in the way suggested by the Minister.

[1] *Management of Local Government*, Vol. 1, H.M.S.O., 1967. Ministry of Housing and Local Government. Committee on the Management of Local Government.

[2] *Staffing of Local Government. Report of the Committee*, H.M.S.O. 1967. Ministry of Housing and Local Government. Committee on the Staffing of Local Government.

[3] *Report of the Committee on Local Authority and Allied Personal Social Services, Cmnd.* 3703, 1968.

[4] *National Health Service. The Administrative Structure of the Medical and Related Services in England and Wales*, H.M.S.O. 1968.

This final chapter will briefly describe what action has so far been taken to plan for the future, and to estimate needs and resources; and will discuss how far voluntary bodies and individual citizens are contributing and could further contribute to the formation and implementation of a plan in which the tasks assigned to voluntary workers are acceptable to the general public from which such workers must be drawn. It will then indicate what these tasks are likely to be and the number and nature of the volunteers that will be needed to carry them out: and will conclude by suggesting how the necessary volunteers will be recruited.

1 *Social planning: needs and resources. The role of voluntary work*

Government plans

An interdepartmental review of the social services has been under consideration for some time but no overall plan has yet been announced. Various changes have taken place at national level: the Ministry of Pensions and National Insurance has taken over the work of the National Assistance Board and more recently has itself been merged with the Ministry of Health to form the new Department of Health and Social Security which may later be widened to include parts of the Home Office and of Education. The Ministry of Education has become the Department of Education and Science and has taken over new responsibilities.

The 'Seebohm Committee[1] was appointed in December, 1965, 'to review the organization and responsibilities of the local authority personal social services in England and Wales, and to consider what changes are desirable to secure an effective family service'. It reported in July, 1968, and recommended that there should be 'a new local authority department, providing a community based and family orientated service which will be available to all'.

The terms of reference excluded consideration of the organization of central government, but the committee points out that 'reorganization of services at local level would not

---

[1] *Committee on Local Authority and Allied Personal Social Services, Cmnd. 3703, 1968.*

be effective unless it was accompanied by reorganization at central government level, and in the structure of councils and committees advisory to Ministers in this field'.

The future of the personal social services will also be affected by any local government reorganization which may follow the report by the Royal Commission on Local Government in England which is expected in 1969. The Seebohm Committee is, however, anxious that its own recommendations should be put into effect without waiting for the report of the Royal Commission.

The importance of changes in local government and in the shape of Ministries responsible for the social services for the future of voluntary work lies in the fact that more co-ordination at both levels should make possible better planning for meeting the whole range of social need, and should therefore provide clearer indications as to what demands are likely to be made on voluntary workers.

Local authorities and the social services

The committees responsible for the various branches of social welfare have not halted their planning during the deliberations of the Seebohm Committee. They have been steadily at work extending the scope of their provision and planning for the future, though there is little knowledge outside the localities concerned as to what is going on in different places. From time to time there is mention in the national press of some special development – an experimental scheme for housing the elderly or an educational project for non-English-speaking immigrants, to take two random examples – but for the most part the work of the various authorities receives only local notice. Provision of all kinds varies widely from authority to authority and there is little uniformity either about plans or about their execution. In the field of health and welfare the Ministry of Health has not set clear standards for the development of domiciliary services, so that these depend on what action each local authority decides to take at the present time and to plan for the future. An article by Peter Townsend in 1963[1] showed the variety in actual and planned provision of home

[1] *New Society*, 23rd May, 1963.

helps, home nurses, beds in homes for the old, health visitors and social workers. The list should be studied as a whole to gain a proper idea of relative provision since some authorities do more in one way and less in another, but even so the differences are striking. In the case of home helps, for example, the number per 1,000 of population over sixty-five in the 145 authorities ranges from 11·2 (1962) and 13 (1972) in Rotherham down to 0·6 (1962) and 0·8 (1972) in Plymouth. It is difficult to imagine what alternative provision could adequately bridge so wide a gap.

There is variety, too, in the attitude of local authorities to voluntary workers, and in the use they make of them in their various services. Though all may agree in general terms that volunteers have some part to play, they differ as to what this part should be and how it should be carried out. In some cases a voluntary body is asked to undertake a particular job – the care of unmarried mothers, meals or social facilities for the aged and the handicapped, or clubs for young people – on an agency basis; in others a general grant may be given in recognition of work for the community as a whole; in others again the help is welcomed without financial acknowledgment. The reports of the voluntary bodies describe what work they undertake for local authorities and what grant, if any, they receive from them; and these make it clear that there is no uniform pattern for the whole country, either as regards financial help or as regards consultation, except that regular consultation between statutory and voluntary bodies as a whole about the contribution of volunteers to the overall social needs of the district is everywhere conspicuous by its absence[1].

Planning by voluntary bodies

The voluntary bodies, for their part, have not so far succeeded in getting together at national level to work out overall plans as to what could and should be done by volunteers and how the various organizations could co-operate over recruitment, training and allocation to jobs. Attempts at co-operation have been made by the National Council of Social Service but

---

[1] See above, Chapter 1, pp. 3–21.

these have been thwarted by the suspicions of the other organizations of what co-ordination – dreaded word – might involve. The N.C.S.S. was only one among six national bodies called into consultation by the Ministry of Health[1] and the other five seem to have preferred to retain their own responsibility for planning and recruitment. The principal national organizations, not only in the field of health and welfare but throughout the whole range of voluntary action, have been taking stock of their position, planning for the future and undertaking new tasks. Some of this work has been described in preceding chapters. Moreover, although they have been unable to co-operate in working out an overall national plan, some headway has been made over joint basic training schemes, and an important step forward has been taken with the appointment of the Aves Committee on Voluntary Workers in the Social Services with a membership drawn from the statutory and voluntary social services and from the social work departments of the universities. The committee is expected to report in 1969 and should make a major contribution to the subject.

At local level the voluntary bodies have, in some cases at least, been somewhat more successful than their national counterparts in their attempts at co-operation. Something has been done by Councils of Social Service, Rural Community Councils, Community Associations and by Councils of Churches, and something, too, by specially formed neighbourhood groups, both in surveying the needs of their communities and in agreeing how best these needs could be met. Moreover, *ad hoc* bodies composed of representatives of existing organizations and of interested individuals have been formed to help with special problems in every field of social need from the integration of immigrants or the care of the housebound to the neighbourly adoption of a local school, home or hostel[2]. A plan which aims to cover all the social needs of a neighbourhood and can call on all the voluntary manpower available,

---

[1] See above, p. 4.

[2] A variety of schemes carried out by groups of this kind are described in a series of articles in *New Society* beginning on 13th March, 1964. Accounts of other such schemes have also appeared from time to time in *Social Service Quarterly*.

both in existing organizations and outside, is probably an unattainable ideal except in very small communities, but co-operative plans to meet special needs are valuable, too, and of these there seem to be an increasing number.

Social workers

Unlike the national voluntary bodies the professional associations of social workers have managed to unite. They have formed a Standing Conference and are planning to constitute themselves into a national association by the end of 1969. The first sentence of the Annual Report of the Standing Conference for 1966–7 states that one of the three crucial issues facing social workers today is the structuring and staffing of the social work services and that they are giving serious consideration to it both at national and at local level. 'Structuring and staffing', though not as wide a brief as surveying the whole field where social action is needed and working out how and by whom it can best be taken, also bears on the question of voluntary workers, since these are an integral part of its present structure, and perform tasks which would otherwise be left undone. The fact that paid professional workers cannot meet every need without the assistance of volunteers is recognized in the suggestions (which are gaining ground) that consideration of the place of voluntary work and of the relationship between professionals and volunteers should be included in training for social work.

Writings, broadcasting, research and discussion

Planning for the future is not confined to government departments, local authorities, voluntary bodies and professional associations. Sociologists, social scientists, social workers and other interested people are writing articles, books and pamphlets and discussing what ought to be done. Many of the articles describe social experiments which are thus made available for others to copy. Such accounts usually appear in the specialized press, but they sometimes receive wider publicity, at least in local newspapers. Radio and television are opening the eyes of the public to problems of which they were insufficiently aware, and are publicizing what is being done or could be done to meet them. All this, together with discussion in committees, both government and voluntary, in the universities, in adult education, and among the general public, is helping to create a body of opinion which is informed about social needs.

In spite of all the discussion and planning that is going on it is difficult to judge whether an overall plan for the future will really be produced and whether, if produced, it will be carried out. It may be argued that in the end of all this does not matter, or at any rate cannot be avoided, in a country like Britain where people are somewhat averse to plans and are quite prepared to carry on without them, and where, when they have convinced themselves that something wants doing, they take action themselves, and do not wait for those in authority to prepare plans and hand them out for execution.

Certainly volunteers will go on working, both in time-honoured ways and in new ventures, whatever the action or inaction of the planners, but this does not alter the fact that their contribution to the well-being of society would be greater if it were better planned. It is true that there are large numbers of them, and true that much of what they do is valuable, and true, too, that many of them will persevere even if they lack official encouragement and remain unco-ordinated. But it is also true that there might be more of them and that they might do more and better work if they had a clearer idea of what part they ought to be playing, and how they could best equip themselves to play it well.

This clearer idea can only emerge if there is some general acceptance of what should be the respective spheres of statutory and voluntary action. It is this that makes overall planning so important, since some knowledge of the likely extent of statutory provision is essential if the actual tasks to be undertaken by volunteers are to be determined. This information is needed if estimates are to be made of the kind of people best suited to carry them out and the number likely to be required. It is needed, too, if the best methods of recruitment, training and allocation are to be worked out.

Needs and resources: the role of voluntary work in the plan for the social services

It is probably inevitable that voluntary bodies and actual and potential volunteers should be largely excluded in the framing of an overall plan, since this is the business of government, and though some voluntary bodies may be taken into consultation their advice will not necessarily be followed, nor is it likely that they would all speak with one voice or that any group or groups selected could be taken to represent them all. Those taken into consultation are likely to be either co-ordinating bodies, which cannot always speak for their constituent organizations, or the larger national societies whose representatives at headquarters do not always truly mirror the views of their branches, still less of their rank and file. There is, moreover, no obvious machinery for consultation with volunteers who are not linked to organizations. It is because of the absence or inadequacy of machinery for consultation that full publicity should be given to the data on which the plan is based and on the deliberations about the pros and cons of those parts of it which involve the use of voluntary workers, so that the public as a whole from whom these workers will be drawn can have an opportunity of considering it, of forming their own opinions about it, and of making their views known. All citizens have an interest in general policy, and those among them who are actual or potential volunteers have a special interest in those parts of the plan which will depend on voluntary action.

Much of the data on which the plan will be based is common knowledge, since planning must start from what exists today, and must take into account actual needs and resources. About some of these needs and resources there is general agreement, though differences of opinion arise as to which needs are greatest and as to what proportion of available resources should be used to meet which needs. It is generally agreed that more and better houses, schools and hospitals are urgently needed. In spite of expanding programmes, the building of new houses and the rehabilitation of old ones has not kept pace with the demand for homes; most of the hospitals are out-of-date and many are understaffed; many schools are overcrowded and antiquated, and classes are far too large.

In the health and welfare services of the local authorities there are gaps and inadequacies in every section. The most urgent need, according to the Seebohm Report, which was concerned with this field, lies with the very young and the very old – the most vulnerable age groups. To fill these gaps and to raise standards, both building and personnel are needed. There is a shortage of personnel in both educational and social services and recruiting and training is not yet keeping pace with increasing demand. There may be general agreement about all these needs, but the taxpayer might well be appalled at the bill for building the houses, hospitals and schools that are required and for wages and salaries if there were suddenly enough teachers, social workers, doctors, nurses and medical and other auxiliaries to fill all needs.

As far as building is concerned, the help which can be given by voluntary bodies and by volunteers is limited though even here valuable contributions are being made with housing projects, special schools, homes for the elderly, the handicapped, ex-prisoners and others, and with experiments of other kinds. In the case of personnel, however, volunteers can make, and indeed are making, a massive contribution. This has always been so, and will continue in the foreseeable future. It is only necessary to imagine what would happen if all voluntary workers went on strike to realize the extent and importance of what they do. Not only would there be a drastic reduction in the provision of meals on wheels and an end of friendly visiting of the elderly, the sick and the handicapped; work among children and young people would be seriously curtailed, and all the other tasks which have been described in previous chapters neglected, but magistrates, councillors and aldermen, hospital managers and unpaid trade union workers would all stay at home. This massive contribution which is being made here and now by voluntary workers is clearly one of the resources which should be taken into account in any plan which seeks to balance needs on the one hand with the resources available to meet them on the other.

These resources are both human and material. They consist of the people, paid and unpaid, who work in the social services and of the public money which is spent on them. The amount of money made available for this purpose depends not only on national productivity but on the proportion of the total product which is devoted to it. This in turn depends on the relative importance attached to it by public opinion. Voluntary workers can increase the material as well as the human resources available to meet social needs since their presence throughout the social services helps to create a public opinion that is prepared to support and even to press for greater expenditure.

The number of volunteers that will be required to make up the total personnel will, of course, depend partly on the overall need and partly on the number of paid staff, neither of which is easy to estimate. While it is generally accepted that existing numbers of paid staff, full and part-time, trained and untrained, are insufficient for present, let alone for future needs, it would be rash to guess by how much they are insufficient over the whole field. Attempted estimates, even by experts, often prove wildly wrong, as in the case of the Willink Committee on the supply of doctors[1]. It is a safe guess, however, that as they are insufficient here and now when they are supported by volunteers, they would be still more so if all these were removed.

The support of volunteers will still be needed even though the number of trained social workers is increasing, since it is doubtful whether the supply will do more than fill existing gaps, and perhaps meet expected increases in demand due to population growth and to expanding needs. The continued use of volunteers is tacitly accepted in estimates of requirements of trained personnel, since plans for expansion do not as a rule envisage the replacement of volunteers by paid staff. The increased number of trained workers will be needed partly to fill existing posts and partly for new posts that will be created as statutory provision in the social services develops further. For the continued need for volunteers does not imply that they will perform the same tasks in the future as in the past, and that the division between paid and unpaid work will always be the same as it is today. Public opinion largely supports the somewhat haphazard division that now exists, but the division has changed from what it was and will change again.

---

[1] *Report of the Committee to consider the future numbers of medical practitioners and the appropriate intake of medical students.* Joint Publication of the Ministry of Health and the Department of Health for Scotland. Chairman, Rt. Hon. Sir Henry Willink, Bt., M.C., Q.C. (1957).

The question of what is the right division will require continuing careful consideration and the answer cannot be given once and for all, nor will the same answer necessarily be right at any one time for all parts of the country. This is the background against which a consideration of the tasks to be undertaken by voluntary workers must be made.

2 Tasks for voluntary action and the people that will be needed

The tasks

The actual tasks performed by volunteers will vary with time and place, but there are two basic principles which determine the sphere of voluntary action as a whole. *First*, there are some things in all societies and at all times which are better done by volunteers, although what these things are varies from time to time and from place to place; and *second*, volunteers should not be used to save ratepayers' and taxpayers' money in cases where the work to be done has come to be recognized as belonging to the statutory body, where it can be as well or better done by paid labour, and where such labour is available. At the same time, since there is always a limit to government spending, things which ought ideally to be done by paid labour will often be left undone unless they are undertaken by voluntary workers. It is better that they should be done in this way than not at all both for the sake of the people who need the service and because voluntary action of this kind often prepares the way for statutory action.

The acceptance of these two principles does not therefore mean that the interpretation of what they involve in practice is always the same. Agreement that there are some things better done by volunteers does not imply agreement as to what those things are, and the recognition that volunteers should not be used simply to save public money is shared by people with different views as to what limit should be put on government spending. Opinions as to what is government responsibility and how much public money should be spent on social welfare vary at any one time and change as societies evolve. Opinions as to what is the proper sphere of voluntary service also vary and change. In Britain in the sixties there is general agreement that everyone's basic needs should be met from statutory sources if they are unable to meet them by their own efforts. This means that every family should have an income to meet essential needs if retired, sick or unemployed, and that education, housing and medical care should be available for all. There is disagreement as to how much help can still be given from voluntary sources and as to how far overall provision is still inadequate, but few now believe that anyone should be expected to apply to voluntary bodies for food, shelter or medical care or to go without these things. Disagreement also arises, once the basic needs have been met, as to what should be done, and who should undertake it.

This leads to differences in different parts of the country as to what is done by volunteers, but everywhere there is agreement that they should participate in some way and everywhere their participation is a fact. Some indication of what they do and of their numbers has been given in previous chapters and will not be repeated here. Particular reference will, however, be made here to one type of service – work with old people – to show what volunteers are actually doing in one field and how their work is likely to be affected by developments in statutory provision. Work in other fields could also serve as an example, but this is especially suitable because it has expanded so much in recent years and because the elderly are one of the two groups to which the Seebohm Committee gives priority.

Pensions cover basic needs of food, warmth and clothing, the health service gives care in sickness, local authorities provide accommodation for those unable to live at home and home helps to relieve domestic burdens, but is this enough, especially for the very many old people who live alone without family or friends near at hand, since pensions are low, the health service uneven, and local authority provision of residential accommodation and domiciliary help inadequate? Are not the services which are now largely supplied by voluntary effort a tremendous boon, and even in many cases a necessity? Have the local authorities the necessary staff and finance themselves to provide such services as meals on wheels and dinner clubs, centres for social intercourse, holidays and outings, and above all regular home visits, and if they had would this be the best solution? Though a paid worker can be just as good a visitor as a volunteer he must limit the frequency and length of his visits because of the number on his list. The volunteer can give more time, and because he has fewer cases he can take a more personal interest in each. He can bring a neighbour's concern rather than the concern of a professional. He can also act as a valuable check on the working of the various services on which the people he visits are dependent. The factors which make the volunteer especially valuable in the visiting service apply, too, in the case of meals on wheels, but here there are other factors to be taken into account which make it likely that more paid staff will be needed. The provision of regular domiciliary meals could play an effective part in enabling people who are now obliged to seek residential accommodation to go on living comfortably in their own homes, but to do this satisfactorily it will need expansion on a scale that may well be beyond the capacity of voluntary effort. Yet it would be a pity if the contribution made by volunteers, which can be so much greater than the mere delivery of a meal, were lost. This element might be retained if the local authorities took over responsibility and if more of the staff were paid, but the recruitment of volunteers might then become more difficult than it is under present circumstances. Local authorities would have to decide in consultation with the voluntary bodies and with existing volunteers whether unpaid helpers should be used, and would have to work out how many would be needed and how best they could be recruited and retained.

Old people's welfare, taken as a whole, is a good example o a field where the work can be satisfactorily divided between statutory and voluntary effort and where the right kind of tasks are being undertaken by volunteers. In old people's welfare, as in other fields, some of these tasks require special skills, but the distinguishing feature of tasks suitable for voluntary effort is that they involve friendly personal contact of an unhurried kind, a contact that is unofficial yet available in emergency, like the daily call of the good neighbour or the 24-hour emergency service of the Samaritans. Voluntary service of this kind, like that of the extended family, is helping to make community care a reality. Those who render it form part of the human resources available to meet social need, and can be taken into account in future planning. In every field where service of this kind is welcomed by its recipients and generally approved by the statutory authorities and by public opinion it can be expected to continue, though not necessarily along exactly the same lines as at present. It will even continue without the approval of the statutory authorities, wherever there are people concerned to play a personal part in making the services work and in pressing for their improvement.

The example of old people's welfare shows that the expansion of statutory provision is not likely to mean that fewer volunteers will be needed, and similar evidence could be found in every field in which they are now playing a significant part. In some cases, too, developments in professional social work are involving the participation of a greater number of volunteers – as, for instance, in the after-care of prisoners for which it is hoped to enlist voluntary workers as 'associates'.

The inadequacy of present provision is evident in those parts of the social services which are now dependent on voluntary effort no less than in those which are in the hands of paid workers, but the solution will not lie simply in increasing the statutory element. Satisfactory provision will depend on increasing the personnel, both paid and voluntary, throughout the whole field. Some of the tasks now in the voluntary section may be better transferred to paid staff, as was suggested in the case of meals on wheels, but others could and should be expanded by an extended use of volunteers. There will certainly be no shortage of tasks.

The people

What kind of people are best suited to perform these tasks, and how many will be needed? The tasks are so many and so various that they will provide opportunities for people of many different kinds and with a wide variety of skills. Some tasks, like driving or office work, may demand no more than competence at a particular job, but those which involve personal service – and these form the great majority – demand qualities such as kindness, patience, tolerance and above all a concern for other people and a desire to help them. Possessors of these qualities plus the skill which is needed for the more exacting jobs like leadership or counselling, are rare birds, whether paid or unpaid. Perhaps the most that can be expected of volunteers, as of professionals, is that they will be a cross section of the population as a whole, a collection of ordinary men and women of every age and social class, who between them possess a wide range of skills and qualifications. The only thing that will not be ordinary about them is that they will be working without pay, but since at least half the population appears to do this at some time in their lives, they are not perhaps less ordinary than the other half.

The numbers that will be required for the various tasks will have to be worked out locally, with local conditions taken into account. This is the stage of planning at which the voluntary bodies must have a say if they are to continue to 'deliver the goods' in the form of voluntary workers, for their views about what should be done by voluntary labour must be taken into account if they are to recruit the necessary personnel. The extent to which their views will affect local estimates of the total number of volunteers that will be needed will, however, largely depend on their success or failure at agreeing among themselves. Co-operation among themselves is of great import-ance, not only because it will lead to division of labour and harmonious relationships and thus to better service to the public, but also because it will greatly affect the attitude of the statutory bodies. Successful co-operation will disarm the criticism, often made by representatives of the statutory authorities and by professional workers, and often justified, that the voluntary bodies cannot agree among themselves, and cannot therefore be relied upon to cover adequately any field for which they accept joint responsibility. If they cannot agree among themselves on a division of work at local level the authority which needs voluntary help will either have to deal direct with separate voluntary bodies and allocate to each a specific job, or to recruit voluntary workers itself and bypass the voluntary bodies altogether. In both these cases the initiative will pass from the voluntary body to the statutory authority which alone will become responsible for deciding how many volunteers will be needed.

Recruitment

There is little information available about the relative success of different methods of recruitment, nor is there an agreed view among those who wish to use volunteers as to who should be responsible for it. There appear to be several alternatives: recruitment by a voluntary body, by a statutory body, by a combination of the two or by direct action from the volunteers themselves. The last alternative hardly counts as recruitment since it covers those cases where people give neighbourly help not as a result of being asked to do so by a third party but simply because they themselves see a need and feel a call to meet it. Although this is the way in which the greatest volume of voluntary service is given it is not relevant to a consideration of methods of recruitment since the very fact that it is spontaneous and unorganized means that it cannot be controlled by any agency, whether statutory or voluntary.

The voluntary body has long been recognized as the proper agent for recruitment, and the few cases, such as the School Care Committees, in which the authority concerned has itself successfully recruited paid helpers, have been exceptions to the pattern accepted by statutory and voluntary bodies alike. Recent government action and statements have reinforced this view. An important example is the recruitment of women for civil defence in the last war. Instead of its being undertaken by the government departments concerned a special organization, the W.V.S., was set up for the purpose. Although the W.V.S (now W.R.V.S.) is strictly speaking a service and not a voluntary body, it is an organization which is itself responsible for the recruitment, allocation and supervision of its workers. It has continued to function in the same way in peace time and now recruits and supervises volunteers in a wide variety of tasks. The tasks are undertaken at the request of the statutory authorities but the workers are recruited by the W.R.V.S. Another example is the action of the Ministry of Health, as recently as 1962, in emphasising that recruitment for voluntary service in hospitals and local authority services should be undertaken through the voluntary bodies and not by direct appeal to the public.

Since then, however, important developments have taken

place, particularly in the hospitals, where, as was seen in Chapter II, schemes for the recruitment and supervision of volunteers by members of staff are growing in number. These schemes are being remarkably successful in increasing the number of voluntary workers, and their example seems likely to be followed by other statutory bodies. Local authorities are increasingly appealing direct to the public for help of various kinds. They are seeking helpers not only for special jobs such as 'adopting' residents in old people's homes and 'befriending' foster children – and, indeed, for fostering itself since the payment offered to foster parents barely covers maintenance[1] – but also for general service in the field of welfare. In Manchester, for example, the Welfare Department is planning to give its District Officers responsibility for voluntary visitors in their districts, and an action research project to develop voluntary service for the elderly financed by the National Corporation for the Care of Old People is being carried out jointly by the District Officers, the Youth and Community Council and the Old People's Welfare Committee of the Council of Social Service. Schemes of this kind are likely to grow in number, especially if the recommendations of the Seebohm Report[2] are carried out. Though it is true that this report stresses the importance of voluntary organizations, it states, too, that local authorities will themselves have to enlist the support of volunteers:

With the continuing growth of the personal social services it will be more and more necessary for local authorities to enlist the services of large numbers of volunteers to complement the teams of professional workers, and the social service department must become a focal point to which those who wish to give voluntary help can offer their services[3].

What will be the effect of such developments on the voluntary bodies? Will they gradually cease to act as agents for the recruitment and supervision of volunteers, or will they continue to function as one source of supply among others? Their position is bound to be affected in some way wherever direct

[1] See 'Should Foster-Mums be Paid?' *New Society*, 22nd August, 1968.
[2] *Committee on Local Authority and Allied Personal Social Services, Cmnd.* 3703 (1968).
[3] *Cmnd.* 3703, para. 498.

recruitment by statutory bodies takes place. This will be so not only in the health and welfare services, but in youth work, in the care and after-care of prisoners, in advice and information, in race relations, and in any other sphere where voluntary workers are required. The way in which it is affected will depend in the long run on which organization or organizations prove most successful at finding and retaining the right number of the right kind of people for the jobs that need doing. To achieve this success three things are necessary – knowledge of needs, efficient administration, and acceptability to prospective volunteers.

Knowledge of needs is more easily acquired by statutory than by voluntary bodies since they have the responsibility for providing the various services, and are in a position to estimate how much can be done by paid labour. The voluntary bodies can share this knowledge if they are taken into consultation and this is clearly an advantage to them, but in any case they have a duty to find out for themselves from the consumer angle what are the main unmet needs, and to form their own views as to which should be met by voluntary labour.

Efficient administration must be achieved by any organization, statutory or voluntary, if volunteers are to be successfully recruited and retained, and if the tasks allocated to them are to be properly carried out. If the voluntary bodies assume this responsibility they must, as has already been stressed, agree among themselves, and this means having effective machinery for making their agreement work. If they cannot do this the statutory body responsible for the work in question will either recruit volunteers direct or delegate the task to a particular body or bodies. This is what seems to be happening in Yorkshire, where there is some co-operation between separate local authority departments and individual voluntary bodies, although there is no machinery for overall co-operation between the local authority on the one hand and the voluntary bodies as a whole on the other.

Whoever assumes responsibility, an important factor in efficient administration is the existence of some kind of central agency which is in touch with organizations and individuals needing help on the one hand and with prospective volunteers on the other. Experience in old people's welfare, in hospitals, in information work, in the youth service, and in many other fields, shows how necessary for the recruitment and placing of voluntary workers is a central bureau or at least a single person in a position both to collect information about openings and to receive offers of help. This central bureau may be part of a local authority or voluntary society[1], or attached to a single institution: what matters from the point of view of efficiency is that it should exist, and should be known to the community.

There are differences, of course, between a central bureau under statutory and one under voluntary control, and differences, too, between one attached to a single institution and one which forms part of a local authority or voluntary society. One difference between control by a statutory or voluntary body is that the former can more easily pay an organizer or second a member of its staff, while the latter, being chronically short of money, cannot usually do so without a special grant. Another difference is that the voluntary body is the more likely of the two to see that volunteers are not used as cheap substitutes for paid labour.

The differences between a bureau which forms part of an organization, whether statutory or voluntary, and one which is attached to an institution are of another kind. The organizer who is attached to a local authority or voluntary society is recruiting for a variety of tasks in different fields, and not just for service in one institution. He draws on a wide public, and can provide a clearing house and allocate people to the work for which they are most suited and which most needs help; he can often persuade uncommitted volunteers to tackle unpopular tasks which badly need doing; he can arrange training courses which are basic to many forms of community service; he can retain contact with recruits after placement and check conditions of service, and can sometimes mediate between volunteers and the staff with whom they are working. The organizer who is attached to an institution has advantages of another kind. He can appeal to people who are attracted to the idea of helping in a particular field or at a particular place – hospital, hostel, school, youth club or prison – but do not want to be involved in membership or other obligation to any

[1] By 1968 at least twenty Cs.S.S. provided a volunteer bureau.

intermediate person or group. He is, moreover, particularly well placed to introduce the new volunteer to his task personally and to maintain constant touch with him, since he is only concerned with one institution.

Whatever the difference, it is the presence of an organizer in each case which leads to successful recruitment and retention of voluntary workers. It is therefore likely that the extent to which such people are appointed will be one of the determining factors in the future pattern of recruitment, and that the relative position of statutory and voluntary bodies will be influenced by the way in which appointments are made. The voluntary bodies will be strengthened if they are grant-aided and left free to make their own appointments, and there is precedent for this since the W.R.V.S. is financed by the Home Office, and some Councils of Social Service and other voluntary bodies receive grants from various central and local government sources; they will be weakened if appointments are made to the staff of statutory authorities, as in the case of the School Care Committees and of some hospitals. The second alternative seems likely to be chosen by at least some local authorities if the advice of the Seebohm Committee is followed. Efficient organization, important though it is, is not the only factor in successful recruitment. It is even more important that the recruiting organization should be acceptable to prospective volunteers. Its acceptability will depend on its being seen to be capable of offering work which is worth doing, and on its ability to rouse the will to volunteer. To do this, it will have to take account of the reasons which lead people to undertake voluntary work. These reasons were discussed in Chapter VIII, and it is only necessary here to re-emphasize how vital it is that they should be taken into account by anyone responsible for recruitment.

Voluntary and statutory organizations have rather different appeals to prospective volunteers. Which of the two is the more successful recruiting agent in any particular place or time will depend on which type of appeal carries most weight with the volunteers it hopes to attract. The voluntary body will be able to call on the loyalty of its members, and their predisposition, by the very fact of membership, to support its undertakings. It may also draw strength from the fact that it has pioneered in the field for which it is seeking helpers, and may have played a part in framing that section of social policy and therefore have a special concern for putting it into action; it may offer special inducements, some trivial, some fundamental, from uniform or social get-togethers to religious or political conviction, which attract and hold supporters.

The statutory body, for its part, will have the advantage, in some cases at least, of offering jobs with social status. Magistrates and members of Royal Commissions, Advisory Committees, Hospital Boards and management committees and of governing bodies of schools, are rarely difficult to find, though they may not always be the best people for the job. There are powerful influences which make people anxious to serve in these capacities which are not always present in other cases. There is the satisfaction of serving on a body to which you have been appointed – you, in preference to anyone else who may also wish to be chosen; there is a status value in belonging to committees which are in the public eye; there may even be a political advantage, for though members may be appointed as individuals and not as party representatives, party balance is often roughly maintained by unwritten law. Active membership of a political party sometimes leads to appointment on statutory committees or to the bench, while holding office of this kind may be an asset in the party. It is true that such factors only operate in the case of the more important offices for which the statutory bodies seek recruits, but there are factors of another kind which help in the case of more ordinary jobs. There is the prestige of an institution for which helpers are needed and the local affection in which it is held, factors which are especially influential in the case of hospitals; there is even the desire felt by some people not to be associated with a voluntary body, though this is a point which the voluntary bodies themselves are slow to recognize.

The growing success of the statutory bodies in recruiting volunteers for jobs which were previously filled through the voluntary bodies is viewed with some anxiety by the latter's representatives. Those of them who conferred with the Ministry of Health in 1962 naturally supported the recommendation that the approach should be made to the responsible body and not to individual members. It was to be expected that they should think that their members would be more likely to volunteer if they knew that the society to which they belonged was taken into partnership, and they quite naturally wanted to have a hand in any further arrangements for recruitment. It appears, however, that they over-estimated the interest of the average volunteer in the role of the voluntary body, since many, even of their own members, seem to obtain satisfaction from the work itself and from their indentification with it and with those it serves, rather than from belonging to an organization which is 'taken into consultation'; while many others neither belong nor wish to belong to any organization at all. Such people can be recruited and retained by a member of staff of the institution or government department concerned without the need for consultation with a voluntary body, and this is what seems to be happening in an increasing number of cases.

In spite of this trend it is most unlikely that the voluntary bodies will everywhere and at all times be superseded as recruiting agents for volunteers. The development of social provision in this country, and the present position of voluntary workers throughout the whole field, make it much more likely that there will be no uniform pattern and that methods of recruitment will vary no less than the tasks for which volunteers will be needed. The position of the voluntary bodies as recruiting agents, and of volunteers as workers, will vary from place to place and from time to time and from one field of service to another, for the extent to which the statutory bodies increase their paid staff and themselves appeal for volunteers will also vary. Thus no general prediction about the future pattern either of recruitment or of voluntary work can safely be made. The only prediction that can be made with confidence is that voluntary workers, however recruited and whatever tasks they undertake, will continue to play a vital part in the life of the community.

They will play a part because there are needs which they alone can adequately meet. They will play a part because of a natural urge to help their neighbours. Finally, they will play a part because their day-to-day experience shows the ordinary citizen how the social services are working, and their personal participation makes them a powerful influence for reform.

Voluntary Workers in Old People's Welfare

As was stated in the text, much of the material collected for the survey which was carried out by the National Old People's Welfare Council in 1965 has not been published. Some of the unpublished material has been transferred to code sheets, but some has not been extracted from the replies to the questionnaires. Even when data have been transferred to code sheets it is not always possible to obtain detailed information from them. A one-in-ten sample has therefore been taken direct from the questionnaires and this has been used to supplement the published material in the following analysis.

The questionnaire was in two parts, Part I dealing with staffing and finance, and Part II with services. The information about voluntary workers was sought partly by means of a direct question about volunteers and partly by asking about services wholly or partly dependent on voluntary workers. The direct question was in Part I and read as follows: 'How many volunteers, i.e., UNPAID people, work directly for the committee?' and the following table for the answer was appended to it.

	Visitors	Office	Meals	Clubs	Others
Full-time					
Part-time					
TOTAL					

The information about services was sought in Part II of the questionnaire under the following headings: Boarding Out, Chiropody, Clubs, Employment and Workshops, Holidays, Homes, Housing, Laundry, Meals, Visiting. Except in the case of visiting the questions did not ask for the number of volunteers involved, but a rough estimate can be made on the basis of the service provided, particularly where additional information is obtainable from other sources.

Visiting

The information about visiting derived from the survey is based on the answers to two questions – first, the question quoted above 'How many volunteers, i.e., UNPAID people, work directly for the committee?' and second, a question in Part II which asked for information about the visiting service under these five headings:

(*a*) Is there a voluntary visiting scheme in your area?
(*b*) If YES please state the organization responsible.
(*c*) How many local organizations co-operate in the service?
(*d*) How many visitors are there altogether, to your knowledge?
(*e*) How many old people are visited regularly (i.e., at least once a fortnight) to your knowledge?

It is not possible to obtain an accurate figure from the answers to the first question because of the way in which these were coded. These answers only give approximate figures for the number of visitors attached to each committee. This information is set out in the following table.

TABLE I

1 *Number of* *visitors*	2 *Number of committees* *with number of visitors* *shown in column 1*
1–9	87
10–19	123
20–49	126
50–99	58
100 or more	34
Don't know	162
No reply	25
TOTAL	615

A rough estimate of the total number of visitors can be obtained from the one-in-ten sample, which contains information direct from the questionnaires.

The sample consisted of eighty-three committees drawn from the 830 which replied to one or both parts of the questionnaire. Seventy-

238

five replied to the question in Part I and sixty-five to that in Part II, though the same figures are only given by twenty-one committees. The difference is explained by the difference in the questions. The first asked 'How many unpaid people work *for the committee* as visitors?' while the second asked 'How many visitors are there altogether?' and went on to ask 'How many local organizations co-operate in the visiting service?' Where organizations other than the O.P.W. Committee share with them the responsibility for the service the number given in answer to the second question must, of course, be higher than that given to the first.

The total number of visitors given by the seventy-five committees which replied to the first question (including twenty which gave the answer 'none') was 1,563, an average of twenty-eight for the fifty-five which had a service. A considerably higher figure emerged from the answers to the second question. Sixty-five committees replied to this (including eleven which gave the answer 'none') and the total number of visitors recorded was 3,335, an average of sixty-two per area for the fifty-four areas in which a scheme was operating.

Six hundred and fifteen of all the respondent committees stated that they had a visiting service in their areas, so if the figures given by the committees in the sample can be taken as representative of the position in the respondent areas there must be 17,220 (28 × 615) voluntary visitors working for O.P.W. committees and 38,130 (62 × 615) visitors altogether in the respondent areas.

These figures are certainly an underestimate for the country as a whole, since they take no account of the visiting schemes known to exist in those respondent areas where the number of visitors is unknown to the committees, or of the non-respondent areas about which there is no evidence in this survey. Fortunately, however, some information about these is available from other sources: from the personal knowledge of the officers of the N.O.P.W.C. and of other bodies at headquarters and in the field, and from various studies which have been carried out. The study which throws most light on the subject is *Visiting Services for the Elderly*, undertaken for the N.O.P.W.C. by Winifred Bayes in 1964. In spite of the fact that its purpose was 'to find out what were the ingredients of a good visiting service' rather than to collect statistical evidence of what was going on – and, indeed, the number of visitors is not given – it revealed the existence of active visiting services in eight areas which had failed to reply to the questionnaire sent out for the N.O.P.W.C. survey. As the Bayes study only covers twenty-four areas in all, eight is a significant number and shows that non-respondency to the N.O.P.W.C. questionnaire cannot be taken as proof of inactivity, and that a true estimate for the country as a whole must make allowance for what is going on in the non-respondent as well as in the respondent areas.

If the non-respondent areas had the same number of visitors as those which replied, the country as a whole would have about double the number calculated from the one-in-ten sample, since the two groups are approximately the same size. In the view of the officers of the N.O.P.W.C. and of the authors of their survey this estimate would be too high, and a total of one and a half times would be nearer the truth. This view is based on their personal knowledge of the position in the non-respondent areas, and is, moreover, supported by the Bayes survey. On this view the number of voluntary visitors in the whole country at the time of the N.O.P.W.C. survey can be estimated at 26,500 working through O.P.W. Committees, and 57,000 including those working through all the other organizations.

Clubs

The survey carried out by the N.O.P.W.C. covered clubs by the same method as it covered visiting, that is to say it sought information by asking two questions: first, a simple question about voluntary workers, 'How many volunteers, i.e., unpaid people, work directly for the committee?' and second, a more complicated question about the clubs themselves. The second question was subdivided as follows:

(*a*) How many social clubs for the elderly are there in the area?
(*b*) Please indicate in the table below how often the clubs open (show number of clubs in each category):—

No. of days	7	6	5	4	3	2	1	Fortnightly	Monthly
No. of clubs									

(*c*) Please list voluntary organizations which are responsible for clubs in your area.
(*d*) How many day centres/clubs are there for:
    (i) The handicapped.
    (ii) The able-bodied.
    (iii) Mainly for the able-bodied but making occasional arrangements for the handicapped.

The answers to the first question have not been coded, so the only information on this point comes from the one-in-ten sample, and this is of limited value since only thirty-five of the eighty-three committees in the sample give figures, and in three of these the number of clubs is not given, though the existence of clubs is recorded in sixty-nine. This lack of information is probably due to the fact that many clubs are not actually run by the O.P.W. committees. Even for the thirty-five cases where the number of workers is given it is not possible to estimate how many there are per club or per club session since in many places some of the clubs known to the committee are run directly by them, while others are run by other organizations, such as the W.R.V.S. or the B.R.C.S. or by independent committees. In the thirty-two cases where both number of workers and number of clubs are given, 796 workers, 169 clubs and 438 sessions are recorded. This makes an average of 4·7 workers per club, and 1·8 per session, but this is certainly too low, since these figures refer only to workers attached to O.P.W. committees, whereas the clubs in question are staffed by other organizations and individuals as well.

The answers to section (*a*) of the second question have been coded and the information shown in the following table (Table 2) has been taken direct from the code sheets. As in the case of visitors, the method of coding makes it possible to give only approximate figures. The figures in Table 2 are based on returns from *local* committees only and those from committees covering geographical

TABLE 2

1 Number of clubs in each area	2 Number of areas having number of clubs in column 1	3 Number of clubs for the whole group in column 2
1– 4	428	$2\frac{1}{2} \times 428 = 1,070$
5– 9	123	$7 \times 123 = 861$
10–19	88	$14\frac{1}{2} \times 88 = 1,276$
20–49	26	$34\frac{1}{2} \times 26 = 897$
50–99	8	$74\frac{1}{2} \times 8 = 596$
100 or more	3	$100 \times 3 = 300$
None	39	$0 \times 39 = 0$
TOTALS	715	5,000

counties have been omitted, since information from geographical counties duplicates information received from committees within the county boundaries.

Column 2 shows the number of committees which recorded the number of clubs shown in column 1. Column 3 gives the approximate total for each group based on a figure midway between the lowest and the highest, viz., $2\frac{1}{2}$ for those having between one and four clubs, 7 for those having between five and nine, 14 for those having between ten and nineteen and $74\frac{1}{2}$ for those having between fifty and ninety-nine. The figure for the three committees with 100 or over has been left at 100.

Further information was again obtained from the one-in-ten sample, and this supported the evidence of the code sheets. Ten of the eighty-three in this sample did not reply to this question; the other seventy-three committees had a total of 529 clubs, which is 5,290 for 730 committees as against 4,810 for the 715 committees recorded on the code sheets. In both cases the average number of clubs per committee is seven. (529 for 73 committees = 7·25 per committee – 4,810 for 715 committees = 6·73 per committee.)

If the non-respondent areas have half as many clubs as those which replied, the total for the whole country will be approximately 7,500.

This estimate is very similar to that given in 1968 by the Seebohm Report (*Cmnd.* 3703), which states (Appendix F, para 184) that there are about 7,000 social clubs mainly run by voluntary organizations.

On the question of sessions (section (*b*)) the figures available from the code sheets show that 56% of the clubs in the respondent areas meet once a week, 23% fortnightly or monthly, 14% five, six or seven days a week and 7% two, three or four days.

In the one-in-ten sample there were 695 sessions for the 529 clubs known to the seventy-three committees which answered the question about clubs. This makes an average of 1·3 sessions per club, and 9·5 sessions per committee.[1]

A summary of the replies to section (*c*) is given in the published report of the N.O.P.W.C. survey. This places the organizations responsible for the clubs in order of the number of times they are mentioned in the completed questionnaires, though it does not record the number of clubs for which each is responsible. The annual reports of the W.R.V.S. and of the B.R.C.S. do, however, give statistics of the work for which they are responsible. The W.R.V.S. runs 2,084[2] clubs in England and Wales, and the B.R.C.S. 518[3]. The N.O.P.W.C. survey lists the organizations running the clubs in the following order:

---

[1] In making this calculation, clubs which meet fortnightly and monthly have been credited with $\frac{1}{2}$ and $\frac{1}{4}$ of a weekly session respectively.

[2] W.R.V.S., *Bulletin*, June, 1968, p. 25.

[3] B.R.C.S., *Annual Report* for 1966 (the most recent available at time of writing).

O.P.W. Committees
W.R.V.S.
Independent local
National Federation of Old Age Pensioners' Associations
Religious groups
B.R.C.S.
Other national
Rotary/Inner Wheel/Inner Circle, etc.
Councils of Social Service

and adds the note that in the respondent county borough areas the W.R.V.S. takes precedence over the others.

The report of the N.O.P.W.C. survey also refers to Day Centres (section (d)). It states that there were 'a considerable number of these' though precise numbers were not available.

It appears from more recent information that provision of this kind is on the increase, since W.R.V.S. alone are now responsible for no less than ninety-three of such centres[1]. The Seebohm Report (*Cmnd.* 3703) states (Appendix F, para. 184) that there are 'about 120 centres provided by local authorities which act as a focus for health and welfare services and sometimes provide opportunities for occupation or employment'. It does not, however, mention whether or not voluntary workers assist at these centres.

Meals

Information comes from the Harris survey described in the text and from the Annual Reports of the Ministry of Health. The Harris survey (1960) estimated that the total number of meals served was 1,250,000 per annum. This included the few which were at that time being served by local authorities. There were five L.A. schemes out of a total of 453, but they were all large (serving 100 or more people) so they must have supplied at least 25,000 meals in a fifty-week year. This reduces the number served by voluntary bodies to 1,225,000, which works out at an average of 300 served by each voluntary worker.

In the case of lunch and dinner clubs, estimates of the number of centres have been made on the basis of the replies to the N.O.P.W.C. survey, and the number of meals now being served at centres has been quoted from the annual report of the Ministry of Health for 1967. Figures supplied by the W.R.V.S.[2] have been of assistance in calculating the overall number of voluntary workers, since they

[1] *Bulletin*, p. 25.
[2] *Ibid.*

243

give the number of centres as well as the number of meals served, which makes it possible to work out the average number of meals served per centre and so to estimate the number of helpers needed to serve them. In 1967 the W.R.V.S. served 1,636,805 meals. This is 32,736 per week for a fifty-week year and works out at an average of seventy-seven meals served per week at each of their 426 centres. There is no information as to whether or not these are all served on the same day. The number of voluntary workers per centre is not given but information from people working in the field suggests that there are at least seven, or one for every ten meals served. There may be more in the bigger centres where meals are served to large numbers several times per week and especially in the few cases where they are cooked by voluntary labour, but there may well be fewer in the smaller clubs and in those where the members themselves help with serving and washing up, though of course they, too, are voluntary workers. The number of meals served in centres by the W.R.V.S., which is quoted in their Bulletin, differs from that given by the Ministry of Health, but this does not affect the estimate of the number of voluntary workers involved, since this has been calculated from the number of meals served in centres by *all* voluntary organizations.

Housing

The distribution of housing schemes between the 144 local committees which supplied information on this point for the N.O.P.W.C. survey is shown in the following table.

TABLE 3

1 *Number of schemes*	2 *Number of committees having the no. of schemes shown in column 1*	3 *Total no. of schemes under committees shown in column 2*
One	75	75
Two	29	58
Three	14	42
Four	8	32
Five	13	65
Six	2	12
Seven	0	0
Eight	1	8
Nine or more	2	80
TOTAL	144	372

If there are 10 workers per scheme there will be 3,720 in the respondent areas. On the assumption that there are half the number of schemes in the non-respondent areas as in those which replied to the questionnaire there will be a total of 5,580 voluntary workers in housing schemes for the elderly in the country as a whole.

APPENDIX II

Voluntary Workers in Youth Work

TABLE I

Membership in national voluntary youth organizations in SCNVYO (U.K. unless otherwise stated) (E. & W. = England and Wales; W = Wales only)

Organization	Membership 1958	Membership 1965–6
1. Army Cadets	43,639	38,089
2. Jewish Youth	20,000	25,000
3. Boy Scouts	422,670	483,439
4. Boys' Brigade	152,000	142,000
5. B.R.C.S. (E. & W.)	63,753	59,543
6. Cath. Y.M.S.[1]		
7. Church Lads (E. & W., N. Ireland)	18,644	12,424
8. Co-op. Union	24,703	16,601
9. Girl Guides	501,596	586,608
10. Girls' Brigade	64,169	60,315
11. Girls' Guildry (E. & W.)[2]	5,544	
12. G.F.S.[2]	22,227	19,709
13. Grail	10,500	14,000
14. Methodist Youth	96,561	92,456
15. N.A.B.C.	145,949	158,119
16. N.A.Y.C.	156,000	239,000
17. N.C. Cath. Y.C.[3]		37,169
18. N.F.Y.F.C.	65,702	56,551
19. Pony Club	26,366	30,021
20. St. John Amb.	71,498	60,165
21. Salvation Army (E. & W.)[2]	85,800	90,233
22. Sea Cadets	18,032	17,504
23. Welsh League of Y. (W.)	20,280	19,796
24. Y. Christian Workers	16,230	17,748
25. Y.M.C.A.	84,457	83,974
26. Y.W.C.A.	14,232	17,790
27. Y.H.A. (E. & W.)	124,225	135,796
TOTALS	2,274,777	2,514,050

APPENDICES

1. No figures were supplied for 1958 and those for 1965–6 (15,000 members) have been omitted from the table since this apparently is not a youth organization. 'Catholic Young Men's Society' is a misnomer.
2. In these three cases the figures were supplied from the Annual Reports of SCNVYO for 1961–2 (the first year in which a report was published) and 1965–7 and not direct from the organizations concerned.
3. This organization was not formed until 1964.
4. The figures in Table 1 include the under-11's, of whom according to SCNVYO there were 609,000 out of a total for all age groups of 2,141,000 (England and Wales) in 1960 (the first year SCNVYO published statistics); and 646,000 in 1965–6. Assuming that there were the same number under 11 in 1958 as in 1960 the figures supplied for this table could be amended to exclude the under-11's as follows:

> 1958 2,275,000 – 609,000 = 1,666,000
> 1965–6 2,514,000 – 646,000 = 1,868,000

The percentage increase for those over 11 is 12.

NOTES TO TABLE 2

1. Not formed until 1964.
2. The general secretary was not able to supply figures for voluntary workers, but suggests that there may be about $2\frac{1}{2}$ for each club. This works out at 2,857 for 1958 and 2,537 for 1965. (Letter to the author, 22nd Nov., 1966.)
3. The figures supplied (38 for 1958 and 59 for 1965–6) cannot be compared with those supplied by other organizations. An explanatory letter from the general secretary to the author (4th January, 1967) reads: 'We only include in our statistics of voluntary workers those who actually take the place of professional workers. As far as I know, we have never calculated the number of those who help through committee work, money-raising, etc., but they must total several thousands all over the country.' It is difficult to decide whom to include as voluntary workers in the field of youth work. Those who are merely concerned with high level committee work and money-raising are not strictly speaking youth workers, and will probably not be counted as such by those compiling the statistics for the organizations, but many who do committee work locally are in close touch with the day-to-day work of the clubs and the activities of their members and may well be included.

TABLE 2

Voluntary Workers in National Voluntary Youth Organizations in SCNVYO

Organization	1958		1965–6	
	No. of vol. workers	*No. of members per vol. worker*	*No. of vol. workers*	*No. of members per vol. worker*
1. Army Cadets	4,920	8	5,367	7
2. Jewish Youth				
3. Boy Scouts	58,855	7·2	62,329	7·7
4. Boys' Brigade	23,000	6·6	27,000	5·3
5. B.R.C.S.	3,000	21	4,000	15
6. Cath. Y.M.S.				
7. Church Lads	1,929	9·8	1,545	8·2
8. Co-op. Union				
9. Girl Guides	44,402	11·3	57,626	10·2
10. Girls' Brigade	3,938	16·4	4,751	12·8
11. Girls' Guildry				
12. G.F.S.				
13. Grail	300	35	470	30
14. Methodist Youth	6,000	16·7	5,500	16·8
15. N.A.B.C.	7,350	19·8	8,000	19·8
16. N.A.Y.C.	4,860	32·1	11,410	20·9
17. N.C. Cath. Y.C.[1]			1,021	37
18. N.F.Y.F.C.[2]				
19. Pony Club	2,738	9·6	3,264	9
20. St. John Amb.				
21. Salvation Army				
22. Sea Cadets	2,484	7·2	3,149	5·6
23. Welsh League of Y.	752	26.5	621	31.9
24. Y. Christian Workers	212	75	272	65
25. Y.M.C.A.	Not available		9,298	9·1
26. Y.W.C.A.[3]				
27. Y.H.A.				
TOTALS	164,740		205,623	

TABLE 3

Membership in 1965–6 of organizations which give members of voluntary workers for that time. (U.K. unless otherwise stated.)

1.	Army Cadets	38,089
3.	Boy Scouts	483,439
4.	Boys Brigade	142,000
5.	B.R.C.S. (E. & W.)	59,543
7.	Church Lads	12,424
9.	Girl Guides	586,608
10.	Girls' Brigade	60,315
13.	Grail	14,000
14.	Methodist Youth	92,456
15.	N.A.B.C.	158,119
16.	N.A.Y.C.	239,000
17.	N.C.Cath. Y. C.	37,169
19.	Pony Club	30,021
22.	Sea Cadets	17,504
23.	Welsh League of Y. (W.)	19,796
24.	Y. Christian Witness	17,748
25.	Y.M.C.A.	83,974
	TOTAL	2,092,205
	Total of voluntary workers (see Table 2)	205,623

On these figures there is one voluntary worker for every ten members. The reports from Accrington and Bury to which reference is made in the text show that the ratios there are considerably lower, being one to fifteen in Accrington, and one to twenty-seven in Bury.

TABLE 4

Information furnished to the Scottish Education Department in October, 1965, by S.S.C.V.Y.O. (Scottish Standing Conference of Voluntary Youth Organizations)

	No. of units or centres	Total membership	Headquarters' staff leaders, organizers and specialist instructors			
			Paid Full time	*Paid Part time*	*Unpaid*	*Total*
Youth Organizations	12,697	434,933	181	801	37,697	38,679
Education Authorities	534	44,152	65	3,400	253	3,718
TOTALS	13,231	479,085	246	4,201	37,950	42,397

Voluntary Work in Bradford

A survey was carried out in the spring and early summer of 1967 by students in the School of Studies in Applied Social Studies in the University of Bradford under the supervision of Mr. J. W. McCulloch, Lecturer in Research Methods, in conjunction with the author. The purpose of the survey was to 'discover the involvement of ordinary people in social interaction'; to find out, that is to say, how many people were doing voluntary social work of any kind and who those people were. The schedule was arranged to include neighbourly help as well as action taken through voluntary bodies, since it was felt that a completely inadequate picture of the extent of voluntary work would result if questions were restricted to the activities of members of organizations. And this would indeed have been the case since nearly a third of the sample were giving neighbourly help while less than 8% were members of voluntary organizations. There is a possibility that some people may be acting through organizations, such as the Women's Royal Voluntary Service or an Old People's Welfare Committee, without thinking of themselves as members, but people of this kind are unlikely to be numerous since the schedules were filled in by the interviewers, who checked facts during the interview.

The method adopted was by random sample, every hundredth name being drawn from the electoral register for the whole city. The total number drawn was 2,727. A letter of introduction was sent to these people, and this was followed by a visit from a student who filled in the schedule at the interview.

The schedule was made as simple as possible and only contained these four questions:

1 *In the past month have you regularly helped any friends or neighbours with tasks which, for any reasons, they have been unable to accomplish themselves?* YES/NO

If *yes* please give details of help given; the time involved with each recipient; why help was necessary (i.e., the nature of the recipient's infirmity).

2 *Are you a member of any voluntary social work organization(s)?*
YES/NO
If *yes* please give details of each including:

(i) Its title; (ii) Its functions; (iii) Time spent by respondent;
(iv) Nature of respondent's participation; (v) Duration of membership; (vi) Origin of interest.

3 *Are you a member of any committee?*   YES/NO
If *yes* please give details of *each*, including:
(i) Its title; (ii) Its function; (iii) Its parent body; (iv) Time spent
by respondent; (v) Duration of membership.

4 *Is there a need for voluntary helpers (social work) in our country which
runs Welfare Services?*   YES/NO/DON'T KNOW
If *yes*, do you see this as a desirable permanent feature?   YES/NO
Comments:

The number of schedules completed was sufficient for the purpose
of the survey, and the fall out was a random one as far as social class
was concerned, though the age distribution was about 8% low for
the under-forties, and 7% high for those over sixty. Overall completion was rather disappointing as only 1,072 (for 505 m. and
567 f.) (39%) were completed. These small numbers were due to

TABLE I

Interview Response Rate (percentages)

Failure to contact after repeated calling	=	18·4
Untraced, 'gone away'	=	14·6
Refused to co-operate	=	8·6
No effort made to contact	=	19·1
Questionnaire satisfactorily completed	=	39·3
		100·0

people having been rehoused, to refusal to co-operate and to the
fact that students had insufficient time to make more than two
visits in their efforts to interview. (Table 1)

The completed schedules were processed for sex, age, and social
class[2] by Mr. J. W. McCulloch and the following picture emerged.

[1] I am grateful to Miss E. M. Beermann for permission to use data for
this table from her dissertation *The organisation of data collection* (1968). The
University of Bradford B.A. (Hon.) Degree in Applied Social Studies.

[2] The reference used for social class analysis was *Classification of Organisations*, 1966, H.M.S.O.

Overall involvement   Questions 1 and 2

Some 36% of the sample are involved in giving neighbourly help or in membership of voluntary organizations or both. This figure is reached by adding the totals in Table 2 (32%) and Table 5 (4%). People who only do committee work (i.e., those answering *yes* to question 3 and *no* to questions 1 and 2) have been excluded – there

TABLE 2

All persons who give neighbourly help (percentages)

	Males (n = 505)	Females (n = 567)	Both sexes (n = 1,072)
Neighbourly help only (1)	1·6	1·9	1·8
(1) and vol. social work (2)	0·4	0·2	0·3
(1) and committee work (3)	0·4	0·4	0·4
(1) and acknowledgment of continued need for vol. social work (4)	16·2	27·3	22·1
(1) + (2) + (3)	—	0·2	0·1
(1) + (2) + (4)	1·2	1·1	1·1
(1) + (3) + (4)	4·9	3·0	3·9
(1) + (2) + (3) + (4)	1·6	3·2	2·4
Totals	26·3	37·3	32·1

TABLE 3

All persons who work through voluntary organizations

	Males	Females	Both sexes
Voluntary organizations only (2)	2	1	3
(2) and neighbourly help (1)	2	1	3
(2) and committee work (3)	0	1	1
(2) and acknowledgment of future need for vol. social work (4)	9	11	20
(2) + (1) + (3)	0	1	1
(2) + (1) + (4)	6	6	12
(2) + (3) + (4)	8	8	16
(2) + (1) + (3) + (4)	8	18	26
Totals	35 (7%)	47 (8%)	82 (7·7%)

TABLE 4

Persons who give neighbourly help but do not work through organizations

	Males	Females	Both sexes
Neighbourly help only (1)	8	11	19
(1) and committee work (3)	2	2	4
(1) and acknowledgement of need for vol. social work (4)	82	155	237
(1) + (3) + (4)	25	17	42
Totals	117 (23%)	185 (32%)	302 (28%)

TABLE 5

Persons who work through voluntary organizations but do not give neighbourly help

	Males	Females	Both sexes
Vol. organizations only (2)	2	1	2
(2) and committee work (3)	0	1	1
(2) and acknowledgement of need for vol. social work (4)	9	11	20
(2) + (3) + (4)	8	8	16
Totals	19 (3·7%)	21 (3·7%)	40 (3·7%)

are in fact only seven of them (5 m. and 2 f.) (0·65% of the total), and these may well be members of committees not connected with social work since question 3 asked about all committees.

Who are these 36% who are involved in voluntary social work and what differences are there between those who give neighbourly help and those who belong to voluntary organizations? It will be seen that by far the greater number do not belong to organizations, and it is interesting to consider how far these differ from those who do belong.

The sample contained more women than men, so if they were equally involved there would in any case be more women than men. The numbers, however, show a wider gap. One hundred and fifty-two men and 232 women were involved. One hundred and fifty-two men is 30% of the men in the sample and 14% of the whole sample. Two hundred and thirty-two women is 40% of the women in the sample and 21·6% of the whole sample. Thus while there are three women to every two men in the whole sample who are involved in voluntary work, the ratio is only 4 to 3 if the imbalance of the sexes in the sample is taken into account.

There was no age bias in the distribution of men who answered *yes* to questions 1 and 2. In the case of women, however, there was an age bias in both sets of respondents. In the case of Question 1, more women in the 40–59 age group and fewer over 60 answered *yes*. In the case of Question 2 fewer of the under-forties answered *yes*. These were statistically significant findings. This means that neighbourly help is more often given by women under 60, and that female membership of voluntary organizations is more frequent among the over-forties.

As far as social class is concerned there is a definite distinction between those who give neighbourly help and those who belong to voluntary organizations in the case of both men and women. In the case of neighbourly help (Q. 1) men in social classes I and II responded 'yes' *much more often* than could have been expected by chance, whereas there was no class bias in the case of women. In the case of membership of voluntary organizations (Q. 2) men in social classes I and II again responded 'yes' *more often* than could be expected by chance, while those in classes IV and V responded 'yes' *less often*. Women in social classes I and II were even more likely to answer *yes* to Question 2. This finding was highly statistically significant. Women in classes I and II are therefore the section of the population most likely to belong to voluntary organizations.

TABLE 6

Percentage of respondents who answered 'yes' to questions (1) and (2) comparing the total sample with respondents from social class III

	Yes to Q. 1		Yes to Q. 2	
	Males	*Females*	*Males*	*Females*
Total sample	$(n = 505)$	$(n = 567)$	$(n = 505)$	$(n = 567)$
	26·3	37·2	6·9	8·3
Social class III	$(n = 252)$	$(n = 287)$	$(n = 252)$	$(n = 287)$
	22·6	39·4	6·7	7·0

Class III is represented in overall involvement almost exactly in proportion to its numbers in the sample, but though it is not over-represented, it is most important numerically since it comprises almost exactly half the sample. The figures are shown in Table 6. More detailed figures are given in Table 7, which show that the

TABLE 7

Percentage of total respondents belonging to social class III shown in Tables 2, 3, 4 & 5

	Males (n = 252)	*Females* (n = 287)	*Both sexes* (n = 539)
Table 2	22·6	39·0	31·5
Table 3	7·0	7·0	7·0
Table 4	22·0	36·0	29·0
Table 5	5·5	3·4	4·5

Class III woman is the backbone of voluntary work. Though she plays a less than average part in voluntary organizations, this hardly affects her overall contribution, since membership of such organizations only affects a small proportion of the volume of voluntary work, and she gives a more than average amount of neighbourly help. Class III men, on the other hand, are more often members than might be expected, but give a rather less than average amount of neighbourly help.

Committee membership   Question 3

One hundred and forty-eight respondents, 14% of the sample, answered *yes* to this question, considerably more men (8% of the sample, 17% of the men in the sample) than women (6% of the sample, 11% of the women in the sample). When *non-social work* committee membership is considered this trend is much more marked and more significant statistically. Women, however, play a much greater part than men in voluntary social work committees. (Table 8).

In committees of all kinds there were more men found in the middle age group (40–59) and fewer in the 60+ group than could be explained by chance distribution. This is a statistically significant finding. For women there was no age bias.

The social class of male members of committees is predominantly I or II. There are very few men from classes IV and V. In the case of women, the concentration in classes I and II is even more marked. The findings for both sexes are statistically significant.

How stands class III? As in the case of overall voluntary work it is numerically important, as it contains half of all committee members. Moreover, class III is nearly as well represented as the average (viz., 13% as against 14%, the percentage of members of all classes who are members of committees). Again, the men are very much in the majority. Committee membership as a whole

TABLE 8

Committee Membership

		Males		Females		Both sexes	
		no.	%	no.	%	no.	%
In sample	All social classes	505	100	567	100	1,072	100
	Social class III	252	49·9	287	50·6	539	50·3
Involved in Committee Work	All social classes	85	16·8	63	11·1	148	13·8
	Social class III	[2]43	17·1	+26[1,2]	9·1	+69	12·8
All social classes who are members of non-social work committees		69	81·2	33	52·4	102	68·9
All social classes who are members of social work committees		16	18·8	30	47·6	46	31·1

(i.e., not deducting non-social work committees) is very much a male occupation. This is clearly shown in Table 8.

Are voluntary helpers needed?   Question 4

The people who answered *yes* to this question and *no* to all the others are those who believe in the value of voluntary social help but do not themselves give it. There were no less than 496 (224 m. and 252 f.) in this category, 46% of the total.

There was no great difference here between the sexes, 48% of the men and 44% of the women answering *yes*, and there was no age bias. There was no class bias in the case of women, but men in social classes I and II who believe in social work tend to do it more than those in other classes. These were the men who answered *yes* to questions 1 and 2 as well as to question 4.

Very few people (8 m. and 19 f., or 27 in all) were active in all the ways covered by questions 1, 2, and 3. These people answered *yes* to questions 1, 2, and 3, and to questions 1, 2, 3, and 4. Taking the sexes together because of the small numbers there are extremely few under forty—about a third of the chance expectation; exactly the chance expectation for those over sixty and almost twice the chance expectancy for the middle group (40–59). This is a significant finding. As far as social class is concerned there were

[1] This is a minimal figure since the social class of 4 females was not known.

[2] Percentages of social class III population.

almost none in classes IV and V, about half what might be expected by chance in class III and three times the chance expectancy in classes I and II.

The 'doers' in the sense of those who belong to committees as well as being members of voluntary organizations and undertaking neighbourly tasks are therefore concentrated in the upper social groups and in the middle age range (40–59). But as the findings for those in membership of organizations and even more for those who give neighbourly help show, this is only part of the picture. The other classes, especially the numerically large class III, are of great importance in the overall picture of voluntary work.

Neighbourly help[1]

This is the most usual form of voluntary service since four times as many people are giving neighbourly help as are voluntary workers in the social service agencies. This help is of many different kinds and involves several hours' work every week. It is all regular help, since no information was sought or recorded in the schedules about occasional acts of neighbourliness. Regular help most often given, is, as might be expected, to those who need it most—the old, the sick, the handicapped, the very young and the immigrants. Friendly visiting, doing odd jobs, housework and shopping, baby-sitting and interpreting are some of the tasks most often mentioned, among the thirty different kinds of help which are recorded. The extent of the help given varies from brief visits to undertakings of some magnitude and taking a long time. 'Helping a widow, aged seventy-one, re-decorate her kitchen, put in a sink unit, do her garden, made her a new gate and put railings up' (52-year-old machine fitter): 'taking an elderly neighbour to visit his wife in hospital three times a week' (64-year-old railway goods checker): 'helps two elderly neighbours, baking, shopping, gardening, chatting' (57-year-old housewife): 'minding children, helping mother' (26-year-old housewife): 'shops for a blind lady every day' (60-year-old housewife): 'help to other immigrants with language and other problems' (30-year-old Pakistani fitter). These are some examples picked at random from among comments made by those who answered *yes* to question 1.

Membership of voluntary bodies

Over forty different voluntary organizations were mentioned in the

[1] Help given to members of the respondents' family was excluded. In this respect the Bradford survey differs from that carried out in Portsmouth, to which reference was made in Chapter I, section 1, pp. 17-18.

replies to Question 2, many of them several times. Most often mentioned were those like the Women's Royal Voluntary Service, Townswomen's Guild or Rotary, which are concerned with general social needs, or those like Scouting or Old People's Welfare which are mainly devoted to one category of people. A considerable number of the smaller societies which only rated an occasional mention were connected with work for the aged. This reinforces the finding from the replies to Question 1, that service to the aged is the most widely given type of social help.

The most usual pattern of membership is for respondents to belong to one society only, though there are a few instances of multiple membership.

Membership of committees

The committees mentioned were more numerous than the voluntary bodies. This was not unexpected, since Question 3 sought information about committees of *all* kinds, whereas Question 2 only asked about organizations concerned with voluntary social work. No less than eighty committees were mentioned, and of these less than a quarter are primarily concerned with social work. A number of the others, however, especially those connected with the churches, include social work among their activities.

Committee membership, unlike that of the rank and file of voluntary organizations, is often multiple. People who give personal service through a voluntary organization tend to restrict themselves to one society and devote what time and energy they have to helping one category of person—the sick, the elderly or the young. Committee members, on the other hand, are more likely to spread their efforts, and it is common to find them in membership of several committees. This fits in with the experience of most committee members that they themselves and their colleagues tend to have responsibilities to more than one society. There are several reasons for this. Organizations looking for committee members tend, rightly or wrongly, to look first to those who are already known to be successfully engaged in similar activities, rather than to those who are unknown and untried, while people who are already on one committee are often the type who are ready and anxious to take on something else as well. Another reason is the fact that there is a good deal of cross-representation in the field of social work. For example, members of small associations providing a particular form of help to the elderly or the handicapped are appointed as representatives on a larger Old People's Welfare or Handicapped Persons' Committee. Representatives on such co-ordinating bodies are also sought from societies which have a wider range of activities, such as church groups and women's organizations, and it is usually committee members who are chosen for such posts.

People who serve on the committees of social work organizations are likely to give personal service also. The minority of all committee members who do not do this are almost certainly drawn from the much larger number who belong to non-social work committees. (Table 8). In the case of social work, those who are making policy and taking decisions feel an obligation to assist in other ways as well, and this often means that, because of their multiple membership, they are giving personal service through several organizations. The volume of work they do is therefore large in relation to their numbers, but is, of course, small in comparison to that performed by the much larger number of rank and file members, who usually only belong to a single organization.

Attitude to Voluntary Work

The answers to Question 4 show that the great majority (900 out of 1,072, or 84%) believe in the value of voluntary work. The reasons they give for this view are the obvious ones; these three comments are typical: 'Always people who need things, people don't like to ask organizations but will ask ordinary people. It is a good thing to help people and have people in the community to do things.' (60-year-old wife of painter): 'There are still holes in welfare, not enough information and people too independent. Welfare State too sprawling.' (30-year-old female caretaker): 'Voluntary help necessary for elderly who are not sufficiently helped by Welfare State.' (65-year-old male pin setter): The small proportion who hold the opposite view either make a blunt comment like 'Do nowt for nowt unless its family' (30-year-old male driver): 'Should do more for themselves than have things done for them. Too much reliance on National Assistance, Family Allowance, etc.' (50-year-old f. small grocer); or explain that it isn't necessary either in general, as in this remark, 'No need, all found through Labour Party, Trade Unions' (71-year-old f. baker), or personally, 'Any help required given by mother' (26-year-old f. spinner).

In spite of the fact that the great majority approve of voluntary work, less than half of this number do it themselves. Why is this? Few are as frank as the 55-year-old female mill worker who states, 'Voluntary social work would be a very nice thing for those people in the upper classes who have the time and money to carry out such work', or as disarming as the 48-year-old housewife who confesses, 'reluctant to join committees—quickest way to lose friends ... not much of a mixer'. Some suggest that the young should do more, and others, often with justice, think of themselves as at the receiving end as the following comments from widows in the late seventies and eighties show: 'People aren't so neighbourly as they used to be . . . it's not like it was in the good old days.' 'Neighbours necessary. Big need because on the spot and know whether need help or not. More personal.' In these cases people feel they have not been helped enough, but on the other hand a young electrical engineer who does not himself do voluntary work pays tribute to those who do: 'People should help their neighbours, you find this out when you have young children and find out how valuable good neighbours are.'

But examples such as these do not sufficiently explain why so many people of both sexes and all ages who believe in voluntary work do not themselves do any. It is interesting to speculate why this is so, but speculation is all that is possible since few of the completed schedules provide a clue. The fact is that a great many people think voluntary work should be done by others and not by themselves, but more study of human motivation than was possible on the basis of this survey is needed to provide an explanation.

Yet although so many stand aside from voluntary work, the numbers which are involved are considerable. More than a third of this random sample of the adult population of a large city are in fact performing regular voluntary work either on a neighbourly basis or through an organization. They are making an essential contribution to the well-being of their fellow-citizens, and the gaps in welfare provision, serious though they still are, would be far more serious without them. In fact, the persistence of gaps in a highly organized welfare state points to the need for more, rather than less, voluntary service, and for voluntary service of all kinds. The good neighbour can often provide the best answer to the needs of the individual in his own home, but there are social needs which cannot be successfully met by spontaneous neighbourly help, and where organized voluntary work is necessary. This is so in work outside the home, especially in group work of all kinds and in personal work in hospitals, prisons, clubs and other institutions. It is necessary, too, to supplement the work of the good neighbour where this is inadequate because of changing conditions and the break-up of neighbourhoods.

This survey shows that much is being done, but it shows, too, that this is not enough. Much more could be done if more people played a part. It is up to individuals to seek out those who need help in their own neighbourhoods, and to organizations to discover and try to meet the wider needs of society.

Bibliography

GOVERNMENT PUBLICATIONS

Annual Report of the Ministry of Health for 1967, Cmnd. 3702, H.M.S.O., 1968.

Children and their Primary Schools (Plowden Report), Volumes I and II, H.M.S.O., 1967.

Children in Trouble, Comnd. 3601, H.M.S.O., 1968.

Community Service and the Curriculum, The Schools Council, H.M.S.O., 1968.

Findings and Recommendations Following Enquiries into Allegations Concerning the Care of Elderly Patients in Certain Hospitals, Cmnd. 3687, 1968.

The First Hundred Families, H.M.S.O., 1965.

Health and Welfare. The Development of Community Care, April, 1963, Cmnd. 1973.

Health and Welfare. The Development of Community Care, June, 1966, Cmnd. 3022.

HOBMAN, D., *A Guide to Voluntary Service*, H.M.S.O., 1964.

MALLABY, G., *Staffing of Local Government*, Report of the Committee, Ministry of Housing and Local Government, H.M.S.O., 1967.

MAUD, J., *Management of Local Government*, Volume 1, H.M.S.O., 1967, Ministry of Housing and Local Government.

National Health Service. The Administrative Structure of the Medical and Related Services in England and Wales. H.M.S.O., 1968.

The Needs of New Communities, H.M.S.O., 1967.

The Place of Voluntary Service in After-Care, H.M.S.O., 1967.

Report of the Committee on Local Authority and Allied Personal Social Services (Seebohm Report), Cmnd. 3703, 1968.

Report on the Work of the Probation and After-Care Department, 1962–65, Cmnd. 3107.

Residential Provision for Homeless Discharged Offenders, H.M.S.O., 1966.

Royal Commission on the Law Relating to Mental Illness and Mental Deficiency, 1954–57, Cmnd. 169, H.M.S.O., 1957.

Service by Youth, A Report of a Committee of the Youth Service Development Council, H.M.S.O., 1965.

The Youth Service in England and Wales (Albemarle Report), *Cmnd.*
929, 1960.

BOOKS AND OTHER PUBLICATIONS

ABEL-SMITH, B., and TOWNSEND, P., *The Poor and the Poorest*,
Occasional Papers on Social Administration, No. 17, 1965.

Advising the Citizen, N.C.S.S., 1948. (Revised edition, 1964.)

Allen of Hurtwood, Lady, *Design for Play*, The Housing Centre,
13, Suffolk St., London, W.1., 1962.

ARREGGER, C. E., *Graduate Women at Work*, paperback, Oriel Press,
Ltd., 1966.

Attitudes towards Voluntary Social Work in the City of Portsmouth,
College of Technology, Portsmouth, Cyclo., 1965.

BAYNES, W. M., *Visiting Services for the Elderly*, Cyclo., N.O.P.W.C.,
26, Bedford Square, W.C.1, 1964. (Out of print.) Some of
the findings of this survey are incorporated in *Voluntary Visiting*,
N.C.S.S., 1967.

BEER, S. H., *Modern British Politics*, Faber and Faber, 1965.

BOURDILLON, A. F. C., ed., *Voluntary Social Services*, Methuen, 1945.

BRACEY, H. E. *Neighbours on New Estates and Subdivisions in England
and U.S.A.*, Routledge & Kegan Paul, 1964.

BRAITHWAITE, C., *The Voluntary Citizen*, Methuen, 1938.

BRASNETT, M.E., *The Story of the Citizens' Advice Bureaux*, N.C.S.S.,
1964.

British Red Cross Society, *Annual Report, 1966*. B.R.C.S., 14 and 15,
Grosvenor Crescent, London, S.W.1.

BROCKINGTON, F., and LEMPERT, S. M., *Social Needs of the Over-80's*,
Manchester University Press, 1966.

CAMPBELL, M., *Lend a Hand!*, Museum Press, 1965.

The Caring Community, N.C.S.S., 1968.

CLARKE, R., ed., *Working with Communities*, N.C.S.S.

COLE, D., with UTTING, J. E. G., *The Economic Circumstances of Old
People*, Codicote Press, 1967.

Colour and Immigration in the United Kingdom in 1968, Institute
of Race Relations, 36, Jermyn St., London, S.W.1.

Communities and Social Change, Report of the Fifth British
National Conference on Social Welfare, N.C.S.S., 1964.

Community Organisation, An Introduction, N.C.S.S., 1962.

Community Organisation, Work in Progress, N.C.S.S., 1965.

Community Services for Health and Welfare, Conference Report,
1963, Cyclo., Standing Conference of Cs.S.S., 26, Bedford Sq.,
London, W.C.1. (Out of print.)

Co-operation in the Health and Welfare Services, Cyclo., Yorkshire Council of Social Service, 1968.

CRAFT, M., RAYNOR, J., COHEN, L., *Linking Home and School*, Longmans, 1967.

CURTIS, H., and HOWELL, C., *Part-time Social Work*, N.C.S.S., 1965.

DANIEL, W. W., *Racial Discrimination in England*, Penguin Books, 1968.

DENNEY, A., *Children in Need*, S.C.M. Press, 1966.

DICKSON, M., and A., *Count Us In*, Dennis Dobson, 1967.

Educating our Handicapped Children, C.A.S.E., 1967.

Family Planning in the Sixties, Cyclo., F.P.A., 27, Mortimer St., London, W.1, 1963.

GALES, K., and WRIGHT, R. C., *A Survey of Manpower Demand Forecast for the Social Services*, N.C.S.S., 1966.

GANS, H. J., *The Levittowners*, Penguin, 1967.

GAVRON, H., *The Captive Wife*, Routledge & Kegan Paul, 1966. (Penguin, 1968.)

GILLETTE, A., *One Million Volunteers*, Penguin, 1968.

Girls in Two Cities, National Association of Youth Clubs, 1967.

GOETSCHIUS, G. W., and TASH, M. J., *Working with Unattached Youth*, Routledge & Kegan Paul, 1967.

GRAVES, C., *Women in Green*, Heinemann, 1948. (Out of print.)

GRIFFITH, J. A. G., *Central Departments and Local Authorities*, Allen & Unwin, 1966.

HALL, M. P., *The Social Services of Modern England*, Routledge & Kegan Paul, 1952.

HARE, E. H., and SHAW, G. K., *Mental Health on a New Housing Estate*, O.U.P., 1965.

HARRIS, A., *Outlines of a Survey on the Meals on Wheels Service*, N.C.C.O.P., Nuffield Lodge, Regent's Park, London, N.W.1, 1960.

HEIMLER, E., *Mental Illness and Social Work*, Penguin, 1967.

Help for the Handicapped, An Enquiry into the Opportunities of the Voluntary Services, N.C.S.S., 1958.

Human Rights, A Study Guide for the International Year for Human Rights, Heinemann Educational Books, 1968.

HUNT, P., ed., *Stigma*, Geoffrey Chapman, 1966.

HURST, A., *The Cambridge House Literacy Scheme*, 131, Camberwell Rd., London, S.E.5, 1967.

JACKSON, B., *Working Class Community*, Routledge & Kegan Paul, 1968.

JEFFREYS, M., *An Anatomy of Social Welfare Services*, Michael Joseph, 1965.

JENNINGS, H., *Societies in the Making*, Routledge & Kegan Paul, 1962.

JEPHCOTT, P., *Time of One's Own*, Oliver & Boyd, 1967.

KAHN, A. J., *et al.*, *Neighbourhood Information Centres*, New York, Columbia University School of Social Work, 1966.

KAMER, J., *Voluntary Workers in York*, Cyclo., York Community Council, 1965.

KELLEY, J., *When the Gates Shut*, Longmans, 1967.

KLEIN, J., *Samples from English Cultures: 1. Three Preliminary Studies and Aspects of Adult Life in England; 2. Child-Rearing Practices* and Index, Routledge & Kegan Paul, 1965.

KUENSTLER, P., ed., *Community Organisation in Great Britain*, Faber and Faber, 1961.

LEAPER, R. A. B., *Community Work*, N.C.S.S., 1968.

LOMAS, G. M., ed., *Social Aspects of Urban Development*, U.K. Report for the Thirteenth International Conference of Social Work, 1966, N.C.S.S.

Loneliness, N.C.S.S., 1957, revised 1964.

MANN, P. H., *An Approach to Urban Sociology*, Routledge & Kegan Paul, 1965.

MARSH, D. C., *The Changing Social Structure of England and Wales*, Revised edition, Routledge & Kegan Paul, 1965.

MARSH, D. C., ed., *The Social Sciences, An Outline for the Intending Student*, Routledge & Kegan Paul, 1967.

MARSHALL, T. H., *Social Policy*, Hutchinson University Library, 1965.

MORRIS, M., assisted by G. R. DALBY, *Social Enterprise*, N.C.S.S., 1962.

MORRIS, T. and P., *Pentonville*, Routledge & Kegan Paul, 1963.

MORSE, M., *The Unattached*, Penguin, 1965.

MUSGROVE, F., *Youth and Social Order*, Routledge & Kegan Paul, 1964.

Nacoss Occasional Papers No. 1, A Study of Halifax, by Mary Morris, N.C.S.S., 1965.

National Association for the Care and Resettlement of Offenders, *Manual and Directory*, N.A.C.R.O., 125, Kennington Park Rd., London, S.E.11. Subscription to Directory Service for 1968.

NICHOLSON, J., *Mother and Baby Homes*, Allen & Unwin, 1968.

NICHOLSON, J. H., *New Communities in Britain*, N.C.S.S., 1961.

Notice to Quit, from *Shelter*, 86, Strand, London, W.C.2, 1968.

OAKLEY, R., *New Backgrounds. The Immigrant Child at Home and at School*, O.U.P., 1968.

Old Age, a Register of Social Research, N.C.C.O.P., Nuffield Lodge, Regent's Park, London, N.W.1, 1960 – supplement 1964.

OWEN, D., *English Philanthropy*, O.U.P., 1965.

PARKER, J., *Local Health and Welfare Services*, Allen & Unwin, 1965.

PHILLIPS, M., *Small Social Groups in England*, Methuen, 1965.

PHILP, A. E., *Family Failure*, Faber and Faber, 1963.

REEVES, M., *Eighteen Plus*, Faber and Faber, 1965.

Report of an investigation into the dietary of elderly women living alone, King Edward's Hospital Fund for London, 1965.

Research into the selection, placing and training of voluntary social workers, Cyclo., Camden, formerly Hampstead, C.S.S., 25, Euston Rd., N.W.1, 1966.

ROBB, B., *Sans Everything; A case to answer presented by Barbara Robb on behalf of Aegis*, Nelson, 1967.

ROBERTS, N., *Mental Health and Mental Illness*, Routledge & Kegan Paul, 1967.

ROCHA, J., *Organizers of Voluntary Service in Hospitals*, King Edward's Hospital Fund for London, 1968.

RODGERS, B. N., and DIXON, J., *Portrait of Social Work*, O.U.P., 1960.

ROOFF, M., *Voluntary Societies and Social Policy*, Routledge & Kegan Paul, 1952.

ROSE, G., *Schools for Young Offenders*, Tavistock Publications, 1967.

ROSE, G., *The Struggle for Penal Reform*, Stevens & Sons, London, 1961.

ROSSER, C., and HARRIES, C., *The Family and Social Change*, Routledge & Kegan Paul, 1965.

SANSBURY, K., LATHAM, R., and WEBB, P., *Agenda for the Churches, A Report on the People Next Door Programme*, S.C.M. Press, 1968.

SEGAL, S., *No Child is Ineducable*, Pergamon Press, 1968.

Some Opportunities for Voluntary Social Service in London, London C.S.S., 4, Gower St., W.C.1, 1967.

Stress – report of a Working Party set up by the N.S.M.H.C., 5, Bulstrode St., London, W.1, 1967.

Survey of Services for the Elderly provided by Voluntary Organisations, N.O.P.W.C., 1965.

TITMUSS, R. M., *Essays on the Welfare State*, Allen & Unwin, 2nd impr., paperback, 1963.

TOWNSEND, P., and WEDDERBURN, D., *The Aged in the Welfare State*, 1963. Occasional Papers on Social Administration No. 14, Bell and Son, 1965.

TUNSTALL, J., *Old and Alone*, Routledge & Kegan Paul, 1966.

Two to Five in High Flats, The Housing Centre, 13, Suffolk St., S.W.1, 1961.

VARAH, C., *The Samaritans*, Constable, 1965.

VAUGHAN, P., *Work to be Done*, N.A.M.H., 39, Queen Anne St., London, W.1, 1967.

Voluntary Service and the State, A Study of the Needs of the Hospital Service, Geo. Barber & Sons, for N.C.S.S. and King Edward's Hospital Fund, 1952.

Voluntary Social Services, Handbook and Directory, new edition, N.C.S.S., 1966.

WAINWRIGHT, D., *The Young Volunteers*, Ministry of Overseas Development, Eland House, Stag Place, London, S.W.1, 1965.

WALLIS, J. H., *Someone to Turn To*, Routledge & Kegan Paul, 1961.

WALLIS, J. H., *Marriage Guidance*, Routledge & Kegan Paul, 1968.

Welfare State and Welfare Society, Report of the Sixth British National Conference on Social Welfare, N.C.S.S., 1967.

WHITE, E. E., *Clubs for the Elderly*, N.C.S.S., 1964.

WHYTE, W. H., *Organisation Man*, Penguin, (first published 1956).

WILLIAMS, G. M., *A Preliminary Inquiry into Recruitment and Training by Voluntary Associations in the Social Service Field*, Cyclo., N.C.S.S., 1962. (Out of print).

WILLMOTT, PETER, *Adolescent Boys of East London*, Routledge & Kegan Paul, 1966.

WILLMOTT, PETER, *The Evolution of a Community*, Routledge & Kegan Paul, 1963.

WILLMOTT, PETER, and YOUNG, M., *Family and Class in a London Suburb*, Routledge & Kegan Paul, 1960.

WILLMOTT, PHYLLIS, *Consumer's Guide to the British Social Services*, Penguin, 1967.

Women's Royal Voluntary Service Bulletin, W.R.V.S., 17, Old Park Lane, London, W.1, June, 1968.

WOOTTON, G., *The Politics of Influence*, Routledge & Kegan Paul, 1963.

WYNN, M., *Fatherless Families*, Michael Joseph, 1964.

YOUNG, M., and WILLMOTT, PETER, *Family and Kinship in East London*, Routledge & Kegan Paul, 1957.

Young People To-day, N.C.S.S., 1966.

The reader is also referred to:
    New Society (weekly).
    Social Service Quarterly (N.C.S.S.).
    Annual Reports of Voluntary Bodies, both local and national.

Index

The International Library of

Sociology

and Social Reconstruction

Edited by W. J. H. SPROTT
Founded by KARL MANNHEIM

ROUTLEDGE & KEGAN PAUL
BROADWAY HOUSE, CARTER LANE, LONDON, E.C.4

CONTENTS

PRINTED IN GREAT BRITAIN BY HEADLEY BROTHERS LTD
109 KINGSWAY LONDON W C 2 AND ASHFORD KENT

GENERAL SOCIOLOGY

Brown, Robert. Explanation in Social Science. *208 pp. 1963. (2nd Impression 1964.) 25s.*

Gibson, Quentin. The Logic of Social Enquiry. *240 pp. 1960. (3rd Impression 1968.) 24s.*

Homans, George C. Sentiments and Activities: Essays in Social Science. *336 pp. 1962. 32s.*

Isajiw, Wsevelod W. Causation and Functionalism in Sociology. *165 pp. 1968. 25s.*

Johnson, Harry M. Sociology: a Systematic Introduction. *Foreword by Robert K. Merton. 710 pp. 1961. (5th Impression 1968.) 42s.*

Mannheim, Karl. Essays on Sociology and Social Psychology. *Edited by Paul Keckskemeti. With Editorial Note by Adolph Lowe. 344 pp. 1953. (2nd Impression 1966.) 32s.*

  Systematic Sociology: An Introduction to the Study of Society. *Edited by J. S. Erös and Professor W. A. C. Stewart. 220 pp. 1957. (3rd Impression 1967.) 24s.*

Martindale, Don. The Nature and Types of Sociological Theory. *292 pp. 1961. (3rd Impression 1967.) 35s.*

Maus, Heinz. A Short History of Sociology. *234 pp. 1962. (2nd Impression 1965.) 28s.*

Myrdal, Gunnar. Value in Social Theory: A Collection of Essays on Methodology. *Edited by Paul Streeten. 332 pp. 1958. (3rd Impression 1968.) 35s.*

Ogburn, William F., and **Nimkoff, Meyer F.** A Handbook of Sociology. *Preface by Karl Mannheim. 656 pp. 46 figures. 35 tables. 5th edition (revised) 1964. 45s.*

Parsons, Talcott, and **Smelser, Neil J.** Economy and Society: A Study in the Integration of Economic and Social Theory. *362 pp. 1956. (4th Impression 1967.) 35s.*

Rex, John. Key Problems of Sociological Theory. *220 pp. 1961. (4th Impression 1968.) 25s.*

Stark, Werner. The Fundamental Forms of Social Thought. *280 pp. 1962. 32s.*

FOREIGN CLASSICS OF SOCIOLOGY

Durkheim, Emile. Suicide. A Study in Sociology. *Edited and with an Introduction by George Simpson. 404 pp. 1952. (4th Impression 1968.) 35s.*

  Professional Ethics and Civic Morals. *Translated by Cornelia Brookfield. 288 pp. 1957. 30s.*

Gerth, H. H., and **Mills, C. Wright.** From Max Weber: Essays in Sociology. *502 pp. 1948. (6th Impression 1967.) 35s.*

Tönnies, Ferdinand. Community and Association. *(Gemeinschaft und Gesellschaft.) Translated and Supplemented by Charles P. Loomis. Foreword by Pitirim A. Sorokin. 334 pp. 1955. 28s.*

SOCIAL STRUCTURE

Andreski, Stanislav. Military Organization and Society. *Foreword by Professor A. R. Radcliffe-Brown. 226 pp. 1 folder. 1954. Revised Edition 1968. 35s.*

Cole, G. D. H. Studies in Class Structure. *220 pp. 1955. (3rd Impression 1964.) 21s. Paper 10s. 6d.*

Coontz, Sydney H. Population Theories and the Economic Interpretation. *202 pp. 1957. (3rd Impression 1968.) 28s.*

Coser, Lewis. The Functions of Social Conflict. *204 pp. 1956. (3rd Impression 1968.) 25s.*

Dickie-Clark, H. F. Marginal Situation: A Sociological Study of a Coloured Group. *240 pp. 11 tables. 1966. 40s.*

Glass, D. V. (Ed.). Social Mobility in Britain. *Contributions by J. Berent, T. Bottomore, R. C. Chambers, J. Floud, D. V. Glass, J. R. Hall, H. T. Himmelweit, R. K. Kelsall, F. M. Martin, C. A. Moser, R. Mukherjee, and W. Ziegel. 420 pp. 1954. (4th Impression 1967.) 45s.*

Jones, Garth N. Planned Organizational Change: An Exploratory Study Using an Empirical Approach. *About 268 pp. 1969. 40s.*

Kelsall, R. K. Higher Civil Servants in Britain: From 1870 to the Present Day. *268 pp. 31 tables. 1955. (2nd Impression 1966.) 25s.*

König, René. The Community. *232 pp. Illustrated. 1968. 35s.*

Lawton, Denis. Social Class, Language and Education. *192 pp. 1968. (2nd Impression 1968.) 25s.*

McLeish, John. The Theory of Social Change: Four Views Considered. *About 128 pp. 1969. 21s.*

Marsh, David C. The Changing Social Structure in England and Wales, 1871-1961. *1958. 272 pp. 2nd edition (revised) 1966. (2nd Impression 1967.) 35s.*

Mouzelis, Nicos. Organization and Bureaucracy. An Analysis of Modern Theories. *240 pp. 1967. (2nd Impression 1968.) 28s.*

Ossowski, Stanislaw. Class Structure in the Social Consciousness. *210 pp. 1963. (2nd Impression 1967.) 25s.*

SOCIOLOGY AND POLITICS

Barbu, Zevedei. Democracy and Dictatorship: Their Psychology and Patterns of Life. *300 pp. 1956. 28s.*

Crick, Bernard. The American Science of Politics: Its Origins and Conditions. *284 pp. 1959. 32s.*

Hertz, Frederick. Nationality in History and Politics: A Psychology and Sociology of National Sentiment and Nationalism. *432 pp. 1944. (5th Impression 1966.) 42s.*

Kornhauser, William. The Politics of Mass Society. *272 pp. 20 tables. 1960. (3rd Impression 1968.) 28s.*

Laidler, Harry W. History of Socialism. Social-Economic Movements: An Historical and Comparative Survey of Socialism, Communism, Co-operation, Utopianism; and other Systems of Reform and Reconstruction. *New edition. 992 pp. 1968. 90s.*

Lasswell, Harold D. Analysis of Political Behaviour. An Empirical Approach. *324 pp. 1947. (4th Impression 1966.) 35s.*

Mannheim, Karl. Freedom, Power and Democratic Planning. *Edited by Hans Gerth and Ernest K. Bramstedt. 424 pp. 1951. (3rd Impression 1968.) 42s.*

Mansur, Fatma. Process of Independence. *Foreword by A. H. Hanson. 208 pp. 1962. 25s.*

Martin, David A. Pacificism: an Historical and Sociological Study. *262 pp. 1965. 30s.*

Myrdal, Gunnar. The Political Element in the Development of Economic Theory. *Translated from the German by Paul Streeten. 282 pp. 1953. (4th Impression 1965.) 25s.*

Polanyi, Michael. F.R.S. The Logic of Liberty: Reflections and Rejoinders. *228 pp. 1951. 18s.*

Verney, Douglas V. The Analysis of Political Systems. *264 pp. 1959. (3rd Impression 1966.) 28s.*

Wootton, Graham. The Politics of Influence: British Ex-Servicemen, Cabinet Decisions and Cultural Changes, 1917 to 1957. *316 pp. 1963. 30s.*
Workers, Unions and the State. *188 pp. 1966. (2nd Impression 1967.) 25s.*

FOREIGN AFFAIRS: THEIR SOCIAL, POLITICAL AND ECONOMIC FOUNDATIONS

Baer, Gabriel. Population and Society in the Arab East. *Translated by Hanna Szöke. 288 pp. 10 maps. 1964. 40s.*

Bonné, Alfred. State and Economics in the Middle East: A Society in Transition. *482 pp. 2nd (revised) edition 1955. (2nd Impression 1960.) 40s.*
Studies in Economic Development: with special reference to Conditions in the Under-developed Areas of Western Asia and India. *322 pp. 84 tables. 2nd edition 1960. 32s.*

Mayer, J. P. Political Thought in France from the Revolution to the Fifth Republic. *164 pp. 3rd edition (revised) 1961. 16s.*

CRIMINOLOGY

Ancel, Marc. Social Defence: A Modern Approach to Criminal Problems. *Foreword by Leon Radzinowicz. 240 pp. 1965. 32s.*

Cloward, Richard A., and Ohlin, Lloyd E. Delinquency and Opportunity: A Theory of Delinquent Gangs. *248 pp. 1961. 25s.*

Downes, David M. The Delinquent Solution. A Study in Subcultural Theory. *296 pp. 1966. 42s.*

Dunlop, A. B., and **McCabe, S.** Young Men in Detention Centres. *192 pp. 1965. 28s.*

Friedländer, Kate. The Psycho-Analytical Approach to Juvenile Delinquency: Theory, Case Studies, Treatment. *320 pp. 1947. (6th Impression 1967). 40s.*

Glueck, Sheldon and **Eleanor.** Family Environment and Delinquency. *With the statistical assistance of Rose W. Kneznek. 340 pp.* **1962.** *(2nd Impression 1966.) 40s.*

Mannheim, Hermann. Comparative Criminology: a Text Book. *Two volumes. 442 pp. and 380 pp. 1965. (2nd Impression with corrections 1966.) 42s. a volume.*

Morris, Terence. The Criminal Area: A Study in Social Ecology. *Foreword by Hermann Mannheim. 232 pp. 25 tables. 4 maps. 1957. (2nd Impression 1966.) 28s.*

Morris, Terence and **Pauline,** assisted by **Barbara Barer.** Pentonville: A Sociological Study of an English Prison. *416 pp. 16 plates. 1963. 50s.*

Spencer, John C. Crime and the Services. *Foreword by Hermann Mannheim. 336 pp. 1954. 28s.*

Trasler, Gordon. The Explanation of Criminality. *144 pp. 1962. (2nd Impression 1967.) 20s.*

SOCIAL PSYCHOLOGY

Barbu, Zevedei. Problems of Historical Psychology. *248 pp. 1960. 25s.*

Blackburn, Julian. Psychology and the Social Pattern. *184 pp. 1945. (7th Impression 1964.) 16s.*

Fleming, C. M. Adolescence: Its Social Psychology: With an Introduction to recent findings from the fields of Anthropology, Physiology, Medicine, Psychometrics and Sociometry. *288 pp. 2nd edition (revised) 1963. (3rd Impression 1967.) 25s. Paper 12s. 6d.*
The Social Psychology of Education: An Introduction and Guide to Its Study. *136 pp. 2nd edition (revised) 1959. (4th Impression 1967.) 14s. Paper 7s. 6d.*

Homans, George C. The Human Group. *Foreword by Bernard DeVoto. Introduction by Robert K. Merton. 526 pp. 1951. (7th Impression 1968.) 35s.*
Social Behaviour: its Elementary Forms. *416 pp. 1961. (3rd Impression 1968.) 35s.*

Klein, Josephine. The Study of Groups. *226 pp. 31 figures. 5 tables. 1956. (5th Impression 1967.) 21s. Paper 9s. 6d.*

Linton, Ralph. The Cultural Background of Personality. *132 pp. 1947. (7th Impression 1968.) 18s.*

Mayo, Elton. The Social Problems of an Industrial Civilization. With an appendix on the Political Problem. *180 pp. 1949. (5th Impression 1966.) 25s.*

Ottaway, A. K. C. Learning Through Group Experience. *176 pp. 1966. (2nd Impression 1968.) 25s.*

Ridder, J. C. de. The Personality of the Urban African in South Africa. A Thematic Apperception Test Study. *196 pp. 12 plates. 1961. 25s.*

Rose, Arnold M. (Ed.). Human Behaviour and Social Processes: an Inter-actionist Approach. *Contributions by Arnold M. Rose, Ralph H. Turner, Anselm Strauss, Everett C. Hughes, E. Franklin Frazier, Howard S. Becker, et al. 696 pp. 1962. (2nd Impression 1968.) 70s.*

Smelser, Neil J. Theory of Collective Behaviour. *448 pp. 1962. (2nd Impression 1967.) 45s.*

Stephenson, Geoffrey M. The Development of Conscience. *128 pp. 1966. 25s.*

Young, Kimball. Handbook of Social Psychology. *658 pp. 16 figures. 10 tables. 2nd edition (revised) 1957. (3rd Impression 1963.) 40s.*

SOCIOLOGY OF THE FAMILY

Banks, J. A. Prosperity and Parenthood: A study of Family Planning among The Victorian Middle Classes. *262 pp. 1954. (3rd Impression 1968.) 28s.*

Bell, Colin R. Middle Class Families: Social and Geographical Mobility. *224 pp. 1969. 35s.*

Burton, Lindy. Vulnerable Children. *272 pp. 1968. 35s.*

Gavron, Hannah. The Captive Wife: Conflicts of Housebound Mothers. *190 pp. 1966. (2nd Impression 1966.) 25s.*

Klein, Josephine. Samples from English Cultures. *1965. (2nd Impression 1967.)*
  1. Three Preliminary Studies and Aspects of Adult Life in England. *447 pp. 50s.*
  2. Child-Rearing Practices and Index. *247 pp. 35s.*

Klein, Viola. Britain's Married Women Workers. *180 pp. 1965. (2nd Impression 1968.) 28s.*

McWhinnie, Alexina M. Adopted Children. How They Grow Up. *304 pp. 1967. (2nd Impression 1968.) 42s.*

Myrdal, Alva and **Klein, Viola.** Women's Two Roles: Home and Work. *238 pp. 27 tables. 1956. Revised Edition 1967. 30s. Paper 15s.*

Parsons, Talcott and **Bales, Robert F.** Family: Socialization and Interaction Process. *In collaboration with James Olds, Morris Zelditch and Philip E. Slater. 456 pp. 50 figures and tables. 1956. (3rd Impression 1968.) 45s.*

Schücking, L. L. The Puritan Family. *Translated from the German by Brian Battershaw. 212 pp. 1969. About 42s.*

THE SOCIAL SERVICES

Forder, R. A. (Ed.). Penelope Hall's Social Services of Modern England. *288 pp. 1969. 35s.*

George, Victor. Social Security: Beveridge and After. *258 pp. 1968. 35s.*

Goetschius, George W. Working with Community Groups. *256 pp. 1969. 35s.*

Goetschius, George W. and **Tash, Joan.** Working with Unattached Youth. *416 pp. 1967. (2nd Impression 1968.) 40s.*

Hall, M. P., and **Howes, I. V.** The Church in Social Work. A Study of Moral Welfare Work undertaken by the Church of England. *320 pp. 1965. 35s.*

Heywood, Jean S. Children in Care: the Development of the Service for the Deprived Child. *264 pp. 2nd edition (revised) 1965. (2nd Impression 1966.) 32s.*

An Introduction to Teaching Casework Skills. *190 pp. 1964. 28s.*

Jones, Kathleen. Lunacy, Law and Conscience, 1744-1845: the Social History of the Care of the Insane. *268 pp. 1955. 25s.*

Mental Health and Social Policy, 1845-1959. *264 pp. 1960. (2nd Impression 1967.) 32s.*

Jones, Kathleen and **Sidebotham, Roy.** Mental Hospitals at Work. *220 pp. 1962. 30s.*

Kastell, Jean. Casework in Child Care. *Foreword by M. Brooke Willis. 320 pp. 1962. 35s.*

Morris, Pauline. Put Away: A Sociological Study of Institutions for the Mentally Retarded. *Approx. 288 pp. 1969. About 50s.*

Nokes, P. L. The Professional Task in Welfare Practice. *152 pp. 1967. 28s.*

Rooff, Madeline. Voluntary Societies and Social Policy. *350 pp. 15 tables. 1957. 35s.*

Timms, Noel. Psychiatric Social Work in Great Britain (1939-1962). *280 pp. 1964. 32s.*

Social Casework: Principles and Practice. *256 pp. 1964. (2nd Impression 1966.) 25s. Paper 15s.*

Trasler, Gordon. In Place of Parents: A Study in Foster Care. *272 pp. 1960. (2nd Impression 1966.) 30s.*

Young, A. F., and **Ashton, E. T.** British Social Work in the Nineteenth Century. *288 pp. 1956. (2nd Impression 1963.) 28s.*

Young, A. F. Social Services in British Industry. *272 pp. 1968. 40s.*

SOCIOLOGY OF EDUCATION

Banks, Olive. Parity and Prestige in English Secondary Education: a Study in Educational Sociology. *272 pp. 1955. (2nd Impression 1963.) 32s.*

Bentwich, Joseph. Education in Israel. *224 pp. 8 pp. plates. 1965. 24s.*

Blyth, W. A. L. English Primary Education. A Sociological Description. *1965. Revised edition 1967.*

1. Schools. *232 pp. 30s. Paper 12s. 6d.*
2. Background. *168 pp. 25s. Paper 10s. 6d.*

Collier, K. G. The Social Purposes of Education: Personal and Social Values in Education. *268 pp. 1959. (3rd Impression 1965.) 21s.*

Dale, R. R., and **Griffith, S.** Down Stream: Failure in the Grammar School. *108 pp. 1965. 20s.*

Dore, R. P. Education in Tokugawa Japan. *356 pp. 9 pp. plates. 1965. 35s.*

Edmonds, E. L. The School Inspector. *Foreword by Sir William Alexander. 214 pp. 1962. 28s.*

Evans, K. M. Sociometry and Education. *158 pp. 1962. (2nd Impression 1966.) 18s.*

Foster, P. J. Education and Social Change in Ghana. *336 pp. 3 maps. 1965. (2nd Impression 1967.) 36s.*

Fraser, W. R. Education and Society in Modern France. *150 pp. 1963. (2nd Impression 1968.) 25s.*

Hans, Nicholas. New Trends in Education in the Eighteenth Century. *278 pp. 19 tables. 1951. (2nd Impression 1966.) 30s.*
   Comparative Education: A Study of Educational Factors and Traditions. *360 pp. 3rd (revised) edition 1958. (4th Impression 1967.) 25s. Paper 12s. 6d.*

Hargreaves, David. Social Relations in a Secondary School. *240 pp. 1967. (2nd Impression 1968.) 32s.*

Holmes, Brian. Problems in Education. A Comparative Approach. *336 pp. 1965. (2nd Impression 1967.) 32s.*

Mannheim, Karl and **Stewart, W. A. C.** An Introduction to the Sociology of Education. *206 pp. 1962. (2nd Impression 1965.) 21s.*

Morris, Raymond N. The Sixth Form and College Entrance. *231 pp. 1969. 40s.*

Musgrove, F. Youth and the Social Order. *176 pp. 1964. (2nd Impression 1968.) 25s. Paper 12s.*

Ortega y Gasset, José. Mission of the University. *Translated with an Introduction by Howard Lee Nostrand. 86 pp. 1946. (3rd Impression 1963.) 15s.*

Ottaway, A. K. C. Education and Society: An Introduction to the Sociology of Education. *With an Introduction by W. O. Lester Smith. 212 pp. Second edition (revised). 1962. (5th Impression 1968.) 18s. Paper 10s. 6d.*

Peers, Robert. Adult Education: A Comparative Study. *398 pp. 2nd edition 1959. (2nd Impression 1966.) 42s.*

Pritchard, D. G. Education and the Handicapped: 1760 to 1960. *258 pp. 1963. (2nd Impression 1966.) 35s.*

Richardson, Helen. Adolescent Girls in Approved Schools. *Approx. 360 pp. 1969. About 42s.*

Simon, Brian and **Joan** (Eds.). Educational Psychology in the U.S.S.R. *Introduction by Brian and Joan Simon. Translation by Joan Simon. Papers by D. N. Bogoiavlenski and N. A. Menchinskaia, D. B. Elkonin, E. A. Fleshner, Z. I. Kalmykova, G. S. Kostiuk, V. A. Krutetski, A. N. Leontiev, A. R. Luria, E. A. Milerian, R. G. Natadze, B. M. Teplov, L. S. Vygotski, L. V. Zankov. 296 pp. 1963. 40s.*

SOCIOLOGY OF CULTURE

Eppel, E. M., and M. Adolescents and Morality: A Study of some Moral Values and Dilemmas of Working Adolescents in the Context of a changing Climate of Opinion. *Foreword by W. J. H. Sprott. 268 pp. 39 tables. 1966. 30s.*

Fromm, Erich. The Fear of Freedom. *286 pp. 1942. (8th Impression 1960.) 25s. Paper 10s.*
The Sane Society. *400 pp. 1956. (4th Impression 1968.) 28s. Paper 14s.*

Mannheim, Karl. Diagnosis of Our Time: Wartime Essays of a Sociologist. *208 pp. 1943. (8th Impression 1966.) 21s.*
Essays on the Sociology of Culture. *Edited by Ernst Mannheim in co-operation with Paul Kecskemeti. Editorial Note by Adolph Lowe. 280 pp. 1956. (3rd Impression 1967.) 28s.*

Weber, Alfred. Farewell to European History: or The Conquest of Nihilism. *Translated from the German by R. F. C. Hull. 224 pp. 1947. 18s.*

SOCIOLOGY OF RELIGION

Argyle, Michael. Religious Behaviour. *224 pp. 8 figures. 41 tables. 1958. (4th Impression 1968.) 25s.*

Nelson, G. K. Spiritualism and Society. *313 pp. 1969. 42s.*

Stark, Werner. The Sociology of Religion. A Study of Christendom.
Volume I. Established Religion. *248 pp. 1966. 35s.*
Volume II. Sectarian Religion. *368 pp. 1967. 40s.*
Volume III. The Universal Church. *464 pp. 1967. 45s.*

Watt, W. Montgomery. Islam and the Integration of Society. *320 pp. 1961. (3rd Impression 1966.) 35s.*

SOCIOLOGY OF ART AND LITERATURE

Beljame, Alexandre. Men of Letters and the English Public in the Eighteenth Century: 1660-1744, Dryden, Addison, Pope. *Edited with an Introduction and Notes by Bonamy Dobrée. Translated by E. O. Lorimer. 532 pp. 1948. 32s.*

Misch, Georg. A History of Autobiography in Antiquity. *Translated by E. W. Dickes. 2 Volumes. Vol. 1, 364 pp., Vol. 2, 372 pp. 1950. 45s. the set.*

Schücking, L. L. The Sociology of Literary Taste. *112 pp. 2nd (revised) edition 1966. 18s.*

Silbermann, Alphons. The Sociology of Music. *Translated from the German by Corbet Stewart. 222 pp. 1963. 32s.*

SOCIOLOGY OF KNOWLEDGE

Mannheim, Karl. Essays on the Sociology of Knowledge. *Edited by Paul Kecskemeti. Editorial note by Adolph Lowe. 352 pp. 1952. (4th Impression 1967.) 35s.*

Stark, W. America: Ideal and Reality. The United States of 1776 in Contemporary Philosophy. *136 pp. 1947. 12s.*

The Sociology of Knowledge: An Essay in Aid of a Deeper Understanding of the History of Ideas. *384 pp. 1958. (3rd Impression 1967.) 36s.*

Montesquieu: Pioneer of the Sociology of Knowledge. *244 pp. 1960. 25s.*

URBAN SOCIOLOGY

Anderson, Nels. The Urban Community: A World Perspective. *532 pp. 1960. 35s.*

Ashworth, William. The Genesis of Modern British Town Planning: A Study in Economic and Social History of the Nineteenth and Twentieth Centuries. *288 pp. 1954. (3rd Impression 1968.) 32s.*

Bracey, Howard. Neighbours: On New Estates and Subdivisions in England and U.S.A. *220 pp. 1964. 28s.*

Cullingworth, J. B. Housing Needs and Planning Policy: A Restatement of the Problems of Housing Need and "Overspill" in England and Wales. *232 pp. 44 tables. 8 maps. 1960. (2nd Impression 1966.) 28s.*

Dickinson, Robert E. City and Region: A Geographical Interpretation. *608 pp. 125 figures. 1964. (5th Impression 1967.) 60s.*

The West European City: A Geographical Interpretation. *600 pp. 129 maps. 29 plates. 2nd edition 1962. (3rd Impression 1968.) 55s.*

The City Region in Western Europe. *320 pp. Maps. 1967. 30s. Paper 14s.*

Jackson, Brian. Working Class Community: Some General Notions raised by a Series of Studies in Northern England. *192 pp. 1968. (2nd Impression 1968.) 25s.*

Jennings, Hilda. Societies in the Making: a Study of Development and Redevelopment within a County Borough. *Foreword by D. A. Clark. 286 pp. 1962. (2nd Impression 1967.) 32s.*

Kerr, Madeline. The People of Ship Street. *240 pp. 1958. 28s.*

Mann, P. H. An Approach to Urban Sociology. *240 pp. 1965. (2nd Impression 1968.) 30s.*

Morris, R. N., and **Mogey, J.** The Sociology of Housing. Studies at Berinsfield. *232 pp. 4 pp. plates. 1965. 42s.*

Rosser, C., and **Harris,** C. The Family and Social Change. A Study of Family and Kinship in a South Wales Town. *352 pp. 8 maps. 1965. (2nd Impression 1968.) 45s.*

RURAL SOCIOLOGY

Chambers, R. J. H. Settlement Schemes in Africa: A Selective Study. *Approx. 268 pp. 1969. About 50s.*

Haswell, M. R. The Economics of Development in Village India. *120 pp. 1967. 21s.*

Littlejohn, James. Westrigg: the Sociology of a Cheviot Parish. *172 pp. 5 figures. 1963. 25s.*

Williams, W. M. The Country Craftsman: A Study of Some Rural Crafts and the Rural Industries Organization in England. *248 pp. 9 figures. 1958. 25s. (Dartington Hall Studies in Rural Sociology.)*

The Sociology of an English Village: Gosforth. *272 pp. 12 figures. 13 tables. 1956. (3rd Impression 1964.) 25s.*

SOCIOLOGY OF MIGRATION

Humphreys, Alexander J. New Dubliners: Urbanization and the Irish Family. *Foreword by George C. Homans. 304 pp. 1966. 40s.*

SOCIOLOGY OF INDUSTRY AND DISTRIBUTION

Anderson, Nels. Work and Leisure. *280 pp. 1961. 28s.*

Blau, Peter M., and **Scott, W. Richard.** Formal Organizations: a Comparative approach. *Introduction and Additional Bibliography by J. H. Smith. 326 pp. 1963. (4th Impression 1969.) 35s. Paper 15s.*

Eldridge, J. E. T. Industrial Disputes. Essays in the Sociology of Industrial Relations. *288 pp. 1968. 40s.*

Hollowell, Peter G. The Lorry Driver. *272 pp. 1968. 42s.*

Jefferys, Margot, with the assistance of Winifred Moss. Mobility in the Labour Market: Employment Changes in Battersea and Dagenham. *Preface by Barbara Wootton. 186 pp. 51 tables. 1954. 15s.*

Levy, A. B. Private Corporations and Their Control. *Two Volumes. Vol. 1, 464 pp., Vol. 2, 432 pp. 1950. 80s. the set.*

Liepmann, Kate. Apprenticeship: An Enquiry into its Adequacy under Modern Conditions. *Foreword by H. D. Dickinson. 232 pp. 6 tables. 1960. (2nd Impression 1960.) 23s.*

Millerson, Geoffrey. The Qualifying Associations: a Study in Professionalization. *320 pp. 1964. 42s.*

Smelser, Neil J. Social Change in the Industrial Revolution: An Application of Theory to the Lancashire Cotton Industry, 1770-1840. *468 pp. 12 figures. 14 tables. 1959. (2nd Impression 1960.) 50s.*

Williams, Gertrude. Recruitment to Skilled Trades. *240 pp. 1957. 23s.*

Young, A. F. Industrial Injuries Insurance: an Examination of British Policy. *192 pp. 1964. 30s.*

ANTHROPOLOGY

Ammar, Hamed. Growing up in an Egyptian Village: Silwa, Province of Aswan. *336 pp. 1954. (2nd Impression 1966.) 35s.*

Crook, David and **Isabel.** Revolution in a Chinese Village: Ten Mile Inn. *230 pp. 8 plates. 1 map. 1959. (2nd Impression 1968.) 21s.*

The First Years of Yangyi Commune. *302 pp. 12 plates. 1966. 42s.*

Dickie-Clark, H. F. The Marginal Situation. A Sociological Study of a Coloured Group. *236 pp. 1966. 40s.*

Dube, S. C. Indian Village. *Foreword by Morris Edward Opler. 276 pp. 4 plates. 1955. (5th Impression 1965.) 25s.*
India's Changing Villages: Human Factors in Community Development. *260 pp. 8 plates. 1 map. 1958. (3rd Impression 1963.) 25s.*

Firth, Raymond. Malay Fishermen. Their Peasant Economy. *420 pp. 17 pp. plates. 2nd edition revised and enlarged 1966. (2nd Impression 1968.) 55s.*

Gulliver, P. H. The Family Herds. A Study of two Pastoral Tribes in East Africa, The Jie and Turkana. *304 pp. 4 plates. 19 figures. 1955. (2nd Impression with new preface and bibliography 1966.) 35s.*
Social Control in an African Society: a Study of the Arusha, Agricultural Masai of Northern Tanganyika. *320 pp. 8 plates. 10 figures. 1963. (2nd Impression 1968.) 42s.*

Ishwaran, K. Shivapur. A South Indian Village. *216 pp. 1968. 35s.*
Tradition and Economy in Village India: An Interactionist Approach. *Foreword by Conrad Arensburg. 176 pp. 1966. (2nd Impression 1968.) 25s.*

Jarvie, Ian C. The Revolution in Anthropology. *268 pp. 1964. (2nd Impression 1967.) 40s.*

Jarvie, Ian C. and **Agassi, Joseph.** Hong Kong. A Society in Transition. *396 pp. Illustrated with plates and maps. 1968. 56s.*

Little, Kenneth L. Mende of Sierra Leone. *308 pp. and folder. 1951. Revised edition 1967. 63s.*

Lowie, Professor Robert H. Social Organization. *494 pp. 1950. (4th Impression 1966.) 50s.*

Mayer, Adrian C. Caste and Kinship in Central India: A Village and its Region. *328 pp. 16 plates. 15 figures. 16 tables. 1960. (2nd Impression 1965.) 35s.*
Peasants in the Pacific: A Study of Fiji Indian Rural Society. *232 pp. 16 plates. 10 figures. 14 tables. 1961. 35s.*

Smith, Raymond T. The Negro Family in British Guiana: Family Structure and Social Status in the Villages. *With a Foreword by Meyer Fortes. 314 pp. 8 plates. 1 figure. 4 maps. 1956. (2nd Impression 1965.) 35s.*

DOCUMENTARY

Meek, Dorothea L. (Ed.). Soviet Youth: Some Achievements and Problems. *Excerpts from the Soviet Press, translated by the editor. 280 pp. 1957. 28s.*

Schlesinger, Rudolf (Ed.). Changing Attitudes in Soviet Russia.
2. The Nationalities Problem and Soviet Administration. Selected Readings on the Development of Soviet Nationalities Policies. *Introduced by the editor. Translated by W. W. Gottlieb. 324 pp. 1956. 30s.*

Reports of the Institute of Community Studies

(*Demy 8vo.*)

Cartwright, Ann. Human Relations and Hospital Care. *272 pp. 1964. 30s.*

Patients and their Doctors. A Study of General Practice. *304 pp. 1967. 40s.*

Jackson, Brian. Streaming: an Education System in Miniature. *168 pp. 1964. (2nd Impression 1966.) 21s. Paper 10s.*

Jackson, Brian and **Marsden, Dennis.** Education and the Working Class: Some General Themes raised by a Study of 88 Working-class Children in a Northern Industrial City. *268 pp. 2 folders. 1962. (4th Impression 1968.) 32s.*

Marris, Peter. Widows and their Families. *Foreword by Dr. John Bowlby. 184 pp. 18 tables. Statistical Summary. 1958. 18s.*
Family and Social Change in an African City. A Study of Rehousing in Lagos. *196 pp. 1 map. 4 plates. 53 tables. 1961. (2nd Impression 1966.) 30s.*
The Experience of Higher Education. *232 pp. 27 tables. 1964. 25s.*

Marris, Peter and **Rein, Martin.** Dilemmas of Social Reform. Poverty and Community Action in the United States. *256 pp. 1967. 35s.*

Mills, Enid. Living with Mental Illness: a Study in East London. *Foreword by Morris Carstairs. 196 pp. 1962. 28s.*

Runciman, W. G. Relative Deprivation and Social Justice. A Study of Attitudes to Social Inequality in Twentieth Century England. *352 pp. 1966. (2nd Impression 1967.) 40s.*

Townsend, Peter. The Family Life of Old People: An Inquiry in East London. *Foreword by J. H. Sheldon. 300 pp. 3 figures. 63 tables. 1957. (3rd Impression 1967.) 30s.*

Willmott, Peter. Adolescent Boys in East London. *230 pp. 1966. 30s.*
The Evolution of a Community: a study of Dagenham after forty years. *168 pp. 2 maps. 1963. 21s.*

Willmott, Peter and **Young, Michael.** Family and Class in a London Suburb. *202 pp. 47 tables. 1960. (4th Impression 1968.) 25s.*

Young, Michael. Innovation and Research in Education. *192 pp. 1965. 25s. Paper 12s. 6d.*

Young, Michael and **McGeeney, Patrick.** Learning Begins at Home. A Study of a Junior School and its Parents. *About 128 pp. 1968. 21s. Paper 14s.*

Young, Michael and **Willmott, Peter.** Family and Kinship in East London. *Foreword by Richard M. Titmuss. 252 pp. 39 tables. 1957. (3rd Impression 1965.) 28s.*

The British Journal of Sociology. *Edited by Terence P. Morris. Vol. 1, No. 1, March 1950 and Quarterly. Roy. 8vo., £3 annually, 15s. a number, post free. (Vols. 1-18, £8 each. Individual parts £2 10s.*

All prices are net and subject to alteration without notice